A COOKBOOK
TO KEEP YOU SLIM FOR LIFE!

Complete with 600 mouth-watering recipes for all occasions—hors d'oeuvres, hearty soups and vegetables, crispy cool salads and tangy dressings, relishes, superb and succulent entrees, sauces, fruits, beverages and creamy light desserts . . . PLUS plan-ahead menus, money-and-calorie-saving tips, ideal weight and calorie charts, a guide-list of herbs and spices, descriptions of three famous quick weight loss diets and how to choose the one for you!

THE SAFE, SLIMMING, SATISFYING, "MIRACLE WORKING" DIET COOKBOOK— BY THE BESTSELLING AUTHORS OF *THE DOCTOR'S QUICK WEIGHT LOSS DIET!*

ABOUT THE AUTHORS

IRWIN MAXWELL STILLMAN, M.D., D-IM, has treated and succesfully reduced more than 10,000 men, women, and teenagers in his private practice, and is undoubtedly the best known physician in this field, having practiced medicine for over 45 years. He is a Diplomate in Internal Medicine, Attending and Consulting Physician of Medicine at Coney Island Hospital and Harbor Hospital, Fellow in the American Geriatric College, Fellow in the American College of Angiology, and Clinical Instructor of Medicine at Long Island College Hospital.

SAMM SINCLAIR BAKER is the author of over twenty books, numerous articles, in many fields, and has appeared extensively on radio and television. Mr. Baker presents Dr. Stillman's findings and recommendations in clear, simple, usable form. Together they co-authored the famous bestsellers *The Doctor's Quick Weight Loss Diet* and *The Doctor's Quick Inches-Off Diet* . . . books which have literally changed the shape of millions of Americans.

The Doctor's Quick Weight Loss Diet Cookbook

By
Irwin Maxwell Stillman, M.D., D-IM
and
Samm Sinclair Baker

BANTAM BOOKS · TORONTO · NEW YORK · LONDON
NEW YORK
A NATIONAL GENERAL COMPANY

Dedicated
to our lovely, slim wives . . .
Ruth Stillman
and
Natalie Baker
invaluable helpmates in the fight
against figure inflation.

*This low-priced Bantam Book
has been completely reset in a type face
designed for easy reading, and was printed
from new plates. It contains the complete
text of the original hard-cover edition.*
NOT ONE WORD HAS BEEN OMITTED.

THE DOCTOR'S QUICK WEIGHT LOSS DIET COOKBOOK
*A Bantam Book / published by arrangement with
David McKay Company, Inc.*

PRINTING HISTORY
*McKay edition published April 1972
2nd printing.......April 1972
3rd printing.........July 1972
Bantam edition published February 1973*

*Bantam Books are published by Bantam Books, Inc., a National
General company. Its trade-mark, consisting of the words "Bantam
Books" and the portrayal of a bantam, is registered in the United
States Patent Office and in other countries. Marca Registrada.
Bantam Books, Inc., 666 Fifth Avenue, New York, N.Y. 10019.*

PRINTED IN THE UNITED STATES OF AMERICA

Contents

A Cookbook to Keep You Slim for Life

This "MIRACLE-WORKING" cookbook is different from any other you've ever seen. It will help you reduce swiftly, surely, and healthfully. It will give you the slimmer, trimmer, more attractive figure you want, and it will reduce you and keep you beautifully slim—*no matter how many times you've failed before.*

This cookbook will change your cooking and eating habits for the rest of your slimmer, healthier life. You'll find recipes for the famous Quick Weight Loss (and Teen QWL) diets, and for the Inches-Off Diet. All three of these diets have helped millions of women, men, and youngsters to get down to their ideal weight in a hurry. With the varied dishes in these pages, no one can ever find the diets monotonous. Here, too, are Stay-Slim recipes so that you need never worry about regaining that unwanted fat.

With the recipes and *proved* rapid-reducing methods here, you can switch from Quick Weight Loss dieting to Inches-Off dieting and back, whenever you want a change of eating pace. And, if you follow the suggested menus for all these programs, you can eat deliciously and healthfully, *and never be heavy again!* This remarkably different and effective reducing and maintenance cookbook can help you for the rest of your better life.

Every word in this book is devoted to "breaking the pound barrier." We know from long, successful experience (over 53 years of medical practice as an internist) that while a word to the wide should be sufficient, it seldom is. The clear instructions here will insure your reducing success. Instead of ineffective generalizations about "eating less," you'll find the exact, tasteful recipes permitted on our noted rapid-reducing diets.

For a detailed breakdown and instructions for the quick reducing programs, you'll wish to read the popular Stillman/Baker diet books for which the menus and recipes here have been designed: *The Doctor's Quick Weight Loss Diet* (Prentice-Hall, Dell) . . . *The Doctor's Quick Inches-Off Diet* (Prentice-Hall, Dell) . . . and *The Doctor's Quick Teenage Diet* (McKay, Paperback Library). (Basic rules for these diets accompany the recipes.)

A Wonderful New Way of Cooking and Eating

Using this book, you have already made the decision to take off those ugly, excess pounds and inches swiftly, and to stay slim from now on. Therefore you must accept this plain fact: The way you have been preparing food and eating has made you overweight. The life-extending recipes here will give you a satisfying alternative to the high-calorie meals that ruin your figure and threaten your health.

Open almost any other cookbook and you'll find recipes loaded with "1 cup butter or margarine" (1600 calories) . . . "2 cups sugar" (1540 calories) . . . "1½ cups mayonnaise" (2400 calories) . . . "1 cup cream" (800 calories) . . . and so on. Such recipes disregard the enormous ingestion of unhealthy calories and fats which pile on pounds and increase the danger of clogging the arteries.

If reading and using this book does nothing more than make you wary of calorie-loaded, high carbohydrate, high cholesterol recipes, it is likely to add healthier years to your life, and to those who eat what you cook and serve.

Cutting 7000 Calories from a Week's Recipes

Just think. With our recipes you can cut out about 1000 calories per day, eating all the foods you're accustomed to, leaving out the dressings, gravies, sugar, butter, and other fats. Thus, you'd drop about 7000 calories a week—the equivalent of 2 pounds of fatty tissue. Also, with this fat loss, you might lose about 2½ pounds of water. Imagine, if you are considerably overweight, you would lose 4 to 5 pounds in a single week just by following the cooking guides in this book.

There is absolutely no question that low fat, low-calorie recipes and meals are better for the entire family, youngsters as well as adults. Such food preparation helps to avoid many troubles and to improve general health and vigor.

Which Taste: "Light and Clean" or "Rich and Greasy?"

Our experience proves that dieters who switch to cooking without, or with an absolute minimum of rich greases and other high-calorie ingredients, soon prefer the light, clean taste of such dishes. You will soon be convinced after following our recipes, that heavy fats and rich dressings kill the natural flavors of fine meats, poultry, fish, vegetables, and salads.

Millions of our successful dieters have come to detest greasy foods, just as many epicures feel that adding heavy cream and sugar spoils the flavor of fine coffee and tea. One superb cook asks: "Why bother to start with excellent ingredients if you're going to 'drown' their delicious natural tastes?"

It's a matter of taste habits which you can readily change. Consider a magazine cartoon showing a scowling, skinny husband staring distastefully at his plate as his angry wife says, *"That 'yellow scum' on your asparagus is the finest hollandaise sauce!"* The point is that the slender gentleman is cutting out loads of calories by preferring the unadulterated fine flavor of the naturally low-calorie food.

The number of calories you can save by avoiding rich additives is startling. Frying an egg in a no-stick pan, instead of using a tablespoon of butter, margarine, or bacon fat, *saves 100 calories*. Six fresh cooked asparagus with a dash of your favorite seasonings, and perhaps a sprinkle of fresh lemon juice, are less than 25 calories

. . . but if you add only 4 teaspoons of hollandaise sauce, the same dish totals about 225 calories—*about 10 times more calories per serving!*

Furthermore, the taste of the fattening sauce has hidden the luscious flavor of the natural fresh vegetable. Ask yourself which are the real "masterpieces of culinary art"? Are they recipes that bring out the food's own flavor best . . . or high-calorie concoctions which cover up naturally fine flavors, add hundreds of calories, and pile pounds of unhealthy, unattractive blubber on your figure?

Once you "discover" the fine non-greasy flavors in most foods, you're likely to prefer such recipes by far. And you'll be healthier, slimmer, and more "alive," thanks to the switch.

The Stomach Has No Taste Buds

Your stomach operates like a marvelously intricate piece of machinery. It uses some food elements directly, and converts others if necessary. For example, your body is able to turn extra protein into carbohydrates if needed. It packs excess fat into fat-storage pockets, swelling your dimensions, tending to clog and mess up your internal "machinery," often causing serious, even fatal troubles, as in some heart attacks.

Your taste buds, "end-organs of the sense of taste," are cells of the tongue. It couldn't matter less to your innards whether or not the food you ingest has a "gourmet taste." The stomach only reacts negatively if quantities of fat or sharp seasonings and other harmful elements in the food thicken the blood and harm the delicate tissues and organs.

How Dangerous Is High Calorie, Fattening Eating?

Is overweight really dangerous? Consider this: before World War II, the incidence of heart attacks was high in many European countries where high-fat foods such as butter, cream, oils, and other rich additives and greases were part of the usual diet, causing overweight.

During the war when such rich ingredients were scarce *heart troubles diminished drastically*, as many people slimmed down. After the war, overweight and the rate of heart attacks zoomed again!

Horrifying facts that have made being overweight "the nation's No. 1 health problem" (according to a past president of the American Medical Association) could fill a book shelf. The Heart Association warns that "more than 3 times as many sudden deaths occur in middle-aged men who are 20 percent or more overweight."

Another medical report states that "overweight produces 2½ times greater risk of coronary (heart) trouble than normal weight." High blood pressure is found twice as often in overweights; hardening of the arteries 3 times as often. People who are overweight are more inclined to suffer from diabetes, arthritis, stomach troubles, and many more painful health hazards.

Keep those dangers in mind when preparing foods. "Gourmet recipes" need not be high in fats. Brillat-Savarin, the noted French gourmet, bitterly denounced those who eat too richly and overeat: "Well, go ahead and grow fat, become ugly, heavy, have asthmatic attacks, and die choked by your own fat."

Healthful Foods, Not "Health Foods"

When reference is made here to "fresh, natural flavor" and "healthful foods"—this doesn't necessarily mean "organically grown," "naturopathic," "macrobiotic (long life)," or other so-called "health foods." There is no evidence that "health foods," such as those sold in special "health food stores" or by mail, and usually priced higher than comparable foods without the "health food" tag, are actually better for you.

Comparing the nutritional values of foods "grown with organic fertilizers (of animal or vegetable matter) rather than chemical fertilizers," the U.S. Dept. of Agriculture states: "Any difference in their content of essential elements or vitamins that have been noted have been too small to be of any nutritional significance, and have been in favor of the inorganic fertilized plants as often as in favor of those grown with organic materials."

The same is true of "natural vitamins," as compared to synthetic vitamins. If you want to pay more for "natural vitamins" and "health foods," or if you prefer to grow foods organically, go to it. Just don't expect to gain superior nutritional benefits.

Similarly, there are no special virtues in such highly-touted "natural foods" as blackstrap molasses, wheat germ, seaweed, or brewers' yeast. Nor should you be misled by diet fads which may proclaim that a food such as grapefruit or yogurt will in itself take off weight; no single food is a slim-all or cure-all.

The point is not that passionate adherence to "health foods" is particularly dangerous, but that such foods have no better qualities for sustaining life than other natural, processed, or concentrated foods. More important, don't be misguided into foregoing proper care and treatment by a physician for arthritis, cancer, internal pains, and other serious ills because you've been told to consider "health foods" and "natural vitamins" as cure-alls.

In choosing ingredients for your recipes, we recommend reasonably priced quality foods available in most supermarkets and other food outlets. There's no benefit in wasting your money on higher-priced "health foods." Fair warning—the personal decision is up to you.

Double-Check Most "Diet Recipes"

Don't take all so-called "diet recipes" for granted; some can load on excess pounds instead of slimming you. As you use the recipes here, along with the general instructions and calorie tables, you'll learn almost instinctively to be suspicious of certain ingredients which you'll recognize as basically high calorie. Check such a recipe according to calorie tables before using it.

As an example, here's a recipe from the "homemaking page" of a popular newspaper. Under the heading "Diet Supper," the menu includes "Lettuce with Figure-Right Roquefort Dressing . . . using buttermilk in this salad dressing cuts calories." The recipe follows (calorie counts weren't listed in the story):

¼ cup firmly packed Roquefort cheese, at room temperature	230 calories
¼ cup mayonnaise	400 calories
½ cup buttermilk	45 calories
¼ teaspoon paprika; salt and pepper to taste	

TOTAL 675 CALORIES

In this case, using buttermilk instead of whole milk does save 45 calories, but the recipe itself totals close to 700 calories! Instead of that high calorie dressing, you might use fresh lemon juice and herbs, or vinegar with a light dash of vegetable oil, or a bottled diet dressing with as few as 4 calories per tablespoon—and *save hundreds of calories on the salad dressing alone.*

Small to Moderate Portions Only

An overweight patient shook her head in despair and said: "One of the things I want most out of life is to be slim, graceful, beautiful—*and eating my head off!*" It can't be done. You must realize once and for all that food isn't the most important thing in life, and that you can't "eat your cake" and slim down too. To reduce swiftly, you must eat only small or moderate portions even of low calorie recipes. If you follow a recipe totaling 200 calories per moderate serving, and then double your portion, you are taking in 400 calories.

Obviously you're kidding yourself if you're stuffing down oversize servings, yet claim to be using the reducing or Stay-Slim instructions properly. That's as foolish as the fat lady who digs into a huge ice cream sundae topped with gobs of whipped cream and chuckles to a friend: "Lucky me! I'm wearing my electrothermodynamic reducing belt." All she's reducing are her chances for slim, healthy living.

On the other hand, if you want to speed your loss of pounds and inches, consider taking smaller portions, even half-servings. Thus a 200 calorie recipe becomes only 100 calories in intake. You'll not only be losing weight quicker, but also gaining better health, lovelier looks, and greater energy more rapidly as your body devours its own fat more speedily and efficiently.

Medical Checkup Essential

Before you go on any diet, have a medical checkup or get your doctor's approval. He will undoubtedly tell you to take off excess pounds and inches right now to improve your general health and well-being, but if you have any serious medical or mental disorder, you should be guided only by your personal physician's advice.

Apply Your Personal Creativity

Use your own creativity (yes, *everyone* is creative) to vary and improve recipes according to your personal tastes. Be sure to make such changes without adding many calories or any ingredients not permitted on the particular diet that you are following. Otherwise you may slow the reducing process. Always keep in mind that your goal is to be beautifully slim, and *you're going to be* by following instructions in this book.

Adapt your own preferences in herbs, mild spices, and other seasonings if you prefer them to the seasonings listed in any recipe. You may substitute different vegetables, fruits, and other ingredients for those in the recipes, as long as you check the calorie counts.

Be careful not to use rich, high-calorie additives which tend to pile on excess weight. You don't want yourself or any other person in your family to be the too-common "middle-class American" who bulges in the middle. That's why no rich, heavy, or high calorie recipe can be considered a "good" recipe in our book.

Money-Saving, Calorie-Saving Benefits

As you save calories on the recipes here, you will probably find that you're also saving money. Although you may spend more on meats and shellfish, for example, you will not be buying such costly items as butter, cream, high-prized pastries and other rich foods and delicacies.

Even when you entertain, there's no reason to include these items. The following pages provide hundreds of gourmet recipes for delicious company dinners. The same figure-slimming benefits you get can be passed on to your family and guests.

Ecstatic letters from newly slim people of all ages using our quick reducing and Stay-Slim methods enthuse: "Lost 27 pounds in 2 weeks on your diet . . . my overweight husband and teenagers have lost beautifully too . . . thanks from the bottom of my heart for giving us such a wonderful new life . . ."

(RECIPE NOTE: Every Quick Weight Loss Diet and Inches-Off Diet recipe in this book (you don't count calories on these diets) *is also a Stay-Slim Eating recipe.* Simply follow the calorie counts of the QWL and I-O recipes you use for Stay-Slim Eating.)

The Doctor's Quick Weight Loss Diet

The Doctor's Quick Weight Loss Diet is probably the most popular and effective reducing diet of all time. Its phenomenal success is based on two words: *it works!* At this writing, over 7 million copies of the book have been printed worldwide and condensations and variations have appeared in publications reaching additional millions of readers.

On the QWL Diet, *you will lose 5, 10, 15 or more pounds a week,* depending on how overweight you are. Enthusiastic reports of results prove it, as in these typical letters:

Mrs. F.T., age 55: "I went on your diet and started losing as I had never done in my life before, and without feeling hungry. I've lost 80 pounds, getting down to 121 pounds, a weight I hadn't reached since before I was married. When I've gained weight on trips and vacations, I've always been able to lose it immediately on the QWL Diet after getting home. With the weight loss went my disabling back pain. I persuaded my sister who weighed 279 pounds to go on your diet, and she has lost 110 pounds to date. Thank you for giving me a new life."

Mr. W.S., Chef de Cuisine: "Being a chef, I have all the opportunity in the world to get fat. Because of all the foods I work with, tasting them for the right flavoring, I built a big appetite—and big body! For 10 years I tried to lose weight on different diets but found it a waste of time and money. When I started your QWL

Diet I weighed 215 pounds, with 38½ inch wait. Now I'm down to 146 pounds and 31¾ inch waist. The loss of 69 pounds in 74 days can be confirmed by my doctor, as I had a checkup about every 20 days. He was so amazed that he wanted to get his scales checked for accuracy. I really feel great now and will live the life I had before I was so *fat*. I hadn't gone swimming for years because of embarrassment about my overweight. All I can say, with all my heart, is thank you."

Such thrilling success can be yours with the simple Quick Weight Loss Diet. This cookbook gives you the exact, tasteful recipes that will help you diet successfully by providing a wide variety. Eat only from the list of foods and beverages here—*don't eat any foods* not in the following QWL listing or recipes:

BASIC LIST FOR QWL DIET

1. *Lean Meats:* trim off all possible fat.

2. *Lean Poultry—Chicken and Turkey:* don't eat skin or any visible fat.

3. *Fish:* fresh, frozen, or canned fish is excellent (don't eat skin; drain off any oil or heavy sauces on canned fish, and wash off with water).

4. *Shellfish:* all types (with canned shellfish, drain off any oil or heavy sauces, and wash off with water).

5. *Eggs:* made any style without butter or other fat. (If you have a high cholesterol, you can omit eggs from your diet, or limit yourself to 4 per week.)

6. *Cottage cheese:* "creamed" or diet types; also Pot Cheese (dry cottage cheese), and Farmer Cheese (pot cheese compressed in a bar).

7. *Clear Soups:* without fats—meat, chicken, fish or vegetable broth, consommé, bouillon (as long as soup is clear of bits of vegetables; for example, onion or vegetable broth in cubes or powder form is permitted).

8. *Artificially Sweetened Gelatin Dessert:* (no more than 12 calories per half-cup serving; check package).

9. *Coffee, Tea:* no cream, milk, or sugar.

10. *"No Calorie" No-Sugar Beverages:* (that means no more than 1 calorie per ounce, be sure to check labels).

11. *Vitamin-Mineral Tablet:* every day.

12. *Eight (8) Glasses (8–10 ounce) or more of Water Per Day:* (during 16 waking hours, averages ½ glass per hour).

NOTE: Don't go on any diet without your doctor's approval.

GUIDELINES FOR QWL DIETING AND COOKING

(Many of these QWL tips are also available in cooking and eating on the Inches-Off Diet, and for Stay-Slim Eating; all the QWL recipes can be used in Stay-Slim Eating.)

No butter, oils, greases, or other fats should be used in QWL recipes, or in cooking (no-stick pans of all types, and other no-stick cooking vessels are helpful; spray-ons are available to make any pan "no-stick"). You get all the good taste without adding the excessive calories and fats which would interfere with your swiftest slimming. If you "must" have the taste of butter in some dishes, you may use a tiny bit of "butter-flavored salt" or "imitation butter flavoring." Most QWL dieters quickly lose any desire for a buttery, fatty taste.

QWL dieters may eat permitted foods (meat, poultry, fish, others) when prepared with vegetables, fruits, and some other forbidden ingredients (*not* sugar) . . . if they eat the permitted foods only and leave the vegetables, fruits, and extra gravy (as in the New England Beef Stew recipe). Other members of the family, or guests, can eat those ingredients not permitted the QWL dieter. In the New England Beef Stew recipe, QWL dieters eat the meat only, trimming away all possible fat, and skipping gravy; Inches-Off dieters eat the vegetables only; Stay-Slim eaters may have a serving of the entire recipe, both meat and vegetables (if you use the recipe in Stay-Slim Eating, total the calories of *all* ingredients).

Sugar is not to be used in QWL recipes. In addition to piling in unnecessary calories, sugar interferes with the specific dynamic action of protein (SDA) in taking off pounds and inches most rapidly on the QWL Diet. (The "specific dynamic action of protein" is explained in detail in the other Stillman/Baker diet books.)

You may use all herbs and spices, substituting or adding your favorites. Those individuals with a tendency to retain water should avoid salty foods and use little salt in cooking or at the table.

Small quantities of condiments are permitted in QWL dieting, including catsup, chili sauce, cocktail sauce, vinegar, and mustard. In recipes, you may use small amounts of such flavorings as onion flakes or minced onions, parsley flakes or fresh chopped parsley, lemon juice, and other no-sugar ingredients.

IMPORTANT: *Don't use larger quantities of the condiments than are listed in the recipes, as these "extra" flavorings have been figured out in this cookbook to enhance the taste without adding significant calories or interfering importantly with your speedy weight loss.*

A little wine, brandy, or beer, in very small quantities, may be included in some recipes if the alcohol is allowed to cook away so that only subtle flavor and moistness remain.

In cottage cheese recipes, keep in mind that you may use "creamed cottage cheese," "diet-type cottage cheese," "non-fat cottage cheese," or other types of "cottage cheese"—but none that contain fruit or vegetables or any sugar. With the various types of cottage cheese, there is little difference in contents or calories per serving (check the calorie tables on later pages, and then suit yourself).

Remove all possible fat and skin from all meats, poultry, and fish before eating, on both the QWL Diet and Stay-Slim Eating. Make this a lifetime habit.

To remove fat from hot meat juices, gravies, soups, and other liquids, you can refrigerate until fat hardens on top, and then remove it. A quicker method is to pour the liquid into a bowl and add a few ice cubes which soon make fat rise to the top. Spoon off the fat, take out the ice cubes to prevent diluting the flavor, and reheat the food. Another ingenious trick is to float a lettuce leaf on top of a soup or gravy for a few minutes. When you lift the leaf, some of the fat will cling to it and you can skim off the remainder (dispense with the leaf, of course). With some recipes you can simply lift off the fat with a spoon during and after cooking.

"Bouillon" . . . "broth" . . . "consommé" . . . "clear soup" . . . all mean about the same thing, whether "instant mix" or homemade. One may be substituted for another in a recipe, as long as all possible fat has been removed.

How "well" you cook meat has an effect on the calorie content of the portion. The longer and more thoroughly meat is cooked, the more inner fat and calories disappear. Calorie counts here are all calculated for "medium." Add about 20 calories for a four ounce portion of meat if it is cooked "rare," deduct about 25 calories if the same portion is "well done."

In using "instant broth" in recipes, make a cupful if you're using 1-cup cubes or envelopes, even if you only use a tablespoon or so in the recipe. Drink the rest if you wish, since it's invigorating and has practically no calories. Or, reserve it in the refrigerator for use later.

Artificially sweetened gelatin dessert—if you can't find a no-sugar gelatin dessert of no more than 12 calories per half-cup in the stores, buy unflavored gelatin, prepare according to package directions, and flavor with your favorite no-sugar syrup.

If you wish to make a QWL recipe for 4 (or whatever number is stated in the recipe) just for yourself, you can either make one-fourth the recipe, or cook the entire 4 portions, serve 1 and divide and wrap the remaining 3 individually to keep in the freezer for future meals.

To brown meats and other foods, you don't have to use high-calorie oil, butter, margarine, or other fats. You can brown the food in a little bouillon in the skillet; place it under the broiler; or sprinkle the bottom of a no-stick skillet with coarse salt, then sauté the food over a moderate flame.

With canned tuna, salmon, sardines . . . get water-packed when available, or drain off all possible oil by placing the fish in a strainer and washing it under slow running water.

QWL sauces and marinades listed in recipes may be used for other meats, chicken, fish, and so on. For example, the sauce in the recipe for Frankfurter Kabobs is also delicious with hamburgers. Apply your own good judgment and creativity.

Smoked or dried beef should be "desalted" before cooking or eating, by rinsing with boiling-hot water, and then draining (use a strainer).

Have meat ground to your order, or grind it at home, to make sure all possible fat is removed before grinding. When you buy the usual "hamburger meat" in the store, it is usually loaded with fat and excess calories.

Check the printed calorie count on packages of "low calorie" foods such as artificially sweetened gelatin dessert, "diet sodas," instant broth, and others, to be sure each serving hasn't more calories than specified. For example, no more than 12 calories per cup for broth; no more than 12 calories per half-cup serving of artificially sweetened gelatin dessert. Sodas and other beverages must be no more than 1 calorie per ounce, and contain absolutely no sugar. Just because a product is labeled "low calorie," or "lower in calories," or "diet," doesn't mean that it's *really* low in calories—you can only be sure by counting the number of calories per portion.

When using soy sauce which is permitted in small quantities, be sure to select a brand that doesn't contain sugar—again, check ingredients on the label. There are "leading brands" made without sugar.

In many QWL recipes, you may substitute other types of lean meat, fish, seafood, and so on for those not readily available or too costly at the time.

Don't eat bigger portions than specified in QWL recipes. If you eat larger amounts, you'll just be fooling yourself because you won't be slimming down as swiftly and beautifully as you could. Although you don't count calories on the QWL Diet, they are listed per serving to help you use the QWL recipes (and Inches-Off recipes) in your Stay-Slim Eating, after you're down to your desired weight.

You may prefer half-servings in order to lose weight extra quickly. Or you may increase portions for a meal if you have eaten little during the day. For example, the recipe for Poached Eggs in Chicken Broth specifies 1 egg per cup of broth, but you might prefer 2 eggs in the broth if you've eaten skimpily during the last 24 hours. Just use good judgment, and don't overeat lest you interfere with your sure quick weight loss.

Cut portions in half, and spread over 6 meals a day if you wish to lose weight even more speedily on QWL dieting. In this case, you would eat the same total quantity of food daily, but spread over 6 feedings instead of three. You'll find the pounds dropping off more rapidly. It's not known exactly why this happens, but it's a fact of reducing life that you can use to your advantage if you wish, to become slim sooner.

Teenagers on QWL diets may use all the QWL recipes here, noting also a few recipes which are for QWL Teen dieters only since they contain skim milk, buttermilk, or yogurt.

In buying meats, keep in mind that the number of calories in cooked meats is a little less than the "raw" calories listed in this book.

Where measured servings are noted in recipes, such as "Rib Roast . . . 4-ounce servings (260 calories per serving)," these are small recommended portions for dieters—other diners may have larger servings if desired. Usually what most people consider an "average" serving may be up to twice the size of a recommended QWL portion. When purchasing a large cut of meat, poultry, or fish, ask the number of "average servings."

In a very few recipes, such as Rib Roast, the number of servings cannot be given accurately because of variations in size of bones, visible fat, and shrinkage. It would be misleading to list "8 to 12 servings," for instance. It's easy to weigh the first 4-ounce serving and make others about the same size for dieters (also providing you with a guide rule for the future).

Getting the Most from Quick Weight Loss . . . Inches-Off . . . and Stay-Slim Eating and Dieting

Use the menus and recipes that follow, either as they are or making up your own from the basic QWL and I-O foods and recipes. While recipe categories are listed according to the order in which they would occur, course by course, in a meal, your main course is the most important for QWL rapid reducing, therefore most recipes are in this category. For the quickest weight loss, you can make your meals just of main course and beverage, skipping appetizers, soups, and desserts entirely.

If you tire of all-protein foods, and long for vegetables and fruits, switch to the Inches-Off Diet for a week or two, then back to QWL eating, alternating as personally suits you best. For example, a successful dieter, L.P. writes: "Let me tell you how happy I am with the results of using your two basic diets, Quick Weight Loss and Inches-Off. I started on QWL and went from 206 to 186 pounds—that's 20 pounds off in 21 days! I switched to Inches-Off and dropped 8 more pounds in a week, and will continue this method. Your diets are great and have changed my eating habits. I'll be forever grateful."

After you are down to your ideal weight, go on Stay-Slim Eating, using the directions, menus, and recipes in this book. Weigh yourself the first thing each morning, and if you are 3 pounds or more over your desired weight, go right back on QWL dieting until you lose enough, then back to Stay-Slim Eating, and so on—for the rest of your slimmer, healthier life.

QUICK WEIGHT LOSS RECIPES

HORS D'OEUVRES AND DIPS

You'll find these recipes desirable not only as hors d'oeuvres and appetizers, but also as satisfying snacks, and many may serve as a main QWL dish in adequate portions. Keep in mind always, as emphasized throughout this book, that the less you eat, the sooner you'll lose pounds and get down to your ideal weight. Therefore, you *don't* need appetizers for every lunch and dinner; the quickest way to a slim figure is to have just a QWL main dish, a QWL dessert or not, and beverage.

These low-calorie, low-fat QWL hors d'oeuvres and appetizers are delicious and more healthful for *everyone* you serve, not just dieters.

Chopped Liver Balls

1 pound beef liver
1 tablespoon unflavored gelatin
⅓ cup cold water
1 packet instant beef bouillon
¼ cup boiling water

1 teaspoon seasoned salt
1 teaspoon dried onion flakes
1 teaspoon dried mixed herbs
Worcestershire sauce, few drops to taste

Cook liver until tender, drain, chop well (in food grinder, blender, or by hand). Sprinkle gelatin over ⅓ cup cold water and add with instant bouillon to ¼ cup boiling water. Combine liver and liquids with other ingredients, and mix well. Refrigerate until thoroughly chilled. Roll into small balls and piece with toothpicks to serve. Makes 6 servings (110 calories per serving).

Seasoned Liver Canapé

1 pound sliced beef liver (carefully trimmed)
Water
2 vegetable bouillon cubes
1 envelope plain gelatin

1 teaspoon salt
2 teaspoons grated onion
1½ teaspoons Worcestershire sauce
Dash pepper sauce

Place liver in water to cover, in saucepan, and cook about 8 minutes, until tender. Pat with paper towels to dry. Run through food chopper (or cut up, and chop in bender). Dissolve bouillon cubes in 2 tablespoons of boiling water. Soften gelatin in ½ cup cold water, and place over heat to dissolve. Add chopped liver and bouillon, then salt, onion, Worcestershire sauce, and pepper sauce. Spoon into 2-cup mold and chill until firm. Unmold and serve cut in slices. Make 10 servings (68 calories per serving).

Chicken Liver Canapés

½ pound fresh (or frozen, thawed) chicken livers
1 medium onion, minced
3 tablespoons chicken bouillon

Celery salt
Black pepper
2 hard-cooked eggs

Sauté minced onion in bouillon over medium heat in no-stick skillet until brown. Add chicken livers (any visible fat removed) and cook 5 minutes. Turn over livers and continue cooking until done (about 5 minutes longer). Mash livers and onion together with fork, adding salt and pepper to taste. Slice eggs lengthwise in egg-slicer. Spoon chopped liver on egg slices and serve with forks as appetizer. Makes 6 servings (80 calories per serving).

Cheese Balls

½ cup cottage cheese
1 teaspoon salad cheese
(available now in shaker top jars)

⅛ teaspoon salt
2 strips lean bacon, well done and crumbled

Mash or blend together cottage cheese, salad cheese, and salt. Add crumbled bacon, and chill mixture for 2 hours. Form into ½ inch balls and roll into little more salad cheese to coat lightly. Makes 4 servings (60 calories per serving).

Cottage Cheese-Sardine Balls

1 can sardines, drained
½ cup cottage cheese
Poppy seeds or caraway seeds

Place sardines into strainer under cold running water to wash off oil. Transfer to small bowl and mash with fork. Add cottage cheese and continue mashing until of desired consistency. Make small balls from each tablespoon of the blend. Serve with poppy seeds or caraway seeds scattered on top. Makes 4 servings (80 calories per serving).

Meat-Cheese Pancake Rolls

4 very thin ½-ounce slices of beef (or lamb, or veal), about 3 inch by 3 inch, all visible fat removed

4 tablespoons cottage cheese
1 teaspoon instant beef broth mix, dry

Mix cottage cheese with the dry broth, then spread thinly on each slice of beef. Roll up slices of meat gently, then refrigerate. When ready to serve, cut into bite-size pieces. Makes 4 servings (50 calories per serving).

All-Purpose Dip

8 ounces creamed cottage cheese
1 teaspoon lemon juice
½ teaspoon chopped fresh dill

½ teaspoon poppy seeds
Dash salt
Dash pepper

Combine all ingredients, except poppy seeds, in blender, and process at low speed until smooth. Place in serving dish. Sprinkle top with poppy seeds. Dip pieces of meat, poultry, fish, shrimp, and other shellfish, cut in thin strips. Makes 8 servings (35 calories per serving, dip only).

Rémoulade Dip

For seafood, cold poultry, or cold meats

½ cup cottage cheese
1 tablespoon lemon juice
1 teaspoon parsley flakes
½ teaspoon seasoned salt

¾ teaspoon prepared mustard
Black pepper
1 teaspoon frozen minced chives (or less to taste)

Process first 6 ingredients together in blender at low speed until smooth and creamy. Fold in chives. Chill for at least 2 hours before using to allow flavors to mingle. Use as sauce or dip. Makes ½ cup (16 calories per tablespoon).

Onion Dip

For QWL TEEN dieters only, contains yogurt

1 pint plain yogurt
2 tablespoons chopped chives
½ teaspoon grated onion

⅛ teaspoon seasoned salt
Dash black pepper

Mix all ingredients together and chill. (Serve on slices of hard-cooked egg, or as filling for rolled dried beef, tongue, cold turkey, chicken, etc.) Makes 2 cups (10 calories per tablespoon).

Dilly Dip

For QWL TEEN dieters only, contains yogurt

1 cup plain yogurt
2 teaspoons chili sauce
1 teaspoon grated onion
1 teaspoon dill powder

2 teaspoons chopped pickle
⅛ teaspoon seasoned salt
Black pepper
Paprika or poppy seeds

Process all ingredients except last in blender until smooth. Serve chilled, topped with a sprinkle of paprika or poppy seeds. (Use as topping for sliced hard-cooked eggs, seafood, or with chicken, turkey, cold meats, etc.) Makes 1 cup (10 calories per tablespoon).

Egg Dip

For QWL TEEN dieters only, contains yogurt

2 hard-cooked eggs
¼ cup plain yogurt
1 teaspoon grated onion

⅛ teaspoon garlic salt
Pepper
Caraway or poppy seeds

Process all ingredients but last in blender. Serve chilled with caraway (or poppy) seeds sprinkled on top. (Use as seafood dip, or with other QWL foods). Makes ½ cup (22 calories per tablespoon).

SOUPS

Homemade Chicken Soup

2 pounds chicken wings, all possible skin and fat removed
2 quarts water
1 large carrot cut into 1" rounds
1 onion in thick slices

1 large rib celery cut into 1" pieces
4 teaspoons chopped parsley
1 tablespoon chopped dill
2 teaspoons salt
1 teaspoon paprika
½ teaspoon savory

In a heavy saucepan with tight cover place all ingredients including chicken. Bring to a strong boil, then cover tightly and simmer for about an hour or until chicken is fully tender to the fork. Remove chicken pieces and take off all meat. Strain out all vegetables to produce clear soup. Let soup cool, remove fat from top. Combine chicken meat and clear soup, heat until close to a boil, then serve. Makes 4 servings (180 calories per serving).

Chef's Bouillon

*QWL dieters eat meat and clear soup only,
no vegetables*

2 pounds very lean beef, all visible fat removed
6 cups water
4 cups canned tomatoes, or cooked fresh tomatoes
4 large or 5 medium carrots, cut up into very small pieces
1 minced green pepper

1 small onion, sliced very thin
3 whole cloves
½ teaspoon whole peppercorns
1 teaspoon chopped fresh parsley
¼ cup tarragon vinegar
Salt and pepper
Thin lemon slices

Simmer beef, cut into small cubes, 2½ hours in water. Add other ingredients except vinegar, salt and pepper and cook together ½ hour. Strain out liquid through 2 layers of cheesecloth. Add vinegar, then salt and pepper to taste. Bring just to boil again and serve hot, floating a thin slice of lemon on top of each serving. Makes 6 servings (325 calories per QWL serving).

Egg Drop Soup

1 medium size egg
1 cup clear soup (broth, bouillon, or consommé)
Celery salt

Beat the egg lightly with a fork, and drop into broth when at the simmering point (don't boil) in saucepan, stirring constantly. When egg has thickened slightly, serve. Season to taste with celery salt. Makes 1 serving (90 calories).

Curry Soup

1 10½-ounce can con-densed beef (or chicken) broth, no fat content

1 soup can water
½ teaspoon curry powder

Heat ingredients together, stirring 2 or 3 times. Serve in bouillon cups if you have them. Makes 3 servings (15 calories per serving).

Jellied Beef Bouillon

1 envelope unflavored gelatin	1 tablespoon lemon juice
3 beef bouillon cubes or packets	⅛ teaspoon rosemary or mixed herbs (optional)
2½ cups water	1 tablespoon chopped parsley

In a saucepan, pour ½ cup of the water, and sprinkle with gelatin slowly to soften. Add bouillon cubes or packets, place saucepan over low heat, and stir slowly until bouillon and gelatin are thoroughly dissolved. Remove saucepan from heat, and stir in remaining 2 cups of water, lemon juice, and herbs. Chill until jelled. Serve with a little parsley sprinkled atop each serving. Makes 4 servings (15 calories per serving).

Jellied Meat-and-Bouillon

1 cup diced lean cooked meat, all visible fat removed, beef, lamb, or veal	1 tablespoon lemon juice
	⅛ teaspoon tarragon or mixed herbs (optional)
1 envelope unflavored gelatin	1 teaspoon caraway seeds (optional)
3 cubes or packets instant beef broth	Paprika
	4 thin lemon wedges
2½ cups water	

In a saucepan, pour ½ cup of the water, and sprinkle with gelatin slowly to soften. Add cubes or packets of beef broth, place saucepan over low heat, and stir until gelatin and broth are thoroughly dissolved and combined.

Remove saucepan from heat, and stir in remaining 2 cups of water, meat, lemon juice, herbs, and caraway seeds. Chill until jelled. Serve with each portion having equal amount of meat, and top with sprinkle of paprika and a lemon wedge. Makes 4 servings (120 calories per serving).

Jellied Chicken/Turkey Bouillon

1 cup diced cooked chicken or turkey, all skin and visible fat removed
1 envelope unflavored gelatin
3 cubes or packets instant chicken broth
2½ cups water

1 tablespoon lemon juice
⅛ teaspoon savory or mixed herbs (optional)
1 teaspoon sesame seeds (optional)
Paprika
4 thin lime (or lemon) wedges

In a saucepan, pour ½ cup of the water, and sprinkle with gelatin slowly to soften. Add cubes or packets of chicken broth, place saucepan over low heat, and stir until gelatin and broth are thoroughly dissolved and combined.

Remove saucepan from heat, and stir in remaining 2 cups of water, chicken or turkey, lemon juice, herbs, and sesame seeds. Chill until jelled. Serve with each portion having equal amount of chicken, and top with sprinkle of paprika and a lime wedge. Makes 4 servings (100 calories per serving).

Jellied Ham and Bouillon

1 cup diced cooked lean ham, all visible fat removed
1 envelope unflavored gelatin
3 cubes or packets instant chicken or onion broth
2½ cups water
1 tablespoon lemon juice

⅛ teaspoon dill or mixed herbs (optional)
1 teaspoon poppy seeds (optional)
Pepper (optional)
4 thin lemon wedges

In a saucepan pour ½ cup of the water, and sprinkle with gelatin slowly to soften. Add cubes or packets of broth, place saucepan over low heat, and stir until gelatin and broth are thoroughly dissolved and combined.

Remove saucepan from heat, and stir in remaining 2 cups of water, ham, lemon juice, herbs, and poppy seeds. Chill until jelled. Serve with each portion having equal amount of ham, and top with sprinkle of pepper and a lemon wedge. Makes 4 servings (125 calories per serving).

Jellied Egged Bouillon

3 hard-cooked eggs, chopped	⅛ teaspoon savory, tarragon, or mixed herbs (optional)
1 envelope unflavored gelatin	1 teaspoon caraway seeds (optional)
3 cubes or packets instant chicken broth	Paprika
2½ cups water	4 thin lemon wedges
1 tablespoon lemon juice	

In a saucepan, pour ½ cup of the water and sprinkle with gelatin slowly to soften. Add cubes or packets of broth, place saucepan over low heat, and stir until gelatin and broth are thoroughly dissolved and combined.

Remove saucepan from heat, and stir in remaining 2 cups of water, lemon juice, herbs, and caraway seeds. Chill for a short time until a little firm, then fold in the chopped eggs to distribute well. Chill further until jelled. Serve each portion topped with a sprinkling of paprika, and a lemon wedge. Makes 4 servings (75 calories per serving).

Cottage Cheese Bouillon

4 cups chicken broth	1 tablespoon parsley flakes
8 ounces cottage cheese	Paprika

Heat broth in a saucepan to the boiling point, then reduce to moderate heat. Add cottage cheese, 1 tablespoon at a time, along with parsley flakes, and stir slowly until cheese is smoothly blended into a thickened soup. Serve hot with a sprinkling of paprika on top. Makes 4 servings (75 calories per serving).

Snowball Onion-Clam Soup

4 cups instant onion-seasoned broth

Lemon pepper marinade, a pinch

10-ounce can whole baby clams, including liquid

8 tablespoons cottage cheese

Prepare 4 cups instant onion-seasoned broth as directed on package. Combine in saucepan with clams and liquid, a pinch of lemon pepper marinade, and heat to boiling point. Divide in 4 serving bowls and add 2 tablespoons cottage cheese to each bowl. Makes 4 servings (80 calories per serving).

Meat-Bits Bouillon

1 cup beef bouillon

½ teaspoon chopped parsley

⅛ cup bits of leftover lean meat (beef, lamb, or veal)

Tarragon, a pinch (optional)

Prepare bouillon according to package directions. Add all other ingredients. Bring just to boil, then simmer 5 to 10 minutes. Makes 1 serving (65 calories).

Chicken-Bits (Turkey-Bits) Bouillon

1 cup chicken bouillon

½ teaspoon finely chopped onion, or onion flakes

¼ cup bits of leftover chicken or turkey

Savory, a pinch (optional)

Prepare bouillon according to package directions (or use homemade chicken broth, all possible fat removed). Add all other ingredients. Bring just to boil, then simmer 5 minutes. Makes 1 serving (100 calories).

Fish-Bits Bouillon

1 cup onion bouillon (or chicken or vegetable bouillon)

½ teaspoon onion flakes, or grated onion

¼ cup bits of leftover fish

Thyme, a pinch (optional)

Prepare bouillon according to package directions. Add all other ingredients. Bring just to boil, then simmer 5 minutes. Makes 1 serving (65 calories).

Shrimp-Bits Bouillon

1 cup chicken bouillon
2 cooked jumbo shrimp cut in bits (or equivalent in smaller shrimp, crabmeat, scallops or lobster)

1 sprig parsley leaves cut into bits
⅛ teaspoon paprika
Marjoram, pinch (optional)

Prepare bouillon according to package directions. Add all other ingredients. Bring just to boil, then simmer 5 minutes. Makes 1 serving (60 calories).

Consommé with "Caviar"

1 can jellied consommé
2 tablespoons whitefish roe caviar (or other)
2 thin lemon wedges

Keep canned consommé in refrigerator to jell. At serving time, spoon into bouillon cups, and add 1 tablespoon caviar to each serving. Serve a lemon wedge with each portion. Makes 2 servings (30 calories per serving).

Jellied Seafood Bouillon

1 cup diced cooked seafood (shrimp, lobster, crabmeat, or minced clams, or whole baby clams)
1 envelope unflavored gelatin
3 cubes or packets instant broth (chicken, onion, or vegetable)

2½ cups water
1 tablespoon lemon juice
⅛ teaspoon sage or mixed herbs (optional)
4 thin lime or lemon wedges

In a saucepan, pour ½ cup of the water, and sprinkle with gelatin slowly to soften. Add cubes or packets of instant broth of your choice, place saucepan over low heat, and stir until gelatin and broth are thoroughly dissolved and combined.

Remove saucepan from heat, and stir in remaining 2 cups of water, seafood, lemon juice, and herbs. Chill until jelled. Serve with each portion having equal amount of seafood and with a lime wedge atop each serving. Makes 4 servings (55 calories per serving).

Dilled Clam Soup

10-ounce can whole baby clams (or minced clams) including liquid

8 ounces clam juice (bottled or fresh)

8 ounces boiling water

¼ teaspoon dill salt (or celery salt) or more to taste

¼ teaspoon dill weed

Coarse black pepper

In saucepan combine all ingredients, including a few dashes of pepper. Bring to boil, then simmer for 5 minutes. Makes 4 servings (50 calories per serving).

Clam-Shrimp-Onion Soup

8 ounces clam broth

1 package onion-flavored instant broth

1 cup water

8 large cooked shrimp cut in bite-size pieces

1 teaspoon parsley flakes

Combine all ingredients in saucepan. Bring to boiling point, then cover and simmer for 5 minutes. Makes 2 servings (100 calories per serving).

Jellied Clam Consommé

1 can (10 ounce) jellied chicken consommé

1 can (8 ounce) minced clams (drain; reserve juice)

¼ cup cottage cheese

Hungarian paprika

Chill consommé to jell. Gently fold drained clams into jellied consommé. Process cottage cheese and 2 tablespoons of the clam juice in blender at low speed until creamy (use small blender jar if you have one). Spoon consommé into 4 bouillon cups and top with sauce. Sprinkle paprika over sauce. Perfect hot weather combination, or for any time of year. Makes 4 servings (55 calories per serving).

Creamy Chicken Soup

For TEEN QWL dieters only, contains skim milk

1 pint skim milk	1 teaspoon grated onion
2 cubes chicken bouillon	1 tablespoon minced parsley
1 tablespoon flour	Pepper (optional)
½ cup cubed cooked chicken	

Heat the milk just to boiling, then stir in the bouillon cubes until dissolved. Remove from heat. Slowly stir in the flour. Return to heat, add chicken, onion, parsley, and seasonings, and stir until mixture thickens a little. Serve piping hot. Makes 3 servings (160 calories per serving).

BEEF

Beef Steak Broiled

2 pounds steak (weight without bone)—club, filet mignon (tenderloin), porterhouse, or sirloin, all visible fat removed before eating
Salt (plain, garlic salt, or seasoned salt)
Pepper

Have lean steak cut about 1 inch thick. Score fat edges with knife about 1 inch apart, cutting into fat but not into meat. Place steak on rack in broiler in preheated oven, about 3 inches from broiler heat. Broil on one side for about 5 minutes, season to taste with selected salt and pepper, then turn to other side and place under broiler. Should take about 8 minutes total for rare steak, 12 minutes for medium, up to 20 minutes for well-done (check by making small slit in center of surface and noting extent of doneness). When finished, remove steak, season just-broiled surface with salt and pepper, and serve. (QWL dieters be sure to remove all possible fat before eating steak.) (230 calories per 4-ounce serving.)

Beef Steak Panbroiled

2 pounds lean steak (your choice of available varieties)
Salt
Pepper

Place lean steak, about 1 inch thick, in heavy no-stick skillet, sprinkling a little coarse salt and pepper in pan first. Brown lightly on one side and season with salt and pepper to taste. Turn on other side, turning every few minutes over medium-high heat, no cover. Varying with thickness of steak, it usually takes about 9 minutes for rare, 12 minutes for medium, 20 minutes for well-done (slit center of meat in shallow cut to check for color desired). Season with salt and pepper to taste, and serve. (QWL dieters trim off all possible fat before eating steak.) (230 calories per 4-ounce serving.)

Baked Sirloin Steak

2½ pounds sirloin steak, 1–1½ inches thick, all visible fat removed
3 tablespoons beef bouillon
½ teaspoon salt
¼ teaspoon pepper
½ teaspoon rosemary, ground
¼ teaspoon garlic salt

Mix the beef bouillon with all the herbs and spices. Brush liberally on both sides of the steak. Let steak sit on a rack for about 15 minutes on the kitchen counter. Place the bouillon mixture in a skillet over high heat, and add the steak, browning about 5 minutes on each side.

Place the browned steak on rack in a shallow roasting pan, pour over it any remaining bouillon mixture. Insert a meat thermometer in side of steak, pushing point to about middle of the meat. Bake in top part of preheated 350° oven until thermometer reaches 130° for medium rare (less or more for rare or well done), probably about 15 minutes. Serve on heated platter. (230 calories per 4-ounce serving.)

Steaks Flambé

4 small shell steaks or club
   steaks (8 ounces each, ½
   inch to ¾ inch thick),
   all visible fat removed
1 tablespoon coarse pepper

1 cup beef bouillon
1 small onion, minced
3 tablespoons brandy
Salt

Rub dried steaks well with coarse pepper, on both sides. Heat 3 tablespoons of the bouillon in large no-stick skillet, and sauté steaks about 2 or 3 minutes on each side for rare, a little longer for medium, and still longer for well done.

Meanwhile, in another pan, sauté onions over medium heat in 2 tablespoons of the bouillon until tender, then add balance of bouillon and simmer for 10 minutes or less if bouillon cooks away.

When steaks are ready, lower heat under them, spoon brandy over them, stand back and light, waiting for flame to go out. Remove steaks, salt to taste, slice and place on warm serving dish. Spoon sautéed onions over them, and serve. Makes 6 servings (300 calories per serving).

Quick Beef Minute Steak

4-ounce minute steak, very lean
Seasoned salt

Heat a no-stick pan, keep heat high, and cook steak for 1 minute. Turn, sprinkle with seasoned salt, and cook for 1 minute on that side. (If well-done steak is desired, turn again and cook 1 minute longer before serving.) Place on plate, hottest side up, and sprinkle with seasoned salt. Makes 1 serving (230 calories, with all visible fat removed).

Beef Tenderloin

4 pounds whole beef tenderloin
Salt (garlic salt or seasoned salt if preferred)
Pepper

When buying, have the butcher remove all possible fat and visible connective tissue from a whole 4-pound beef tenderloin. Season it well with salt (or garlic salt or seasoned salt) and pepper, to taste. Place on a rack in a shallow roasting pan. Insert meat thermometer into center of meat. Roast at 325° oven to 140° on thermometer for rare, to 170° if wanted well done, usually 45 minutes to 1 hour. Cut leftovers into separate amounts for future meals and place in freezer. (230 calories per 4-ounce serving.)

Beef Japanese Style

1¼ pounds sirloin steak, ½ inch thick, all visible fat removed, cut into bite-size pieces
½ clove garlic, minced (or garlic salt to taste)

Artificial sweetener equal to 2 teaspoons sugar
⅓ cup no-sugar soy sauce
2 tablespoons dry sherry
¼ teaspoon rosemary

In a shallow pan, combine all ingredients except the meat, mixing well. Marinate the meat in the mixture and set on counter for about an hour, turning it over about every 10 minutes in the mixture. Place pan about 3 inches from broiler, heat for about 5 minutes. Baste meat with marinade, then turn it over and baste with marinade again, and cook for about 3 minutes more. Remove from broiler, baste with mixture again, and serve. Makes 4 servings (310 calories per serving).

Steak on Skewers

1½ pounds lean flank steak, cut in ⅛ inch to ¼ inch strips
¼ cup no-sugar soy sauce
3 tablespoons bouillon
½ teaspoon ground ginger
½ clove garlic, minced
1 teaspoon parsley flakes
Artificial sweetener equal to 1 teaspoon sugar
Salt
Pepper

Mix all ingredients except salt and pepper in bowl. Marinate the strips of steak in the sauce for 1 or more hours, turning several times. Pierce and twist strips of steak on skewers. Brush with the marinade sauce and sprinkle lightly with salt and pepper. Broil about 4 minutes on each side, about 3 inches from heat, brushing again with the marinade when turning skewers over. Remove and serve. Makes 6 servings (245 calories per serving).

London Broil

1¼ pounds lean prime beef flank steak or London broil
2 tablespoons bouillon
1 teaspoon vinegar
1 teaspoon Worcestershire sauce
⅛ teaspoon garlic salt (or seasoned salt)
Salt and pepper

Combine all ingredients except meat and salt and pepper in a bowl and mix thoroughly. Place the meat in a shallow pan and brush thoroughly with all the sauce. Cover and let stand on the kitchen counter for 2 hours, turning and brushing all over with the sauce every half hour. Brush again with sauce, then place meat on cold rack in broiler pan in pre-heated oven, about 3 inches from heat source. Broil for about 4 minutes, then season with salt and pepper. Turn on other side and broil about 5 minutes more until medium rare (check with partial cut down the middle). Salt and pepper unseasoned side lightly, then cut in thin diagonal slices, and serve. Makes 4 servings (300 calories per serving, all visible fat removed).

Beef Rollarounds

2 pounds lean round steak, all fat trimmed off, cut about ¼ inch thick
½ teaspoon light or dark prepared mustard
1 tablespoon onion flakes
1 tablespoon parsley flakes (or fresh parsley), chopped fine
1 large dill pickle cut into 3 pieces lengthwise, then halved
2 sweet pickles, cut in thirds lengthwise
1 cup beef bouillon, double-strength
Salt and pepper to taste

Pound steak until flattened to about ⅛ inch thick, then cut into 6 equal pieces. Sprinkle pieces with salt and pepper, spread on mustard, and sprinkle with onion and parsley flakes. Place a piece of dill pickle and a piece of sweet pickle across the narrow end of each piece of steak, then roll up each piece and fasten into rolls with string.

In a no-stick skillet place 2 tablespoons of the bouillon, heat, then brown the rolls of steak on all sides; takes about 15 minutes. Add the rest of the bouillon, cover, lower heat until simmering, then cook for ¾ to 1 hour, removing any top fat occasionally, until meat is tender to the fork. Transfer rollarounds to hot serving plate and remove string. Makes 6 servings (320 calories per serving).

Flank Steak Ham Rolls

1 pound beef flank steak, trimmed of visible fat, pounded and flattened tender
2 thin slices boiled ham, all visible fat removed
3 tablespoons chili sauce
1 teaspoon Worcestershire sauce
1 tablespoon bouillon
Salt

Place slices of ham on the flattened steak, and brush with sauce made from the chili sauce, Worcestershire, and bouillon, mixed in a bowl. Roll up the meat with ham and fasten securely with skewers. Cut rolls into 1 inch to 1½ inch segments. Brush liberally on all sides with the sauce and sprinkle lightly with salt. Place on rack in preheated broiler pan, about 4 inches from heat. Broil for 5 minutes. Turn rolls and brush exposed surfaces with the sauce. Broil for about 5 minutes more. Makes 4 servings (240 calories per serving).

Rib Roast

QWL dieters are to trim away all visible fat from portion, and not eat the ribs, only the solid meat of the roast

6 pounds rib roast   Pepper
Salt   Marjoram (optional)

Place the roast in a shallow roasting pan, resting on the ribs with rounded side up. Season all sides of meat with salt and pepper to taste, adding a sprinkle of marjoram for extra seasoning zest if desired. Insert meat thermometer right in center of roast. Uncovered, roast in 325° oven for about 1½-2 hours, checking thermometer: 140° rare, 160° medium, 170° well done. (260 calories per 4-ounce serving.)

Rolled Rib Roast

4 pounds rolled rib roast   Pepper
Salt   Tarragon (optional)

Select a lean boned and rolled rib roast. Salt and pepper all surfaces well, adding sprinkling of tarragon for extra zesty flavor if desired. Keeping fat side up, place meat on rack in shallow roasting pan. Insert meat thermometer in top center of roast. Don't cover. Roast for 1½ to 2 hours in 325° oven, checking thermometer: 140° rare, 160° medium, 170° well done. (260 calories per 4-ounce serving, all visible fat removed.)

Freezer-to-Table Roast

4 pounds boneless beef roast
Seasoned salt to taste
Lemon pepper marinade

This simple recipe cooks lean roast beef right in the heavy aluminum foil in which it was wrapped for freezer. Remove roast from freezer, open foil, and sprinkle meat well with seasoned salt and lemon pepper marinade. Re-wrap, leaving foil loose around the roast as you crimp ends closed. Place roast in a shallow pan in preheated 400° oven for 2½ hours. Turn back foil to leave meat open at top and sides, and let brown in oven for another ½ hour. Transfer to serving platter, slice and serve. (QWL dieters trim off all fat from portions, and don't use juice unless fat has been removed.) (240 calories per 4-ounce serving.)

Pot Roast in "See-Through Bag"

3 pounds beef roast, all visible fat removed
Flour
Salt
Pepper
3 carrots, cut in 2 inch pieces
3 medium onions, quartered
2 ribs celery, cut in 1 inch pieces
⅓ cup water

Rub flour, salt and pepper over outside of beef and place in "see-through bag for oven roasting." Add salted vegetables and water. Secure bag 2 inches from food with twist-tie, cut off end, and puncture 4 holes in top of bag. Place carefully in shallow baking pan and cook in 400° preheated oven about 1½ hours.

When ready, snip corner off bag and pour out juice (may be used by non-dieters). Then slit top of bag to remove meat and vegetables. Makes 8 servings (375 calories per QWL serving, meat only).

Family Beef Stew

QWL dieters eat meat only

1½ pounds boneless stew meat, all visible fat trimmed off, then cut in 1 to 1½ inch cubes
1½ cups water
1 packet instant beef broth

1 tablespoon onion flakes
1 tablespoon parsley flakes
½ teaspoon salt
¼ teaspoon paprika
1 package frozen mixed vegetables

Brown the beef cubes in a pan under the broiler for a few minutes, turning to brown all sides. Combine the water and all other ingredients except the vegetables, and cook with meat in a tightly covered skillet over slow to moderate heat for about 2 hours (check several times and add a little water if needed). Add the vegetables and cook for 20 to 30 minutes longer until meat and vegetables are done, tender to the fork. Makes 6 servings (280 calories per QWL serving, meat only).

New England Beef Stew

QWL dieters eat only the meat

1¼ pounds very lean beef, all visible fat removed
1 8-ounce can tomato sauce
1 cup water
¾ teaspoon steak salt
½ bay leaf

⅛ teaspoon thyme
10 small onions
6 medium carrots, scraped and cut in 1 inch pieces
1 8-ounce can peas, drained

Cut meat into 1 inch cubes and place in shallow no-stick pan in broiler, 2½ inches from heat, turning until all sides are brown. Transfer to saucepan and add tomato sauce and water, salt, bay leaf, and thyme. Simmer, covered, for 1¼ hours. If liquid dries out, add a little more water. Meat should be almost tender. Add onions and carrots, cook another ½ hour, or until vegetables are done. Then add peas. Cook a few moments longer until peas are heated through. Add more salt if desired.

Makes 4 servings (230 calories per QWL serving, meat only).

Stewed Beef, English Style

1½ pounds lean eye round, all visible fat removed, cut into 1 inch cubes
1 vegetable bouillon cube
1 cup boiling water

1 tablespoon wine vinegar
1 bay leaf
½ teaspoon salt
2 ground peppercorns

Dissolve bouillon cube in boiling water in heavy saucepan. Add meat and other ingredients and cover pan very tightly. Simmer over very low heat for 2½ hours, longer if necessary, until meat is tender. If liquid should cook away, add a little hot water or tomato juice, just enough to prevent meat from sticking to pan. Makes 6 4-ounce servings (230 calories per serving).

Beef Ragout

QWL dieters eat only the meat

2 pounds very lean beef, all fat removed, cut into 1 inch cubes
2½ cups water
2 beef bouillon cubes
1¼ teaspoons garlic salt (or 1 clove chopped garlic and 1 teaspoon salt)
1 teaspoon thyme

Black pepper
3 sprigs parsley tied together
3 cups sliced celery
½ pound fresh mushrooms, sliced
½ pound very small white onions
1 package frozen green beans

Broil beef cubes 3 inches from heat, turning until all sides are browned. Place in heavy saucepan with water, bouillon cubes, garlic salt, thyme, pepper and tied parsley. Mix, bring to boil, then simmer covered for 1½ hours. Add celery, mushrooms, onions and green beans. Simmer ½ hour longer, adding a little water if necessary, or until meat is tender and vegetables just done. Remove parsley, then serve. Makes 8 4-ounce servings (230 calories per QWL serving, meat only).

Braised Beef

QWL dieters eat only the meat

3 pounds lean boneless chuck, all possible fat removed
1 scant teaspoon lemon pepper marinade
1 medium onion, sliced thin
2 carrots, pared, then sliced very thin
4 celery stalks, sliced crosswise
1 beef bouillon cube
1 cup boiling water
1½ teaspoons seasoned salt
2 tablespoons chopped parsley
1 garlic clove, crushed
½ teaspoon thyme
2 bay leaves
2 whole cloves

Wipe meat with damp paper towel and sprinkle with lemon pepper marinade. Place in center of large piece of heavy foil in shallow roasting pan. Place pan under preheated broiler, turning meat until all sides are browned. Discard fat. Place onion, carrots, and celery slices in separated piles around meat. Sprinkle with a little salt. Broil 5 minutes. Dissolve bouillon cube in boiling water and add salt, parsley, garlic, thyme, bay leaves, and cloves. Mix thoroughly and spread over meat. Fold edges of foil over all and seal together on top. Roast in preheated 350° oven 1¼ hours or more, according to desired doneness. (To hasten cooking, open top of foil during last 15 minutes.) Cut in diagonal slices for serving. Makes 10 4-ounce servings (245 calories per QWL serving, meat only).

Home Boiled Beef

QWL dieters eat meat only

3 pounds very lean beef brisket, all visible fat removed
2 sliced carrots
½ cup chopped celery
1 tablespoon salt
¼ teaspoon black pepper
4 whole cloves
Water to cover

Place beef in deep saucepan with other ingredients and add water to cover. Simmer covered for 3 hours. Allow to cool and remove any fat which rides to top. Reheat to serve (do not boil). Save stock for later use in soup. Serve a little prepared horseradish with the beef. Makes 10 4-ounce servings (260 calories per QWL serving).

Farm Boiled Beef

QWL dieters eat only the meat, with a touch of horseradish, and broth

2½ pounds lean flank steak, all visible fat removed
7 cups boiling water
2 teaspoons salt
1 package frozen green beans (thawed first)

2 carrots, cut into thirds
1 pound fresh whole mushrooms
1 small onion quartered
4 sprigs fresh parsley
3 stems fresh dill
Horseradish (prepared)

Cook meat in salted boiling water, skimming off top until water is quite clear. Add thawed green beans, carrots, mushrooms and onion. Tie together washed parsley and dill with white thread and add to pot. Simmer covered, 1½ to 2 hours, until meat is very tender. Allow to cool, remove fat from top, reheat and serve with a little horseradish. Makes 8 4-ounce servings (260 calories per QWL serving).

Corned Beef Farm Style

QWL dieters eat the meat only, not fruit or vegetables

2 pounds lean corned beef, all possible fat removed
¼ cup water
1 tablespoon pickling spice
1 small orange, sliced

1 small onion, sliced
1 carrot, sliced
1 stalk celery, including leaves
3 parsley stalks

Soak corned beef in water that covers surface, for about ¾ hour. Pat corned beef dry, then place in center of a sheet of heavy duty foil in a shallow pan. Slowly pour on the ¼ cup water. Sprinkle on the pickling spice, and arrange orange and vegetable slices and stalks on top of and around meat on the foil. Cover meat tightly with the foil, folding all edges so no juice can run out. Bake in 325° oven for 3 or more hours until tender to work. Serve in fairly thin slices. (Trim off all visible fat when eating.) Makes 8 4-ounce servings (260 calories per QWL serving, meat only).

Corned Beef Home Style

QWL dieters eat meat only, no vegetables

3 pounds corned beef, lean,
    trimmed of all possible fat
Water to cover
2 tablespoons finely chopped
    onion
½ teaspoon powdered
    tarragon

2 bay leaves
5 peppercorns
1 package frozen sliced
    carrots
2 packages frozen Brussels
    sprouts

Place corned beef brisket in heavy pot that has a tight-fitting cover. Cover with water to top of beef only. Add onion, tarragon, bay leaves, and peppercorns. Stir. Cover tightly, and simmer about 2½ hours, or until almost tender (test with fork). Add carrots, cover with lid, cook 10 minutes more. Add Brussels sprouts and cook for 10 more minutes. Discard bay leaves. Serve. (If you want to get rid of more fat, cook in morning, let cool, then skim fat off top shortly before serving, and reheat.) Makes 10 4-ounce servings (260 calories per serving, meat only).

Glazed Cold Beef

3 cups cooked cubed lean
    beef, all visible fat
    removed
1 teaspoon mixed herbs
1 envelope unflavored
    gelatin

1 cup cold water
1 packet instant beef
    bouillon
1 tablespoon lemon juice
1 tablespoon minced
    parsley

Arrange beef cubes in serving bowl. Sprinkle with mixed herbs. Soften gelatin in the cold water. Add instant beef bouillon and heat, stirring until dissolved. Add lemon juice and parsley, stir in well, and pour over herbed beef cubes. Chill in refrigerator until jelled. Makes 6 servings (240 calories per serving).

Meat Jell

1 envelope unflavored
gelatin
1¾ cups water
2 cubes or packets of
instant beef broth
1 cup diced cooked beef
(or lamb, veal, or ham),
all visible fat removed

1 tablespoon minced
parsley or parsley flakes
1 teaspoon grated raw
onion

In ¾ cup of the water in a saucepan, sprinkle the gelatin. Add instant beef broth. Over low heat, stir until broth and gelatin are dissolved and combined. Add remaining 1 cup water, stir. Chill until mixture is thickened but not set, then fold in remaining ingredients. Turn into 4 individual molds, or 1 large mold. Chill until set. Unmold and serve. Makes 4 servings (135 calories per beef serving).

LAMB

Simple Roast Leg of Lamb

3 pounds lean half leg of
lamb (with bone)
1 clove garlic, cut into 8
slivers

1 teaspoon crushed mint
½ teaspoon salt
⅛ teaspoon pepper

Wipe meat with damp cloth. Cut 8 shallow slashes in top, and insert a sliver of garlic in each slash. Combine mint, salt, and pepper, and rub well into all surfaces of meat. Leave on kitchen counter for about an hour. Roast in 325° oven for about 1½ hours. Dieters should trim all fat from portion before eating. Makes 8 servings (330 calories per serving).

Thymed Leg of Lamb

QWL dieters eat the meat only, no vegetables, trimming off all visible fat

3 pounds half leg of lamb (before boning)
1 teaspoon powdered thyme
Salt, pepper to taste
1 large carrot, cleaned and cut into thin discs

1 small onion, peeled and diced
1 tablespoon chopped parsley
1 cup celery, diced (include leaves)
1 clove garlic, crushed (optional)

Have leg of lamb boned, and all visible fat removed. Rub meat (unrolled) lightly with the thyme and with salt and pepper. Place lamb flat outer side down, in a shallow roaster pan, and cook uncovered for 15 minutes in preheated 400° oven. Then turn lamb over, still flat, and sprinkle the remaining ingredients on and around the lamb. Roast for 25 to 30 minutes longer, or until lamb is medium rare or well done, as you like it. Remove lamb from drippings, and serve, discarding vegetables. Makes 8 servings (330 calories per QWL serving).

Minted Roast Lamb

5 pounds leg of lamb (with bone)
Mint or parsley leaves
2 tablespoons chopped mint (can use parsley if no mint available)

1½ teaspoons salt
1 teaspoon mixed herbs
1 teaspoon lemon rind
¼ teaspoon ground ginger
Pepper to taste

Prepare lamb by cutting small shallow slits in surface 2-3 inches apart. Place mint or parsley leaf in each slit. Combine all other ingredients in a mixture, and rub all over the lamb.

After inserting a meat thermometer into lamb (not touching the bone), place on rack in roasting pan in 325° oven, uncovered. Roast about 30 minutes per pound (about 180° on thermometer) for well-done meat, about 25 minutes per pound (165°) for medium, about 20 minutes per pound (150°) for pink. QWL dieters trim off any visible skin or fat. Makes 12 servings (330 calories per serving).

Lamb Chop Broil

4 average 6-ounce loin lamb chops, all possible fat removed
1 glove garlic

½ teaspoon mixed herbs
½ teaspoon parsley flakes
½ teaspoon salt
2 tablespoons herb vinegar

The day before cooking chops, add garlic, herbs, parsley flakes, and salt to vinegar, mix thoroughly in a covered bowl, and place in refrigerator. An hour before cooking, place the trimmed chops in a large shallow bowl, brush with the seasoned vinegar and let marinate. Remove chops from bowl and broil about 3 inches from heat for about 12 minutes on each side, or until done to your liking. Makes 4 servings (290 calories per serving).

Baked Lamb Chops

QWL dieters eat only the meat, no sauce

4 shoulder lamb chops ½ inch to ¾ inch thick (about 1½ pounds), all visible fat removed
Lemon pepper marinade

½ teaspoon salt
1¼ cups tomato juice
½ green pepper, chopped
1 small onion chopped

Place chops on rack in broiler 2½ inches from heat and brown both sides (about 4 minutes each side).

Sprinkle with lemon pepper marinade and salt and place in skillet. Add tomato juice, green pepper, and onion. Cover and simmer 25 to 30 minutes, until tender. Makes 4 servings (240 calories per QWL serving, meat only).

Marinated Lamb Chops

4 shoulder lamb chops,
    about ¾ inch thick
    (about 1½ pounds)
¼ cup no-sugar soy sauce

¼ cup beef bouillon,
    double-strength
1 teaspoon lemon juice
¼ teaspoon garlic salt

Trim all visible fat possible from chops, and place in a shallow baking dish. Combine all other ingredients, mix well, and pour over chops. Cover dish and place in refrigerator for at least 2 hours, turning meat about every ½ hour. Place chops on preheated broiler about 3 inches from heat, and broil about 8 minutes on one side, then turn and broil about 8 minutes on other side. Makes 4 servings (240 calories per serving).

Curry-Flavor Lamb Chops

4 shoulder lamb chops,
    about ¾ inch thick
    (about 1½ pounds)
½ cup beef bouillon,
    double-strength

1 teaspoon curry powder
¼ teaspoon garlic salt

Place chops on rack over shallow pan under preheated broiler, so tops of chops are about 3 inches from heat. Broil about 6 minutes, or until browned. Turn and broil other side 2 minutes. Meanwhile, combine curry and garlic salt with bouillon and brush evenly and liberally on both sides of the chops. Broil for about 2 more minutes on second side, or until done to your taste. Makes 4 servings (240 calories per serving).

Lemon-Flavored Lamb Stew

QWL dieters eat the meat only, no vegetables

5 pound leg of lamb, boned and all visible fat removed
Seasoned salt to taste
½ cup lemon juice
4 small onions, peeled and halved
Water to cover
4 medium carrots, peeled and cut in 1-inch pieces

1 stalk celery, including leaves, cut in 1-inch pieces
1 cup green beans cut in 1-inch pieces
2 medium tomatoes, peeled and halved
1 tablespoon green pepper flakes

Cut meat into 1½ inch cubes, trimming off all visible fat. Sprinkle well with seasoned salt. In a large casserole-skillet, heat half the lemon juice, then add onions, and lamb, and brown. Remove onions, setting aside. Add balance of lemon juice, and enough water to cover lamb cubes. Add carrots to lamb, simmer 10 minutes. Add celery, cook 15 minutes more. Add more water if needed. Add onions, green beans, tomatoes, and green pepper flakes; cook 15 minutes more, or until green beans are tender. Serve steaming hot from casserole (only the meat for QWL dieters). Makes 12 servings (330 calories per serving, meat only).

Savory Lamb Stew

QWL dieters eat only the meat

2 pounds very lean lamb, cut into 1½-inch cubes, all visible fat removed
½ teaspoon seasoned salt
Black pepper
Water
4 carrots, peeled and cut into 1-inch discs

8 small onions
3 stalks celery, sliced into 1-inch crescents
½ pound green beans, cut into 1-inch lengths

Arrange the lamb cubes, sprinkled with seasonings and just covered with water, in a saucepan. Top with the prepared vegetables, and add a little more seasoning. Simmer for 2½ hours, tightly covered, until meat is tender, checking occasionally to be certain water does not cook away. If it should, add just a little at a time to keep meat from sticking. Allow to cool, remove any accumulated fat, and reheat to serve. Makes 6 servings (295 calories per QWL serving, meat only).

Seasoned Lamb Steaks

4 lamb steaks, ½ inch thick   ½ teaspoon salt
   (1½ pounds, total)   ⅛ teaspoon paprika
½ teaspoon crushed mint

Trim off all possible visible fat from steaks. Mix the mint, salt and paprika, and rub mixture well into tops and bottoms of steaks. Place steaks on broiler rack about 3 inches from heat, and broil about 8 minutes on one side. Turn and broil about 8 minutes or less on other side, or until steaks are done and still juicy. Makes 4 servings (230 calories per serving).

Curried Lamb Chunks

1½ pounds boneless lamb,   1 tablespoon minced onion
   all possible visible fat re-   or onion flakes
   moved, and cut in   1 teaspoon salt
   1-inch cubes   Coarse pepper
2 tablespoons beef bouillon,   1 bay leaf
   double-strength   1 teaspoon curry powder
1 cup water

In no-stick skillet, heat the bouillon, then brown the lamb chunks lightly. Mix all other ingredients in the water, pour all over the lamb in the skillet, cover and cook slowly for about an hour or until meat is tender to the fork. Makes 4 servings (330 calories per serving).

Lamb Steak Kabobs

QWL dieters eat meat only

1 pound lamb steak, cut in
¾-inch cubes, all visible
fat removed
2 tablespoons grated onion
3 tablespoons lemon juice

½ teaspoon salt
3 slices canned pineapple,
packed in its own juice
⅓ pound small
mushrooms, stems removed

Mix together onion, lemon juice and salt and marinate in this mixture for at least 2 hours, turning meat at least once. Cut pineapple into 1-inch pieces. Alternate lamb, pineapple, and mushroom caps on thin skewers, and broil 3 inches from heat for 12 to 15 minutes, turning occasionally. Makes 4 servings (225 calories per QWL serving).

Herbed Lamb Kabobs

1½ pounds lean boneless
lamb, visible fat trimmed
off, cut in 1-inch cubes
½ cup beef bouillon,
double-strength

1 teaspoon lemon juice
½ teaspoon garlic salt
½ teaspoon rosemary
1 tablespoon fine chopped
parsley flakes

Place lamb cubes slightly separated in shallow baking dish. Combine all other ingredients, mix well, and pour over meat. Let stand about 2 hours at room temperature, turning chunks every ½ hour. Drain off liquid into bowl. String lamb chunks on broiler skewers, separated. Brush with marinade. Broil about 4 inches from heat, turning about every 4 minutes and brushing with marinade, for total of about 15 minutes. Remove from skewers and serve. Makes 4 servings (330 calories per serving).

Glazed Cold Lamb

3 cups cold cooked lamb,   1 cup cold water
   cut into ¾-inch cubes   1 packet instant beef broth
1 tablespoon minced mint   1 tablespoon lemon juice
   leaves
1 envelope unflavored
   gelatin

Remove all visible fat from lamb. Arrange cubes in serving dish. Top with mint.

Soften gelatin in 1 cup cold water. Add instant beef broth and heat, stirring until dissolved (do not boil). Combine with lemon juice and pour over lamb. Chill in refrigerator until jelled. Makes 4 servings (345 calories per serving).

VEAL

Simple Roast Veal

3 pounds boneless rolled   ½ teaspoon coarse black
   veal roast   pepper
1 teaspoon salt   ½ cup chicken broth,
                          double-strength

Remove all visible fat from veal. Rub all over with mixture of the salt and pepper, adding more if desired. Place meat, flattest surface down, on a rack in a shallow roasting pan. Insert meat thermometer into center of roast. Cook in 325° oven 1½ to 2 hours, or until thermometer registers 170° (about 35 minutes per pound). While roasting, brush top and sides of meat occasionally with the double-strength chicken broth to keep meat moist. Serve in thin slices cut with very sharp knife. Makes 8 servings (300 calories per serving).

Juicy Roast Veal

3 pounds rolled lean veal
   roast, all visible fat
   removed
1 teaspoon garlic salt
Paprika

Parsley leaves
Lemon pepper marinade
1 chicken bouillon cube
   1 cup boiling water

Wipe veal with damp cloth; place in baking dish. Rub on all sides with garlic salt, paprika, parsley leaves, and lemon pepper marinade. Dissolve bouillon cube in boiling water and pour over the seasoned veal. Roast in preheated 350° oven 1½ to 2 hours, basting occasionally with pan juices. Turn over after 1 hour of roasting. If liquid cooks away, add more bouillon. Slice to serve. Delicious with a poached egg on each slice (just decrease amount of meat). Makes 8 servings (300 calories per serving).

Mediterranean Veal

2 pounds boneless veal
   rump, all visible fat
   removed, then cut into
   1½ to 2-inch cubes
4 tablespoons no-sugar soy
   sauce
½ teaspoon powdered
   ginger
½ teaspoon anise extract

½ teaspoon Worcestershire
   sauce
1 teaspoon onion salt
¼ teaspoon garlic salt
Artificial sweetening equal
   to 1 teaspoon sugar
½ cup beef bouillon,
   double-strength

Combine the soy sauce with all the seasonings, but not the bouillon. Place the veal in a baking dish and brush the seasoned sauce on all sides of the pieces of meat, then let stand on kitchen counter for ½–1 hour.

Remove the meat and brown all surfaces over high heat in a no-stick skillet. When browned, return meat to the baking dish; slowly pour the bouillon over all pieces. Bake in 350° oven for about 30 to 40 minutes or until meat is tender to the fork. Makes 4 servings (320 calories per serving).

Italian Veal

QWL dieters eat only the veal, no juice or vegetables

1½ pounds lean veal, all visible fat removed, cut in cubes

¾ teaspoon garlic salt

¼ teaspoon lemon pepper marinade

3 fresh green peppers, cut into thin strips

1 small onion, chopped

¾ cup tomato juice

6 ounces Italian plum tomatoes (fresh or canned), cut in halves

3 tablespoons minced parsley

¼ teaspoon oregano

Season veal cubes with garlic salt and lemon pepper marinade, place in shallow pan. Brown under broiler, stirring so all sides brown evenly. Transfer to large no-stick skillet, and add pepper and onion. Cook together for 3 minutes, stirring, then add other ingredients. Cover skillet and cook over low heat for 45 minutes. (If more liquid is needed, add a little tomato juice.) If fat rises to surface while cooking, skim it off. Serve piping hot. Springle a little grated Italian cheese on top if desired. Makes 4 servings (310 calories per QWL serving, meat only).

Veal Scaloppine with Wine Sauce

4 veal scaloppine (1 pound) pounded Italian style

Salt and pepper to taste

2 tablespoons beef bouillon, double-strength

¼ teaspoon garlic salt

¼ cup Marsala wine or sherry wine

2 tablespoons tomato sauce, no oil content

⅛ teaspoon oregano

1 tablespoon chopped parsley

Rub the scaloppine with salt and pepper. Combine the bouillon and garlic salt,, and place in heated no-stick skillet over fairly high flame. Add the scalloppine and brown the meat lightly on both sides.

Meanwhile, in another small skillet, combine the wine, tomato sauce and oregano, and simmer for 5 minutes or more (alcohol evaporates but flavor remains).

Transfer the scalloppine to a hot platter, pour the sauce over the meat, sprinkle on parsley, and serve. Makes 4 servings (210 calories per serving).

Pan Fried Veal Loin Chops

4 loin veal chops, 6 ounces each

½ teaspoon salt

¼ teaspoon black pepper

¼ teaspoon powdered tarragon

½ cup chicken bouillon, double-strength

Trim all visible fat possible from chops. Mix salt, pepper, and tarragon, and rub well into tops and bottoms of chops. Pan fry over moderate heat in no-stick pan. After browning both sides a little, brush surfaces occasionally with the double-strength bouillon. Cook until meat is done through but still tender to the fork. Makes 4 servings (300 calories per serving).

Egged Veal Cutlets

4 small veal cutlets (4 ounces each)

2 eggs, beaten

¼ teaspoon salt

Black pepper to taste

2 tablespoons chicken bouillon, double-strength

Dip the cutlets in the beaten eggs to which have been added salt and pepper. Coat well on both sides of cutlets. Cover bottom of no-stick baking dish with bouillon, set in the cutlets, pour any remaining egg mixture over cutlets. Place in preheated 350° oven to bake 20 to 25 minutes. Turn cutlets about every 5 minutes until done through but not dry. Makes 4 servings (238 calories per serving).

Veal Scallops and Ham

1 pound veal scallops, all
    visible fat trimmed off
Salt and pepper to taste
1 teaspoon mixed herbs
⅛ pound prosciutto or boiled
    ham, in very thin slices,
    remove all fat possible

1 teaspoon lemon juice
2 tablespoons beef
    bouillon

Pound the veal until flattened, then cut into 4- to
5-inch squares (or rectangles). Season each side with
salt, pepper and mixed herbs. Top each piece with same
size slice of the ham, and fasten together with toothpicks, keeping flat as possible.

Combine bouillon and lemon juice in a large no-stick
skillet. Brown the meat in this mixture for a few minutes, with veal side down. Turn pieces over and brown
ham side for a few minutes until veal is cooked through.
Drain and serve. Makes 4 servings (220 calories per
serving).

Veal-Ham-Cheese Rolls

1 pound lean veal scallops
    4 inches wide, all visible
    fat removed
4 thin slices of lean boiled
    ham (¼ pound), all
    visible fat removed

4 very thin slices of skim
    milk mozzarella cheese
    ¼ cup bouillon
Salt and pepper to taste

On each slice of veal, place a slice of cheese topped
with a slice of ham. Roll and hold the rolls together by
piercing with wooden toothpicks. Dust with salt and
pepper to taste. Brown the rolls in bouillon in no-stick
frying pan over medium heat. When browned, serve
piping hot. Makes 4 servings (230 calories per serving).

Glazed Cold Veal

3 cups cold cooked lean
   veal, cut into cubes
Paprika
1 envelope unflavored
   gelatin

1 cup cold water
1 packet instant beef (or
   vegetable) broth
1 tablespoon lemon juice

Remove all visible fat from veal and place cubes in
serving bowl. Sprinkle with paprika.

Soften gelatin in 1 cup cold water. Add instant broth
and heat, stirring until dissolved. Combine with lemon
juice and pour over veal. Chill in refrigerator until
jelled. Makes 4 servings (310 calories per serving).

Spiced Jellied Veal Loaf

1½ pounds boned veal
   rump, all visible fat
   removed
2 cups water (or more—
   to cover veal)
1 tablespoon finely chopped
   onion (or onion flakes)
2 teaspoons celery salt

¼ teaspoon coarsely
   ground pepper
2 teaspoons pickling spice
¼ teaspoon tarragon
¼ teaspoon basil
2 envelopes unflavored
   gelatin
1 tablespoon minced
   parsley

Place the veal in a heavy saucepan that has a tight
cover. Add all other ingredients except parsley and gelatin. Cover, bring to boil, lower heat and simmer for 1½
hours, or until veal is tender.

Remove the veal, and chill. Chill broth separately,
then skim off all solidified fat. Soften the gelatin in a
little cold water and add to broth. Heat until gelatin is
completely dissolved, about 5 minutes. Chill mixture
until consistency of unbeaten egg white.

Meanwhile, cut veal into thin strips. Fold veal strips
and parsley into thickened gelatin mixture. Turn into
a loaf pan about 6 inches long. Chill until firm, then
unmold gently on serving plate. Makes 4 servings (252
calories per serving).

HAM / PORK / BACON

Open-Baked Ham with Fruit

QWL dieters eat ham only, no fruit

5 pounds (half) ham,
including bone, precooked
or uncooked
Cloves

No-sugar pineapple slices
Drained bottled cherries

Score ham fat in checkerboard squares in shallow cuts with very sharp knife. Make pattern of spaced cloves, and with cherries and pineapple slices fastened with wooden toothpicks. Place ham, fat side up, on rack in roasting pan without any cover. Insert meat thermometer in thickest part of meat, not resting on bone or fat. Roast "precooked" ham in 325° oven about 20 minutes per pound, or until thermometer registers 140°. Roast "uncooked" ham about 25 minutes per pound, or until thermometer registers 160°. QWL dieters don't eat pineapple or cherries, and make sure to trim away every bit of visible fat. Makes 10 servings (390 calories per serving).

Baked Canned Ham

2-pound canned ready-to-eat ham
1½ teaspoons prepared mustard

½ cup orange juice
10–12 whole cloves

Remove ham from can, remove all possible fat. Place ham on rack in small baking pan. Mix mustard thoroughly with orange juice and brush half of it over all sides of ham. Stud top and sides with whole cloves. Bake in preheated 350° oven 10 minutes, then brush rest of orange juice-mustard mixture over top and sides of ham. Bake 15 minutes longer, remove from oven, and slice to serve. Don't use drippings. Remove all possible fat before eating. Makes 6 servings (270 calories per serving).

Ham "Quiche"

4 eggs
2 cups cooked lean ham,
   all visible fat trimmed
   off, diced
8 ounces cottage cheese
1 tablespoon chopped green
   pepper

1 teaspoon chopped chives
   or scallions
½ teaspoon dry mustard
Dash of salt (if ham is
   salty, skip this)

Beat eggs slightly and mix with all other ingredients. Spoon into small casserole or 4 small baking dishes and bake in moderate oven until of custard consistency (about 20 minutes, depending upon size of eggs). Do not overcook. Makes 4 servings (340 calories per serving).

Ham 'n Cheese

½ pound lean slice from center of cooked ham, all
   visible fat carefully removed
1 slice part skim mozarella cheese

Place ham on no-stick cookie sheet. Break up mozarella cheese and dot on top. Broil until ham is hot and cheese melts. Makes 2 servings (230 calories per serving).

Deviled Ham-Tuna Salad Combination

4 ounces finely chopped
   cooked lean ham
6½-ounce can drained
   water-packed tuna, broken
   into small flakes
2 hard-cooked eggs,
   chopped

1 tablespoon dill pickle
   relish
1 teaspoon onion flakes
2 teaspoons lemon juice
½ teaspoon paprika
Allspice
Lemon wedges

Combine all ingredients except last two with a fork. Arrange in 4 mounds, dusting tops lightly with a little allspice, and a lemon wedge alongside each. Makes 4 servings (145 calories per serving).

Marinated Pork Roast

3 pounds boned lean rolled pork roast, all possible fat removed

2 tablespoons no-sugar soy sauce

1 tablespoon white cooking wine

½ cup chicken bouillon, double-strength

1 teaspoon unsweetened ginger powder

1 teaspoon ground rosemary

Mix all ingredients except the meat. Place the roast in a heavy plastic bag, pour the marinade mixture into the bag, and seal tightly so bag is leakproof. Turn the bag several times so that marinade covers all surfaces. Marinate for about 3 hours on kitchen counter, turning bag several times to distribute marinade on all surfaces. Remove meat from bag, place on rack in shallow roasting pan, pouring off marinade into a small bowl. Insert meat thermometer in center of roast, and cook in 325° oven until thermometer registers 170° (about 2½–3 hours). Baste every half hour with marinade. Serve in thin slices. (280 calories per 4-ounce serving.)

Oriental Pork Roast

3 pounds lean pork roast, all possible fat removed

1 teaspoon finely chopped nonsweetened ginger

½ teaspoon granulated artificial sweetener

1 teaspoon rosemary

2 tablespoons no-sugar soy sauce

Place roast on rack in a shallow roasting pan. Cut ½-inch deep slits about 1 inch apart in top of roast. Sprinkle mixture of the ginger, sweetener, and rosemary in each slit. Brush surface (not getting into slits) with some of the soy sauce. Place meat thermometer in center of roast. Without covering, roast in 325° oven until meat thermometer registers 170° (about 2½ hours). Brush meat well with soy sauce about every ½ hour (add another tablespoon of soy sauce if needed for brushing). (260 calories per 4-ounce serving).

Baked Pork Chops

4 lean medium thick pork
   chops, all possible visible
   fat trimmed off
½ teaspoon salt

⅛ teaspoon pepper
1 teaspoon prepared
   mustard
½ cup chicken bouillon

Trim chops of all possible excess fat, and wipe with wet paper towels. Combine the salt, pepper, and mustard, and spread over tops and bottoms of chops. Lightly brown chops in a no-stick pan, or under the broiler. Place in baking casserole and pour in the bouillon. Cover casserole and bake in 375° oven for about 45 minutes or until chops are baked through but tender to the fork. Makes 4 servings (310 calories per serving).

Orange Pork Chops

4 lean pork chops, 1 inch
   thick, all visible fat
   removed
2 chicken bouillon cubes
½ cup boiling water

2 teaspoons prepared
   mustard
½ teaspoon grated orange
   rind

Brown chops in large no-stick skillet. Stir bouillon cubes in boiling water until dissolved and pour over the chops. Cover, and simmer for ¾ hour, basting frequently with juice in pan, or until chops are tender.

Remove chops from pan, pour juice into a bowl. Chill for a few minutes and skim off any fat which comes to the top. Return juice to pan. Stir in mustard and orange rind. Replace chops in pan, bring juice to boil, and serve. Makes 4 servings (235 calories per serving).

Snowcapped Canadian Bacon

12 slices lean Canadian bacon
Mozzarella part skim milk cheese
Paprika

Trim all possible visible fat off bacon. Place slices on broiler rack. Cut thin 1/8-inch slices of cheese into 1-inch squares, and place one square in center of each slice of bacon, then sprinkle lightly with paprika. Broil 5 inches from heat for about 3 minutes. Makes 4 servings (120 calories per serving).

GROUND MEAT

Basic Hamburgers

1 pound lean coarse-ground beef, all visible
  fat removed before grinding
1/2 teaspoon salt*
Dash black pepper*

Add salt and pepper to the meat, distributed evenly with fork, then shape gently into four patties about 3/4 inch thick (don't squeeze meat into close texture lest hamburgers tend to be tough and dry). Broil 3 inches from heat about 4 minutes, then turn patties and broil other side for about 4 more minutes (more or less depending on doneness desired). (To shape patties equal size, form meat into a sausage-like roll about 3 inches in diameter, then cut into 4 equal size slices.) Makes 4 servings (250 calories per serving).

Chili-Beef Burgers

1 pound lean coarse-ground
  beef, all visible fat
  removed before grinding
1 tablespoon minced raw
  onion or onion flakes

2 tablespoons water
2 tablespoons chili sauce
1 teaspoon chili powder

Combine all ingredients (but only 1 tablespoon chili sauce) thoroughly with meat, mixing gently in a bowl.

* You may use 1 teaspoon instant beef bouillon instead of salt and pepper.

Form into 4 patties. Spread other tablespoon chili sauce in no-stick pan. Brown patties about 6 minutes on each side, more or less depending on doneness you prefer. Serve with a little more chili sauce if desired. Makes 4 servings (250 calories per serving).

Italian Meatballs

1 pound lean ground beef, all visible fat removed before grinding
¼ cup beef bouillon, double-strength
1 tablespoon minced parsley
½ teaspoon garlic salt
¼ teaspoon oregano
1 egg slightly beaten
2 tablespoons water

Heat the bouillon in no-stick skillet. Meanwhile combine the meat and all other ingredients, mixing until moisture is absorbed. Form mixture into 1-inch meatballs. Brown meatballs in the skillet over moderate heat, and cook for about 20 minutes, turning meatballs often until cooked through. Makes 4 servings (270 calories per serving).

Miniature Meatballs

QWL dieters eat with a minimum of sauce. These small meatballs also make delicious hors d'oeuvres

1 pound lean ground round, all visible fat removed
1 egg, lightly beaten
2 springs parsley, cut up small
½ small onion, grated
¾ teaspoon seasoned salt, more or less to taste
Black pepper, to taste
Pinch oregano
6 ounces catsup
¾ can beer (low-carbohydrate beer, if available)

Combine first 7 ingredients with fork and form into about 20 tiny meatballs. Combine catsup and beer in saucepan and bring to boiling point. Drop meatballs into catsup and beer sauce and simmer ½ hour. QWL dieters shake off as much sauce as possible before eating meatballs. Eat with fork as main dish; serve hot meat-balls with toothpicks, as hors d'oeuvres. Makes 4 serv-ings, main dish (290 calories per serving).

Tiny Tartare Steak Balls

¾ pound very lean twice-
  ground steak, all visible fat
  removed before grinding
½ teaspoon herb mix salt
Salt (to taste)
⅛ teaspoon freshly ground
  black pepper

1 raw egg, lightly beaten
¼ cup cottage cheese
2 teaspoons pickle relish
2 tablespoons minced
  parsley
Sesame seeds (optional)

Place ground meat in bowl; use fork to blend in all other ingredients except sesame seeds. Keep light and fluffy. Gently roll meatballs between palms of hands, using 1 tablespoon of mixture for each.

Coat balls by rolling over sesame seeds, if you like, or roll in minced parsley.

Serve on toothpicks as main serving or as hors d'oeuvres. If you prefer, cook for a few minutes, rolling balls in no-stick skillet until brown. Or, make patties instead of balls, and cook as you would hamburger meat. Makes 4 servings (210 calories per serving).

Ground Beef Loaf

1 pound ground beef, all
  visible fat removed be-
  fore grinding
1 egg lightly beaten
1 tablespoon minced onion
  or onion flakes
1 tablespoon minced parsley

3 tablespoons beef bouillon,
  double-strength
1 tablespoon catsup
¼ teaspoon salt
¼ teaspoon sage powder
Grated cheese

Combine all ingredients except grated cheese well with a fork, so that moisture is all absorbed in meat. Place the meat in a small no-stick loaf pan. Sprinkle top of meat loaf lightly, with grated cheese. Bake uncovered in 350° oven about an hour until meat is cooked through, but not dried out. Makes 4 servings (280 calories per serving).

Meat Loaf Surprise

Only for TEENAGERS on QWL Diet

1 pound lean ground beef, all visible fat removed before grinding	1 teaspoon garlic salt
	⅛ teaspoon basil
	½ teaspoon paprika
2 tablespoons grated onion	Seasoned pepper (or lemon pepper marinade)
1 raw egg, slightly beaten	Pinch of dried rosemary
⅓ cup skim milk	1 hard-cooked egg
2½ tablespoons chopped parsley	

With fork, gently mix all ingredients except hard-cooked egg. Form into loaf in no-stick baking pan. Open center of loaf and insert hard-cooked egg in lengthwise direction; close again. Bake in 350° oven one hour. When cut for serving, slices of egg will appear in center portions. Makes 4 servings (295 calories per serving).

Chinese Chopped Beef

1 pound lean ground beef, all visible fat removed before grinding	1 tablespoon finely chopped parsley
1 teaspoon grated onion	1 tablespoon no-sugar soy sauce
	¼ cup water
	½ teaspoon garlic salt

Combine all ingredients well in a bowl, then place in a preheated no-stick skillet over moderate heat. Cook to brown, breaking up mixture occasionally with a wooden spatula until thoroughly browned. Serve immediately from skillet or hot serving plate. Makes 4 servings (250 calories per serving).

Chopped Beef-Cheese Patties

1 pound lean ground hamburger meat, all visible fat trimmed from meat before grinding
Salt and pepper to taste
4 tablespoons cottage cheese

1 tablespoon finely minced onion (or parsley)
1 teaspoon sesame seeds
¼ teaspoon paprika

Season the chopped meat with salt and pepper to taste. Form into 8 flat patties. Combine the cottage cheese, onion, sesame seeds, and paprika, and mix together well. Place one-fourth of the cheese mixture flat on a patty, leaving about ⅜ inch of edge of meat uncovered. Place a patty on top of the cheese, and pinch edges of the top and bottom patties together to look like the usual hamburger. Repeat to make 3 more double patties. Broil about 5 inches from heat, and turn after top side is browned. Broil other side to the doneness you prefer. Makes 4 servings (265 calories per serving).

Lamb Burgers

1 pound lean coarse-ground lamb, all visible fat removed before grinding
¼ cup chicken bouillon

½ teaspoon celery salt
½ teaspoon salt
¼ teaspoon crushed mint

Mix spices in bouillon, then, using fork, combine gently with meat, until thoroughly distributed. Form into 4 patties about ½ to ¾ inch thick. Broil about 4 inches from heat for about 8 minutes. Turn patties and broil about 8 minutes more, depending on doneness you prefer. Makes 4 servings (225 calories per serving).

Pickled Lamb Patties

1 pound lean coarse-ground lamb, all visible fat removed before grinding
1 tablespoon chopped raw onion or onion flakes

1 tablespoon chopped parsley
1 tablespoon sweet pickle relish
½ teaspoon salt

Using fork, combine all ingredients gently with meat to distribute thoroughly. Shape into 4 patties. In no-stick pan, cook patties about 8 minutes on one side over moderate heat, then turn and cook about 8 minutes on other side, more or less depending on doneness desired. Makes 4 servings (225 calories per serving).

Ground Lamb Curry

1 pound very lean ground lamb
1 teaspoon grated onion

½ teaspoon curry powder (more or less, to taste)
¾ teaspoon seasoned salt

Combine ingredients together lightly with fork and form into 4 thin patties. Cook in hot no-stick skillet until browned, about 8 minutes on each side. Makes 4 servings (225 calories per serving).

Veal Burgers

1 pound lean coarse-ground veal, all visible fat removed before grinding
1 tablespoon water
1 teaspoon lemon juice
1 tablespoon catsup

¼ teaspoon celery salt
½ teaspoon paprika
¼ teaspoon marjoram
1 egg, slightly beaten
2 tablespoons beef bouillon

Combine all ingredients (except bouillon), stir, then mix gently with the meat. Form into 4 patties. Cook in no-stick pan containing the bouillon for about 6 minutes on each side, a little longer if desired well done. Makes 4 servings (222 calories per serving).

Veal Meat Loaf

1 pound ground lean veal, all possible fat removed before grinding
1 egg, beaten
¾ cup cottage cheese

1 teaspoon onion flakes
1 teaspoon seasoned salt
Black pepper
½ teaspoon basil

Mix veal and egg lightly in bowl with fork. Add cottage cheese, then other ingredients. Transfer to no-stick loaf pan, and bake in preheated 350° oven 45 to 55 minutes, until firm and brown. Makes 4 servings (280 calories per serving).

Ground Ham Loaf

1 pound ground lean ham, all visible fat removed before grinding
1 egg beaten lightly
2 tablespoons chicken bouillon, double-strength

1 tablespoon chili sauce
1 tablespoon minced onion or onion flakes
1 tablespoon minced parsley
12 cloves

Combine all ingredients (except cloves) thoroughly with fork until liquid is absorbed. Place mixture in small no-stick loaf pan. Press cloves into top of loaf, spacing out over surface. Bake uncovered at 350° for about an hour. Makes 4 servings (280 calories per serving).

Ground Pork Loaf

¾ pound ground lean fresh pork, all visible fat removed before grinding
1 egg beaten lightly
2 tablespoons chicken bouillon, double-strength
2 tablespoons chili sauce

½ teaspoon salt
½ teaspoon rosemary
1 tablespoon chopped parsley
1 tablespoon minced onion or onion flakes
½ teaspoon Worcestershire sauce

Combine all ingredients with fork except for 1 tablespoon of the chili sauce. Mix until moisture is all absorbed. Press mixture into small no-stick loaf pan. Spread remaining tablespoon of chili sauce over top of loaf. Bake uncovered in 350° oven about 30 to 40 minutes until cooked through but still moist. Makes 4 servings (250 calories per serving).

VARIETY AND MISCELLANEOUS MEATS

Franks in Bouillon

4 all-beef frankfurters   1 beef bouillon cube or packet
2 cups water   ½ teaspoon prepared mustard

In 2 cups boiling water in saucepan, place bouillon cube or powder, and prepared mustard. Stir well while water is boiling until ingredients are dissolved. Place franks in the boiling water, cover saucepan tightly, and simmer 5 minutes. Serve franks with a little pickle relish. Makes 4 servings (153 calories per serving).

Franks in Barbecue Sauce

4 all-beef frankfurters   1 teaspoon Worcestershire
½ cup water   sauce
3 tablespoons beef bouil-   1 teaspoon wine vinegar
   lon, double-strength   1 teaspoon catsup
1 teaspoon chopped onion   1 tablespoon chili sauce
1 tablespoon chopped   1 teaspoon prepared
   celery   mustard
1 tablespoon chopped   Artificial sweetening equal
   parsley   to 1 teaspoon sugar

Combine all ingredients except frankfurters in saucepan. Cover pan and simmer 15 minutes. Make shallow cuts along each frank about 1 inch apart, place franks in sauce, cover pan, and simmer 15 minutes more. Serve franks complete with sauce. Makes 4 servings (160 calories per serving).

Chili-Flavored Franks

4 all-beef frankfurters   ⅛ teaspoon chili powder
2 slices lean bacon   1½ teaspoons grated onion
½ cup beef bouillon   1 tablespoon chopped parsley
1 tablespoon chili sauce

Cook bacon until very well done, blot with paper towel, crumble bacon into bits. Place bits in saucepan, add all other ingredients except for franks, and stir well to combine thoroughly. Cover pan and simmer 10 minutes. Make shallow cuts along each frank about 1 inch apart, place in sauce, cover pan, and simmer 15 minutes more. Serve franks complete with sauce. Makes 4 servings (180 calories per serving).

Frankfurter Kabobs

4 all-beef frankfurters, cut in 1-inch pieces	1 tablespoon catsup
	1 teaspoon prepared mustard
¼ cup no-sugar soy sauce	1 teaspoon wine vinegar
¼ cup beef bouillon, double-strength	½ teaspoon tarragon

In a shallow broiler pan, combine all ingredients except the franks. Place meat pieces in the marinade. Chill in refrigerator 2 to 3 hours, turning pieces several times to expose all surfaces to marinade. Then place pan about 4 inches from broiler heat for about 8 minutes, turning pieces about every 2 minutes to cover with marinade at each turn. Makes 4 servings (155 calories per serving).

Diced Frankfurter Casserole

4 all-beef frankfurters, diced in about ⅜-inch pieces	1 tablespoon chopped parsley
2 hard-cooked eggs, chopped	1 teaspoon sesame seeds
1 tablespoon chili sauce	1 teaspoon prepared mustard
1 tablespoon sweet pickle relish	Grated cheese

Combine all ingredients well, except cheese, with a fork. Place in a casserole or no-stick baking dish. Sprinkle top surface with a little grated cheese. Bake in 350° oven for about 15 minutes, and serve in casserole dish. Makes 4 servings (200 calories per serving).

Low-Fat Knackwurst

*Knackwurst must be cooked this special way for
QWL dieting*

4 all-beef knackwurst
Water

Pierce a few holes in casing of knackwurst with fork
to allow fat to come out. Place in boiling water to cover
and cook until casings burst open. Remove from water
and split in halves lengthwise. Cook further in no-stick
skillet, open sides down, for about 4 minutes to allow
more fat to escape. Blot with paper towels before serving. Serve with a little prepared mustard. Makes 4
servings (150 calories per serving).

Bologna-Egg Rolls

4 slices bologna
2 hard-cooked eggs, chopped
Salt

Heat bologna in no-stick pan for a few minutes to
cook fat out. Pat dry with paper towel. Add salt to taste
to chopped eggs. Spread egg evenly over the bologna
slices and roll like a jelly-roll. Secure with toothpicks.
Make 2 servings (155 calories per serving).

Dried Beef Combination

8 thin slices dried beef   ½ teaspoon Worcestershire
3 tablespoons cottage cheese   sauce
2 teaspoons chopped chives   Paprika

Combine the cottage cheese, chives, and Worcestershire sauce. Spread ¼ of the mixture on 1 slice of dried
beef, sprinkle lightly with paprika, then cover with another slice of dried beef, and roll up slowly, fastening

well with toothpicks. Make 3 more rolls in the same
way. Makes 4 servings (135 calories per serving).

Herbed Tongue

3 pounds lean beef tongue   ½ teaspoon marjoram
3 quarts water   ¼ teaspoon paprika
12 cloves   1 teaspoon celery salt
10 black peppercorns   ¼ cup wine vinegar
4 bay leaves

Place tongue in 3 quarts water in heavy pot with a
tight cover. Add all other ingredients to water and stir
well. Cover pot, bring to boil and then simmer for 3
hours (1 hour per pound). Plunge cooked tongue into
very cold water, trim off all visible fat, including gristle
from end, then slit skin with very sharp knife from end
to tip, and pull off skin. Cut thin slices. QWL dieters
trim off any remaining skin and visible fat. Makes 4
servings per pound (280 calories per serving).

Tongue Roll-Ups

For QWL TEEN dieters only, contains yogurt

¼ pound lean tongue (or   1 tablespoon yogurt (or
  lean ham, fewer calories),   buttermilk)
  sliced into 8 slices (1   Salt
  ounce each)   Lemon pepper marinade
2 hard-cooked eggs, chopped

(QWL adult dieters use, instead of yogurt, 1 tablespoon
creamed cottage cheese and 1 teaspoon water.)

Separate slices of tongue and remove all possible fat.
Lay slices flat side by side on wax paper. Mash together
chopped eggs and yogurt, seasoned to taste with salt
and lemon pepper marinade, using fork. Spread each
slice of tongue with egg mixture, roll up slices and
secure with toothpicks. Makes 4 servings (100 calories
per serving).

Sautéed Liver

QWL dieters eat liver only

1 pound calves' liver, thinly sliced	Black pepper
2 tablespoons chicken bouillon, double-strength	2 tablespoons dry white wine
1 large onion, sliced thin	3 tablespoons parsley, minced
1 teaspoon salt	½ teaspoon celery salt

Heat bouillon in no-fat skillet and add sliced onions. Cook slowly until onions are soft and transparent. Turn heat high, add liver, salt and pepper. Cook for 2 minutes, stirring with spoon. Add wine, parsley, and celery salt, stir and cook 3 minutes longer, or until liver is cooked to your liking. Serve immediately. Makes 3 servings (165 calories per QWL serving, meat only).

Southern Calves Liver

QWL dieters eat only the liver

1 pound calves liver, sliced with skin removed	3 tablespoons minced onion
4 tablespoons beef bouillon	½ teaspoon seasoned salt
1 large can peeled tomatoes	Black pepper

Brown liver slices in beef bouillon, using no-stick skillet over a high flame. Cook tomatoes, onion, salt and pepper together for 15 minutes. Add to liver and simmer covered for 15 minutes, remove cover and simmer further, if necessary, until liver is just tender but not bloody. Makes 4 servings (170 calories per QWL serving, meat only).

Liver Julienne

1 pound beef or calves liver, cut into strips about ½ inch wide, 2½ inches long

¼ cup beef bouillon, double-strength

1 egg

Combine egg and beef bouillon, whipping lightly until thoroughly mixed. Place mixture in shallow dish or pan with liver strips. Let liver sit for about 3 minutes, then turn over, and leave another 3 minutes. Pour into preheated no-stick skillet, and cook over moderate heat about 3 minutes. Turn over pieces with wooden spatula, and cook about 2 minutes more on other side, turning if necessary to brown all over. Makes 4 servings (178 calories per serving).

Baked Sweetbreads

1 pound lamb or calf sweet- breads (2 pairs)	1 egg
Water to cover	1 tablespoon chopped parsley
1 teaspoon lemon juice	Celery salt to taste
1 tablespoon salt	Rosemary to taste
	Lemon wedges

Soak sweetbreads in very cold water for 1 hour in a saucepan containing water to cover, lemon juice, and salt, and simmer for 20 minutes. Plunge into cold water to chill. Remove any fibrous parts or skin and cut into 4 portions.

Add 1 tablespoon water to the egg and whip lightly with a fork, then dip sweetbreads into the egg to cover all sides. Place in shallow no-stick baking pan, and bake about 35 minutes in 400° oven. Sprinkle tops with parsley, celery salt, and rosemary (optional), and serve with lemon wedges or adding fresh lemon juice on sweetbreads if desired. Makes 4 servings (135 calories per serving).

Variation: Prepare as above, slice, dip into egg mixture, and sauté in no-stick pan 5 to 6 minutes on each side. Sprinkle minced parsley and onion over tops, season to taste.

BARBECUED MEAT OVER OPEN FIRE

Barbecued Steak over Fire

1½ pounds steak, no bone, ¾ inch thick; all visible fat removed

Barbecue Sauce

½ cup water	1 tablespoon finely chopped
¼ cup lemon juice	parsley
1 clove garlic, sliced	1 teaspoon tarragon
1 tablespoon finely	1 teaspoon rosemary
chopped onion	

Prepare barbecue sauce by mixing all ingredients well and letting stand overnight preferably (if any left over, can keep in refrigerator in covered container for later use).

Brush both sides of steak liberally with barbecue sauce. Place steak on grill over very hot fire. Cook steak on one side until top appears lukewarm to fingertip touch; brush steak liberally with sauce several times while broiling. Turn steak over, brush well with sauce. Cook 1 minute for rare, 2 to 3 minutes for medium, 4 or more minutes for well done. Slice and serve. Barbecue sauce can also be used on hamburgers, lamb, veal. Makes 4 servings (340 calories per serving).

London Broil over Fire

2 pounds London Broil	1 clove garlic, peeled
(flank steak)	2 tablespoons beef bouillon,
Meat tenderizer	double-strength

Remove any visible fat from steak. Apply meat tenderizer about 1 hour before broiling, and let sit on kitchen counter. Just before cooking, crush garlic clove and rub into all surfaces of steak thoroughly. Brush all surfaces liberally with the bouillon. Broil about 5 min-

utes on one side, then about same time on other side, a
little longer on each side if you prefer medium rather
than rare. Slice thinly and slantwise across the grain
with a very sharp knife. Serve with steak barbecue sauce
(Barbecued Steak recipe) if desired. Makes 8 servings
(220 calories per serving).

Barbecued Hamburger over Fire

1 pound lean ground beef,   1 tablespoon finely
  all visible fat trimmed off   chopped parsley
  before grinding   2 tablespoons catsup or
1 tablespoon finely chopped   chili sauce
  onion

Use steak barbecue sauce (recipe given with Barbecued
  Shish Kabobs)

Mix all ingredients except last with the chopped
meat, and form into 4 thick patties. Place on grill over
hot fire. As soon as juice starts to appear on top of patties, turn them over, then brush tops liberally with barbecue sauce. Turn patties every few minutes and repeat
brushing with sauce. Keep checking doneness with a
fork, usually about 10 minutes or less for rare, to 15
minutes or more for well done. Makes 4 servings (250
calories per serving).

Barbecued Franks over Fire

4 large all-beef frankfurters   1 tablespoon very finely
½ cup beef bouillon,   minced green pepper
  double-strength   ¼ teaspoon rosemary
1 tablespoon no-sugar soy   ½ teaspoon prepared
  sauce   mustard
1 tablespoon very finely
  minced onion

Mix all the ingredients except frankfurters in a shallow pan, then heat, simmering covered for about 10
minutes. Score the frankfurters with shallow cuts about

1 inch apart, and place in sauce (not over heat) with cuts soaking in the marinade. Turn franks in sauce after 15 minutes and keep in the marinade for another 15 minutes. Place franks on grill over coals (meanwhile simmering the sauce) and cook through, turning occasionally, until done to your liking but not at all black. Serve franks covered with the heated sauce. Makes 4 servings (170 calories per serving).

Barbecued Beef/Lamb Shish Kabobs over Fire

QWL dieters eat meat only

1 pound 1½-inch cubes top round beef or lamb, all visible fat trimmed off before cutting into cubes

Barbecue Sauce

¼ cup beef bouillon, double-strength	1 teaspoon dried mint
	1 teaspoon onion juice
2 tablespoons dry sherry wine	1 teaspoon oregano
¼ teaspoon pepper	1 teaspoon salt
1 teaspoon tarragon	1 garlic clove, in thin slices

Mix all ingredients of sauce, and marinate all surfaces of meat cubes in the sauce in refrigerator 4 hours or more. String cubes on skewer, close together for rare, with spaces between cubes for well done. Place over low fire, turning about every 5 minutes and brushing surfaces with sauce. Check for doneness by slitting into cube with a very sharp knife—usually takes about 20 minutes or less for rare, to 30 minutes or more for well done. Separate cubes with pieces of tomatoes, onions, mushrooms, and zucchini, for those not on QWL Diet. Makes 4 servings (230 calories per QWL serving, meat only).

Barbecued Lamb Chops over Fire

4 medium lamb chops (or lamb shoulder steaks)

Barbecue Sauce

½ cup water
¼ cup lemon juice
2 teaspoons mixed herbs
1 teaspoon dried mint
1 teaspoon finely chopped parsley

1 teaspoon finely chopped onion
1 garlic clove, in thin slices
¼ teaspoon celery salt

Mix barbecue sauce ingredients well, and let chops stand in it in refrigerator overnight, or at least for a few hours.

Trim all visible fat from meat. Broil slowly over a low fire. Keep turning every 5 to 10 minutes, brushing surfaces with sauce every time you turn meat over. Cook for about 35 minutes, less if you prefer lamb pink in the middle. Makes 4 servings (225 calories per serving).

Barbecued Veal Chops over Fire

4 medium veal chops (or veal steaks)
Barbecue cause (use bottled no-sugar sauce, or make your own using recipe given for pork)

Trim all visible fat from the meat. Broil slowly over a low fire, never a high, hot flame. Keep turning about every 10 minutes, and brush tops liberally with barbecue sauce every time you turn. Cook for about 35 minutes or less for juicy meat (less greasy than lamb or pork). Makes 4 servings (260 calories per serving).

Barbecued Pork Chops over Fire

4 medium lean pork chops (or pork shoulder steaks), about ½ inch thick

Barbecue Sauce

½ cup water
¼ cup chicken bouillon, double-strength
1 tablespoon lemon juice
1 tablespoon finely chopped onion

1 teaspoon mixed herbs
⅛ teaspoon cayenne (red pepper)
½ teaspoon garlic salt

First prepare barbecue sauce by mixing all ingredients thoroughly. Let chops stand in sauce overnight in refrigerator, or at least for a few hours (keep any leftover sauce in a closed container in refrigerator for future use).

Trim all fat possible off meat. Broil very slowly over a low fire for cooking clear through, dousing any flare-ups in a hurry. Keep turning every 5 or 10 minutes. After first 20 minutes, as meat turns brown, baste liberally with barbecue sauce each time you turn meat. Test with fork—should be juicy-tender in less than an hour. Makes 4 servings (310 calories per serving).

Barbecued Liver over Fire

1 pound beef or calves liver, 4 pieces, about ½ inch thick
¼ cup beef bouillon, double-strength

Brush both sides of liver liberally with bouillon. Broil over low open fire (never high, hot flames) for about 5 minutes on one side, then brush top side with bouillon again and turn pieces over. Broil on other side about 5 minutes again, but check midway, by a slit with a very sharp knife, to make sure center meat is pink and juicy, as liver tends to become tough and dry if overdone. Makes 4 servings (165 calories per serving).

POULTRY

Tasty Chicken Breasts

2 boned chicken breasts
(total about 1½ pounds),
skin removed and all
fat scraped off
3 tablespoons chicken
bouillon
½ teaspoon monosodium
glutamate (optional)

½ teaspoon salt
¼ teaspoon ground sage
1 teaspoon tarragon
2 tablespoons dry vermouth
2 thin slices lemon
2 tablespoons chopped
parsley

Cut chicken breasts into strips. Sauté strips in no-stick skillet in bouillon. Add monosodium glutamate, salt, sage, and tarragon. Cook at high heat, stirring occasionally, for 5 minutes. Add vermouth and lemon slices, cover and cook 5 minutes longer. Sprinkle with parsley and serve. Makes 4 servings (255 calories per serving).

Broiler Barbecued Chicken

QWL dieters don't eat skin

1 broiler-fryer (about
3 pounds), cut in pieces
¼ cup tomato juice
¾ cup chicken bouillon
1 tablespoon wine vinegar
1 teaspoon prepared mustard
2 tablespoons minced raw
onion or onion flakes

1 teaspoon Worcestershire
sauce
Pepper sauce, 2 dashes
½ teaspoon salt
⅛ teaspoon pepper
⅛ teaspoon paprika
Artificial sweetening equal
to 1 tablespoon sugar

On rack in preheated broiler pan, place chicken pieces skin side down. In a bowl, combine all other ingredients, and mix well. Brush the marinade liberally over the chicken. Broil about 8 inches from heat 20 minutes, brushing often with sauce. Turn over, brush well and frequently while broiling 20 minutes more, or until chicken is well-browned and tender (don't let dry out). May also be broiled on outdoor barbecue, over low fire. Makes 4 servings (290 calories per QWL serving).

Broiled Breasts of Chicken

2 large boned chicken breasts (total about 1½ pounds)	1 packet instant chicken broth
	2 tablespoons onion flakes
2 teaspoons fresh tarragon, minced (or ½ teaspoon dried)	½ teaspoon mixed herbs
	1 cup boiling water
	2 teaspoons parsley minced
2 tablespoons brandy	

Soak tarragon in brandy overnight, remove, and drain until dry. Cook together instant broth, onion flakes, mixed herbs and water, until about half has boiled away.

Divide chicken breasts in halves lengthwise (skin removed) and arrange in broiling pan. Sprinkle with brandied tarragon and broth mixture. Broil 3 inches from heat in preheated oven until chicken is golden, brushing occasionally with sauce. Turn over and brown the other side, first brushing with sauce from pan. Top servings with a little minced parsley. Makes 4 servings (275 calories per serving).

Roast Chicken

QWL dieters must remove skin before eating

1 whole 3-pound frying chicken (or very lean roasting chicken)	Fresh ground pepper
	Juice of 1 lemon
	1 teaspoon seasoned salt
½ teaspoon dry mixed herbs	½ cup seasoned white cooking wine
¼ teaspoon garlic powder	

Wash chicken and dry thoroughly with paper towels, inside and out. Mix herbs, garlic powder, and a pinch of pepper together and rub on outer surfaces of chicken. Sprinkle a little pepper, lemon juice, and salt into cavities of chicken. Tie legs together. Place seasoned chicken on a rack in roasting pan and brush wine over surfaces. Roast in preheated 350° oven for 1 hour, basting frequently with wine and any pan juices which may accumulate. Don't let surface of chicken dry out. Test for doneness, and if necessary roast a little longer. Makes 4 servings (300 calories per serving).

Chicken Roasted in "See-Through Bag"

QWL dieters remove skin before eating

3-pound fryer or lean   1 small onion, cut up
   roasting chicken   1 rib celery, cut up
Garlic powder   Salt
½ apple, cut up

Wash chicken and remove skin from neck. Sprinkle a little garlic powder on inside and outside surfaces of chicken. Mix apple, onion, and celery, and stuff with neck into cavity.

Slide stuffed chicken into a "see-through bag for oven cooking," tie bag, and punch holes in it according to instructions on bag package. Place on rack in shallow baking pan and roast at 400° for 1 to 1¼ hours, until brown. Remove from bag. Discard apple and vegetables, and sprinkle inside and outside of chicken with salt. Makes 4 servings (290 calories per QWL serving).

Simple Broiled Chicken

*QWL dieters remove skin and all visible fat
before eating*

2 broiler-fryer chickens,   ⅛ teaspoon garlic powder
   ready-to-cook, about   Pepper
   1½ pounds each   Paprika
¼ cup chicken bouillon,
   double-strength

Split broilers in half lengthwise (or have butcher split them). Brush all surfaces liberally with bouillon seasoned with the garlic and pepper to taste. Place in broiler pan about 5 inches from heat, skin side down. Broil 15 to 20 minutes until browned lightly, brushing twice with seasoned bouillon. Turn over and broil 15 to 20 minutes more (brushing twice with bouillon) until browned to your taste (check by slitting with sharp knife at a joint). Makes 4 servings (285 calories per serving).

Baked Chicken Parmesan

1 broiler or fryer (about 2½ pounds), cut up	½ teaspoon sage
Salt, to taste	1 cup chicken broth
Pepper, to taste	Grated Italian Parmesan cheese

Wash and skin chicken parts, removing all possible fat. Season both sides sparingly with salt and pepper. Place parts in shallow casserole or baking pan, and sprinkle with sage. Brush liberally with broth, tops and bottoms. Sprinkle a little cheese lightly over tops. Bake 1 hour or less, depending on size, until chicken is brown and cooked through. Brush with more broth occasionally while baking. Makes 4 servings (260 calories per serving).

Herbed Baked Chicken

1 quartered broiler-fryer, about 2½ pounds	⅛ teaspoon dried crushed thyme
1 lemon, in halves	Salt and pepper to taste
⅛ teaspoon dried crushed basil	

In shallow baking pan, squeeze ½ lemon over chicken quarters. Sprinkle with half the basil and thyme, season with salt and pepper. In preheated 400° oven, bake uncovered 40 minutes, basting occasionally. Turn chicken over, squeeze other ½ lemon, and sprinkle remaining

basil and thyme over quarters. Add salt and pepper.
Bake 30 minutes more or until chicken is tender. Makes
4 servings (250 calories per serving).

Roman Baked Chicken

QWL dieters eat only the chicken

1 3-pound fryer chicken,
cut in 8 parts, skin re-
moved, fat scraped off
¼ cup chicken bouillon
1 teaspoon seasoned salt
½ teaspoon oregano

½ teaspoon paprika
2 sprigs parsley, chopped
1 medium onion, sliced
2 tomatoes, sliced
1 package frozen sliced
zucchini, partially defrosted

Place chicken pieces in shallow baking dish, brush
with bouillon, and brown both sides 3 inches from
broiler heat. Keep moist by brushing pan juice over tops
occasionally. Remove from broiler, sprinkle tops and
bottoms with salt, oregano, and paprika. Add parsley,
sliced onion, tomatoes, and zucchini, and bake in preheated moderate (350°) oven for 1 hour. Makes 4 servings (290 calories per QWL serving, chicken only).

Baked Ginger Chicken

QWL dieters eat only the chicken

2½-pound fryer chicken,
cut in eighths
1 clove garlic, crushed
(optional)
½ teaspoon salt
½ teaspoon paprika
1 bay leaf (remove before
serving)
1 teaspoon parsley flakes
6 peppercorns (remove
before serving)

1 teaspoon onion powder,
or instant minced onion
4 ounces tomato juice
¾ teaspoon powdered ginger
3 celery ribs, cut crosswise
in ½-inch pieces
5 small or 3 large carrots,
cut crosswise in ½-inch
pieces

Remove skin and all visible fat from chicken pieces and arrange in bottom of no-stick baking dish. Top with garlic, salt, paprika, bay leaf, parsley, peppercorns, onion, tomato juice, and ginger. Bake in 350° oven for 1 hour, covered. Add celery and carrots, and bake uncovered about ½ hour longer. Do not allow chicken to dry out. Makes 4 servings (240 calories per serving).

Lemon Chicken

3 pounds broiler chicken thighs and/or breasts
Seasoned salt
Paprika
2 halves of a small lemon
1½ ounces part skim milk mozzarella cheese

Wash chicken parts, removing all skin and scraping off fat. Place in shallow pan and sprinkle with seasoned salt and paprika. Squeeze ½ lemon over tops and place in preheated broiler 3 inches from heat.

After 5 minutes pick up juice from pan with basting brush and moisten chicken.

Broil 5 minutes more, brush again, and turn chicken over. Sprinkle with seasoned salt and paprika, squeeze other ½ lemon over chicken and broil until chicken is brown. Remove chicken from broiler, brush with juice again, and cover with dots of mozzarella cheese. Place in 350° preheated oven, and bake 10 minutes. Do not allow to dry out. Makes 4 servings (295 calories per serving).

Sauterne Chicken

8 chicken thighs and drumsticks (about 2½ pounds)
½ cup sauterne
1 tablespoon minced chives
1 tablespoon minced fresh parsley
½ teaspoon salt
Black pepper
Paprika
Caraway seeds

Remove skin from chicken. Place in bowl, pour wine over it, and refrigerate 3 or 4 hours, turning every ½ hour or so. Lift chicken from wine, and make a sauce of wine, chives and parsley. Sprinkle salt, pepper, and paprika over chicken parts. Place in baking pan, moisten with wine mixture, and bake uncovered in preheated 450° oven for 25 minutes, basting frequently with wine sauce. Turn chicken over, bake 20 minutes longer, keeping moist with wine. Sprinkle caraway seeds over each serving.

(*Note*: 1½-pound boned chicken breasts may be prepared the same way.) Makes 4 servings (250 calories per serving).

Chicken Neapolitan

2½-pound broiler-fryer chicken, quartered, all skin removed and fat scraped off
1 teaspoon butter-flavored salt
⅛ teaspoon black pepper
2 teaspoons oregano flakes
¼ cup lemon juice
½ teaspoon garlic powder
2 tablespoons chopped parsley
2 thin slices part skim mozzarella cheese
Paprika

Rub butter-flavored salt and black pepper into chicken quarters. Moisten chicken, using brush, with combined oregano, lemon juice, garlic powder and parsley. Let sit for 30 minutes. Broil 6 inches from heat 15 to 20 minutes on each side until brown and tender. Brush with pan juice occasionally to prevent drying out. When almost done, dot with mozzarella cheese and continue broiling until cheese melts. Sprinkle a little paprika on top before serving, if desired. Makes 4 servings (280 calories per serving).

Italian Chicken

QWL dieters eat only the chicken

2½-pound broiler-fryer chicken, skin removed and fat scraped off, cut in 8 parts
½ teaspoon oregano
½ teaspoon paprika
4 tablespoons chicken bouillon
2 medium onions, chopped
2 teaspoons garlic salt
½ cup tomato juice
1 bay leaf, crushed
2 green peppers, cut into thin strips
½ pound fresh mushrooms, sliced, or 2 cans sliced mushrooms, drained and butter removed

Rub oregano and paprika into chicken pieces. Moisten bottom of large no-stick skillet with bouillon, and simmer onions and garlic for 5 minutes. Add seasoned chicken, raise flame and brown on all sides. Add tomato juice, bay leaf, pepper strips, and mushrooms. Cook covered over low heat for 1 hour. (If more liquid is needed, add a little tomato juice.) Sprinkle with a little grated Italian cheese if desired. Makes 4 servings (240 calories per QWL serving, chicken only).

Chicken in Red Wine

QWL dieters remove skin before eating chicken

1 3-pound fryer chicken, cut into serving pieces
¾ teaspoon seasoned salt
⅛ teaspoon black pepper
2 tablespoons chicken bouillon
½ teaspoon dried tarragon
¼ teaspoon crushed dried basil
2 tablespoons chopped parsley
1 tablespoon grated onion
¾ cup dry red wine

Sprinkle salt and pepper over chicken pieces and place side by side in narrow baking dish. Mix together bouillon, tarragon, basil, parsley, and onion, and spread over chicken. Pour wine into bottom of dish so it covers part of chicken. Bake uncovered in 375° preheated oven for 50 minutes, or until chicken is browned and tender. Baste occasionally with juice from bottom of baking dish. Makes 4 servings (285 calories per QWL serving).

Hawaiian Chicken

QWL dieters eat chicken only

3-pound fryer chicken, cut into eight pieces
1 teaspoon seasoned salt
2 teaspoons paprika
½ teaspoon crushed oregano
⅛ teaspoon black pepper

¼ cup double-strength chicken bouillon
½ cup water
1 can (13 ounce) pineapple chunks in their own juice (no sugar added)

Mix salt, paprika, oregano, and pepper. Wash chicken and remove skin, scraping off fat, and rub with mixed seasonings. Place in shallow pan. Sprinkle bouillon over top, just enough to moisten. Broil 4 inches from heat in preheated broiler. Occasionally brush with pan juice or more bouillon to prevent drying until chicken is brown. Turn over and brown other side, again brushing with bouillon to keep surface moist.

Reduce oven heat to 350°. Add water to pan and bake tightly covered, until chicken is tender (about 20 minutes). Drain pineapple, and add chunks to chicken. Cover again and bake 10 minutes longer, until pineapple is heated through. Makes 4 servings (310 calories per QWL serving—chicken only).

Spiced Boiled Chicken

QWL dieters eat chicken only, no vegetable, no skin or visible fat

1 3-pound broiling chicken, cut in serving size pieces, skin removed
1 small onion, quartered
1 celery rib with leaves, cut in 1-inch pieces
2 carrots, scraped and cut in ½-inch discs

8 peppercorns
½ teaspoon thyme
2 cloves
⅛ teaspoon paprika
Salt and pepper to taste
4 chicken bouillon cubes
6 cups water (to cover chicken)

In a saucepan, combine the chicken and all other ingredients and bring to a boil, then turn down flame to simmer 45 minutes or until chicken is tender, skimming off all possible foam and fat. Allow to cool, remove fat from top; reheat to serve. Makes 4 servings (290 calories per QWL serving—chicken and clear soup only).

Chicken Cacciatore

QWL dieters eat only the chicken

1 3-pound frying chicken, cut in eighths	1 teaspoon oregano
3 tablespoons chicken bouillon or broth	¾ teaspoon dried basil
	¾ teaspoon garlic salt
1 can (15 ounce) tomato sauce	¼ teaspoon pepper
1 can (1 pound 12 ounces) whole tomatoes, with juice	3 tablespoons minced parsley
1 can (6 ounce) tomato paste	½ pound fresh mushrooms, sliced (or 1 6-ounce can sliced mushrooms, drained)
½ cup dry red wine	

Arrange chicken pieces on flat no-stick broiler pan and brush with some of the bouillon. Brown 3 inches from flame, turn over, brush with bouillon again, and brown other side. Remove from broiler.

Simmer all other ingredients together in a large saucepan for 10 minutes. Then stir in browned chicken pieces. Cover, and simmer 45 minutes, or until chicken is tender, stirring occasionally. QWL dieters remove skin from chicken before eating, and don't eat vegetables or sauce. Makes 4 servings (295 calories per QWL serving).

Cold Chicken with Bacon Sauce

4 ounces white meat of cold chicken, sliced	1 tablespoon water
½ cup cottage cheese	2 strips lean bacon, well done and crumbled
1 teaspoon salad cheese (available in shaker top jars)	

Arrange chicken slices on serving plate. Process cottage cheese, salad cheese and water in blender (use small blender jar if you have one) until smooth. Add crumbled bacon to this mixture and spoon over chicken slices. Serve chilled. Makes 1 serving (350 calories per serving).

Herbed Chicken Fricassee

QWL dieters eat the chicken only, not any skin

3-pound frying chicken, cut in serving size pieces
¼ cup dry white wine
1 tablespoon wine vinegar
1 clove garlic, crushed
⅛ teaspoon saffron
1 teaspoon mixed herbs

1 large onion chopped
2 tablespoons chicken bouillon
1 egg yolk
1 tablespoon lemon juice
2 tablespoons chopped parsley

Combine wine, vinegar, herbs and seasonings, and pour over chicken pieces in a bowl. Let chicken marinate in the sauce on kitchen counter for about an hour, spooning pieces with sauce several times.

In a heavy casserole, cook the chopped onion in the bouillon until tender and browned a little. Place the chicken and remaining sauce in casserole with the onion. Cover and cook over medium heat for about 40 minutes or until done, stirring a few times while cooking.

Mix the egg yolk with lemon juice and chopped parsley, and distribute evenly over the chicken in the casserole. Heat over low flame for about 5 more minutes and serve right from casserole. Makes 4 servings (320 calories per QWL serving).

Simple Chicken (or Turkey) Livers

4 chicken livers (4 ounces)
Lemon pepper marinade (or seasoned salt), to taste

Wash and separate livers, removing any visible fat. Pat dry with paper towel. Sprinkle seasoning in bottom of no-stick skillet. Heat pan for 30 seconds, then put in livers. Sauté over medium flame for 3 minutes, then turn livers over. Sprinkle very lightly with seasoning, if desired. Sauté 2 to 3 minutes longer, until insides of livers are no longer red. (May be served with a little catsup, chili sauce, or a QWL sauce or dressing.) Makes 1 serving (145 calories per serving).

Variations: May use with eggs as omelet, whole livers or cut up. Or, after removing from pan, top livers with a few dots of part skim mozzarella cheese and place under broiler in broiling pan briefly until cheese melts, then sprinkle on a little paprika for color, if desired.

Note: Chicken livers are excellent to use often on QWL Diet, as they're very low in calories as well as delicious.

Seasoned Chicken Livers

1¼ pounds chicken livers
¾ teaspoon seasoned salt
Black pepper
2 tablespoons minced onion
1 tablespoon minced parsley
½ teaspoon dried tarragon
4 tablespoons chicken or onion broth

Wash livers and pat dry with paper towels. Cut in half and remove membrane and any fat. Sprinkle with salt, pepper, onion, parsley, and tarragon.

Heat broth in large no-stick skillet and sauté seasoned livers in it about 8 minutes, turning occasionally; maintain as high heat as possible without burning. Check for doneness before serving. Makes 4 servings (185 calories per serving).

Lemon Chicken Liver Broil

1 pound fresh or frozen chicken livers (if frozen, thaw before cooking)
Seasoned salt
½ lemon, or 2 tablespoons white cooking wine

Separate livers from center membrane, removing fat. Wash gently and dry on paper toweling. Place in very shallow no-stick pan, sprinkling both sides with seasoned salt. Squeeze juice of ½ lemon over livers and cook in preheated broiler 3 inches from heat for 5 minutes until browned. Brush pan juice over liver once during broiling. Turn livers over, brush again with juice, broil 5 minutes longer. Peek inside one to make sure they are done. Don't overcook. Makes 4 servings (155 calories per serving).

Snowtopped Chicken Livers

1 pound fresh chicken livers or 1 pound frozen chicken livers, thawed
Seasoned salt
Pepper
Juice of ½ lemon
4 ounces cottage cheese
Lemon pepper marinade
⅛ teaspoon garlic salt
Paprika (optional)

Cut livers in two, removing membrane and fat from centers. Wash gently, and pat dry with paper towels. Sprinkle with seasoned salt and pepper. Place in shallow no-stick pan and squeeze lemon juice over them. Broil 3 inches from heat in preheated broiler 5 minutes, brushing once with pan juice. Repeat on other sides, broil 3 minutes.

With fork, mix a little lemon pepper marinade and garlic salt into cottage cheese. Spread cheese over tops of livers, return to broiler for 3 minutes. Sprinkle paprika on top for color, if you wish. Makes 4 servings (180 calories per serving).

Chicken Liver-Steak Kabobs

½ pound lean sirloin steak, all visible fat removed
½ pound chicken livers
½ cup lemon juice
½ teaspoon garlic salt
½ tablespoon onion, grated

Mix lemon juice, garlic salt, and onion in bowl. Separate chicken livers, removing membrane and fat in centers. Cut steak into 1-inch cubes. Marinate livers and steak in lemon juice mixture for 2 hours or more on counter top. Alternate liver halves and steak cubes on 4 skewers, place on aluminum foil in preheated broiler pan 2 inches from heat, and broil 4 to 5 minutes on each side, brushing with marinade when turning. Makes 4 servings (205 calories per serving).

Scrambled Eggs with Chicken Livers

¼ pound chicken livers
Salt and pepper
3 tablespoons white cooking wine

6 large eggs or 7 medium
¼ teaspoon seasoned salt
Pinch of dried dill

Wash livers and pat dry. Cut them apart and remove fat and center membranes. Sprinkle with salt and pepper, place in no-stick skillet and sprinkle wine over them. Cook over medium heat until no blood runs out when pierced with fork, brushing occasionally with juice in pan (about 5 minutes).

Beat eggs, adding seasoned salt and dill. Cut livers in half once more (don't scratch finish in pan) and pour eggs over them. Cook, stirring occasionally, until eggs are scrambled "wet" or "dry," to your taste. Makes 4 servings (170 calories per serving).

Chicken Liver Paté

1¼ pounds chicken livers
2 tablespoons chicken broth
3 hard-cooked eggs
2 teaspoons grated onion

1 raw egg, beaten
¾ teaspoon salt
Pepper

Wash livers, pat dry with paper towels, and separate halves, removing membrane and fat. Using no-stick skillet, cook livers in broth for 15 minutes. Grind livers and hard-cooked eggs together. Combine this mixture with onion, raw egg, and salt and pepper. Serve chilled. Makes 4 servings (265 calories per serving).

Chicken (or Turkey) "Quiche"

2 cups cooked chicken
  (or turkey), diced
4 eggs
8 ounces cottage cheese

2 sprigs fresh parsley, chopped
½ teaspoon seasoned salt
Dash black pepper

Beat eggs slightly and mix with all other ingredients. Spoon into small casserole and bake uncovered at 350° until of custard consistency (about 20 minutes or more depending on size of eggs). Top with a sprinkle of paprika before serving, if you wish. Makes 4 servings (295 calories per serving).

Glazed Cold Chicken (or Turkey)

3 cups cold cooked chicken
  (or turkey), cut into
  cubes after all skin and
  visible fat removed
1 envelope unflavored gelatin

1 cup cold water
1 packet instant chicken
  broth
1 tablespoon lemon juice

Place cut-up chicken in serving bowl. Soften gelatin in 1 cup cold water. Add instant chicken broth and heat, stirring until dissolved. Combine with lemon juice and pour over chicken. Chill in refrigerator until jelled. Makes 4 servings (235 calories per serving).

Chicken (or Turkey) Salad

2½ cups diced cold chicken
  (or turkey)
½ cup cottage cheese
1½ teaspoons wine vinegar
½ teaspoon mixed herbs
½ teaspoon salt

Dash lemon pepper
  marinade
1 teaspoon roast pimiento,
  minced
1 teaspoon capers

Place chicken or turkey into small deep serving bowl. Process cottage cheese, wine vinegar, mixed herbs, salt and pepper in blender at low speed until smooth and

creamy. Using fork, combine with chicken or turkey.
Fold in pimiento and capers. Chill before serving.
Makes 4 servings (200 calories per serving).

Turkey (or Chicken) Roll-Ups

For QWL TEEN dieters only, contains yogurt

8 ounces cooked turkey
   white meat (or chicken),
   cut into 8 slices
2 hard-cooked eggs

1 tablespoon plain yogurt
   (or buttermilk)
Salt and pepper to taste

(QWL adult dieters use, instead of yogurt, 1 tablespoon
creamed cottage cheese and 1 teaspoon water.)

Spread out 8 slices of turkey. Process eggs and yogurt,
seasoned with salt and pepper, in blender (use small
blender jar if you have one) at low speed until soft.
Spread on turkey slices, roll up slices, and secure rolls
with toothpicks. Add salt and pepper to taste. Makes
2 servings (250 calories per serving).

Chicken/Turkey Jell

1 envelope unflavored
   gelatin
1¾ cups water
2 cubes or packets of
   instant chicken broth
1 cup diced cooked chicken
   or turkey, all skin and
   visible fat removed

1 tablespoon minced pars-
   ley or parsley flakes
1 tablespoon minced onion
   or onion flakes
2 teaspoons sesame seeds
   or poppy seeds (optional)

Sprinkle the gelatin in ¾ cup of water in a saucepan. Add broth cubes or powder. Over low heat, stir
until broth and gelatin are dissolved and combined.
Add remaining 1 cup water, stir. Chill until mixture is
thickened but not set, then fold in remaining ingredients. Turn into 4 individual molds, or 1 large mold.
Chill until set. Unmold and serve. Sprinkle a few more

sesame seeds on each serving. Makes 4 servings (97 calories per serving).

Basic Roast Turkey

1 young 12-pound turkey (avoid those labeled "self-basting," as they result in extra calories)
1 tablespoon salt
½ teaspoon lemon pepper marinade (or seasoned salt)

1 envelope instant onion broth
½ cup dry white wine
Paprika
3 cups boiling water

Wash turkey with cold water, dry with paper towels. Trim off any visible fat. Tie ends of drumsticks together, and tie wings close to body with white string. Rub inside and outside of turkey with salt and lemon pepper marinade, and brush liberally with mixture of instant onion broth and white wine. Close openings with skewers. Sprinkle paprika liberally over whole turkey.

Pour 3 cups boiling water into bottom of roasting pan, and place turkey, breast side down, on rack in pan. Top loosely with foil. Roast in preheated oven 4¼ to 4½ hours (or until done to your taste). Every 20 to 30 minutes, while roasting, lift foil from turkey, brush liberally with pan juice, and sprinkle on more paprika. If juice in pan dries out, add boiling water. Turn turkey breast side up after 2 hours of roasting. Remove foil for last 45 minutes, but be sure to keep turkey skin moist with basting as necessary.

When turkey is done, drumstick should twist easily in its socket, and meat should feel soft and tender when pinched. (230 calories per 6-ounce serving of meat only; skin and visible fat removed.)

Frozen Turkey Roast in "See-Through Bag"

1 3-pound boneless turkey loaf or roast, frozen
Salt
Pepper

Remove cover from frozen turkey loaf, keeping loaf in the aluminum pan in which it is packed. Sprinkle with salt and pepper and place in "see-through bag for oven cooking." Secure bag 2 inches from roast with twist-tie, cut off end, and puncture 4 holes in bag as instructed on package. Place in shallow pan in preheated 400° oven and roast for 2½ hours. (If you wish to use meat thermometer, insert through bag into turkey after about 1½ hours, and cook until thermometer registers 175°F.)

When finished, take from oven and slit along top of bag to remove turkey. QWL dieters trim off any skin or visible fat. Makes 8 servings (320 calories per QWL serving).

Cornish Game Hen

QWL *dieters do not eat skin*

4 small Cornish game hens	2 chicken bouillon cubes
½ teaspoon salt	1¾ cups boiling water
¼ teaspoon black pepper	¼ cup lemon juice

Gently wash hens with cool water, dry, sprinkle with salt and pepper, and place breast up on rack in small roasting pan. Dissolve bouillon cubes in boiling water and stir in lemon juice. Pour over the Cornish hens and roast uncovered in preheated 425° oven for 1 hour, basting every 10 minutes or so. Remove from oven, pour pan juice into a bowl containing 3 ice cubes. When fat rises to top, remove it, reheat juice and pour some over each hen. Makes 4 servings (360 calories per serving).

Roast Duckling

*Dieters must trim off all skin and visible fat
before eating*

2½-pound duckling, cleaned
   and quartered, ready to
   cook, all visible fat
   removed
½ teaspoon salt
1 teaspoon grated orange rind

½ cup chicken bouillon,
   double-strength
3 tablespoons seasoned
   white cooking wine

Place duckling quarters skin side up on a rack in a
shallow roasting pan, sprinkle with salt and orange rind,
and roast in preheated 425° oven about 20 to 25 minutes or until nicely browned. Drain off fat from bottom
of roasting pan. Combine the bouillon and wine, and
spoon over duckling. Cover pan tight with foil, reduce
heat to 325° and bake for another hour. Remove foil
completely, brush duck with sauce, then continue baking about another 15 minutes, or until meat is tender
to the fork. Serve without juices. Makes 4 servings (230
calories per QWL serving).

FISH

In many of the following fish recipes, you'll find that
you may substitute other more available (and possibly
less costly) types of fish for any of the specific species
stated in the directions. Use your personal preference
and judgment (calories of most types of fish don't vary
greatly; check calorie tables on page 258).

Poached Fish with Herbed Egg

1½ pounds fish fillets
(flounder, sole, or your
choice)
2 cups boiling water
2 tablespoons lemon juice
1 tablespoon finely chopped
onion flakes or onion
1 tablespoon finely chopped
parsley flakes or parsley

1 teaspoon salt
1 bay leaf
2 peppercorns
2 hard-cooked eggs
¼ teaspoon mixed herbs
Paprika, to taste

Cut fish into 4 portions. Place in no-stick skillet. Mix all ingredients except eggs, mixed herbs, and paprika, and add to fish. Cover and simmer fish for 6 to 10 minutes, or until it flakes easily with a fork.

Meanwhile chop hard-cooked eggs fine, adding mixed herbs and paprika (use chopper or cut in quarters and process in blender or "chop" for about 5 seconds).

Place drained fish on hot serving plate, sprinkle chopped egg mixture on surface and color with a little paprika. Makes 4 servings (160 calories per serving).

Fish in "See-Through Bag"

1 2-pound lean fish steak
(red snapper, bass,
halibut, other)
Salt
Pepper

1 tablespoon lemon juice
3 tablespoons double-
strength bouillon
Paprika

Rub fish with salt and pepper, and brush with combined lemon juice and bouillon. Sprinkle liberally with paprika and lift with spatula into a "see-through bag for cooking." Secure bag 2 inches from fish with twist-tie, cut off end, and puncture 4 holes in top of bag as instructed on package. Place in shallow baking pan and cook in preheated 400° oven 35 minutes. Slit top of bag to remove fish when ready to serve. Makes 4 servings (215 calories per serving).

Herbed Fish Fillets

1 pound frozen flounder (or other fish) fillets, thawed (or fresh)
½ cup dry white wine
¼ cup water
1 teaspoon onion flakes or instant minced onion
¼ teaspoon tarragon
¼ teaspoon rosemary

Combine all ingredients, except fish, in skillet. Heat over medium flame, stirring occasionally; bring to boil. Place fillets gently in the pan, cover, simmer over low heat for 8 to 10 minutes or until fish flakes easily. Remove with spatula. Makes 2 servings (220 calories per serving).

Cheese-Flavored Fillets

1½ pounds flounder (or other fish) fillets, fresh or frozen (thawed)
1 tablespoon lemon juice
1 tablespoon grated onion
½ teaspoon butter-flavored salt
⅛ teaspoon lemon pepper marinade
⅛ teaspoon rosemary
⅛ teaspoon marjoram
½ teaspoon parsley flakes
1 tablespoon grated part skim milk cheese

Arrange fillets side by side on no-stick broiling pan. Sprinkle with lemon juice, onion, salt, pepper, and herbs. Broil in preheated oven about 4 inches from heat 10 to 12 minutes, or until fish flakes easily with a fork. Sprinkle cheese on and broil 2 minutes longer. Makes 4 servings (145 calories per serving).

Baked Fillets

1½ pounds sole fillets (or flounder fillets; any lean fish may be used)
1 tablespoon parsley flakes
2 teaspoons onion flakes
3 tablespoons chili sauce
1 teaspoon wine vinegar
1 teaspoon prepared mustard
½ teaspoon celery salt
½ teaspoon paprika

Arrange fish fillets (thawed, if frozen fillets are used) side by side on large shallow no-stick baking pan. Make a paste of all other ingredients and spread over fish. Cook 4 inches from heat in preheated broiler for 5 minutes. Brush sauce in pan over fish again, and broil 5 minutes longer. Lift fish carefully from pan to serving platter, using spatula. Sprinkle with more paprika, or nutmeg, if you like. Makes 4 servings (150 calories per serving).

Parsleyed Fish Broil

1½ pounds lean fish steaks or fillets (salmon, bluefish, flounder, sole, snapper)
½ teaspoon salt
Dash black pepper

1 teaspoon instant vegetable broth
1 teaspoon paprika
1½ teaspoons lemon juice
1 tablespoon minced parsley
(or chives, scallions, or dill)

Arrange fish, skin side down, on no-stick broiler pan. Sprinkle fish with salt, pepper, instant vegetable broth, paprika, and lemon juice. Broil 3 inches from heat in preheated oven until fish flakes easily with a fork, 10 to 15 minutes. Serve sprinkled with parsley, chives, scallions, or dill. Makes 4 servings (135 calories per serving).

Sole Birds

1½ pounds fillet of sole
2 tablespoons lemon juice
½ teaspoon seasoned salt
⅛ teaspoon black pepper

½ teaspoon paprika
Mixed herbs to taste
8 to 10 raw shrimp, shelled and deveined

Split pieces of fillet in halves lengthwise to make strips. Mix seasonings with lemon juice and brush over fish. Roll individual strips, place a shrimp on each and secure each fish roll and shrimp together with a wooden toothpick. Bake in preheated 400° oven for 20 minutes (fish should flake easily with fork). Brush tops of rolls with any lemon juice mixture in pan, and serve sprinkled with paprika. Makes 4 servings (150 calories per serving).

Jelled Cod

12 ounces boiled cod, flaked
1 envelope lemon low-
 calorie gelatin
1 cup boiling water

2 teaspoons onion juice
2 teaspoons lemon juice
1 teaspoon salt

Dissolve gelatin in boiling water; chill until slightly thickened. Mix all other ingredients into chilled gelatin. Place in mold, refrigerate until firm. Unmold to serve. Makes 2 servings (150 calories per serving).

Baked Flounder with Clams

QWL *dieters eat only fish and clams*

2 pounds flounder (or
 sole) fillets
1 can (3 ounce) chopped
 mushrooms, drained
2 cans (8 ounce) minced
 clams, drained
¼ cup celery, chopped

2 teaspoons lemon juice
3 packets instant chicken
 broth
¼ cup hot water
Paprika
Fresh (minced) or dried
 dill weed

Spread a mixture of mushrooms, clams, celery, lemon juice, and 2 packets of broth in the bottom of a shallow casserole. Arrange fillets over this mixture. Dissolve remaining packet of broth in ¼ cup hot water and pour over the fish. Sprinkle paprika and dill over the top and bake 10 minutes in preheated 375° oven. Fish should flake easily with a fork when done. Makes 4 servings (230 calories per QWL serving).

Halibut in Grapefruit Juice

2 halibut steaks (total about
  2 pounds), 1¼ to 1½
  inches thick
½ teaspoon salt
¼ teaspoon mixed herbs

½ cup unsweetened
  grapefruit juice
½ teaspoon paprika
4 thin slices lemon

Preheat broiler. Wipe halibut steaks with wet paper towels and place on foil in broiler pan. Mix together salt, herbs and grapefruit juice, and brush this mixture over fish. Sprinkle with paprika and broil about 3 inches from heat until fish is just browned (about 6 minutes), turn over, brush again with juice, and sprinkle with paprika. Broil 5 minutes, basting with the juice once or twice. Place 2 lemon slices over top of each steak, return to broiler and broil 2 minutes longer. Fish should flake easily with a fork, but do not overcook. Cut steaks in half to serve. Makes 4 servings (240 calories per serving).

Barbecued Halibut Steak

1½ pounds halibut steak (or other fish steaks)
Lemon wedges

Barbecue Sauce

¼ cup wine vinegar
½ cup water
¼ cup chili sauce
1 tablespoon prepared
  mustard
¼ teaspoon cayenne (red
  pepper)

Artificial sweetening equal
  to 1 tablespoon sugar
1 teaspoon onion salt
1 tablespoon finely minced
  parsley
1 tablespoon Worcestershire
  sauce
Lemon wedges

Place all ingredients for sauce in a saucepan, stir thoroughly, and simmer for 15 minutes, then bring to a boil, and let cool. Keep any leftover in covered container in refrigerator for future use.

Cook one side of fish steak over very low fire for 5 minutes, then turn. Brush top side liberally with sauce.

Turn again after 5 minutes and brush top side with sauce. Turn after about 3 minutes, brush with sauce, then 3 minutes on other side, brushing with sauce again. Test with fork to check that center is tender and flaky, then serve, with sauce on table if more is wanted and lemon wedges. Makes 4 servings (180 calories per serving).

Poached Salmon Steaks

4 salmon steaks, about 6 ounces each	½ teaspoon chopped fresh dill
1 cup water	¼ teaspoon seasoned salt
1 cup chicken bouillon	1 bay leaf
½ teaspoon dillseed	Lemon slices

Combine all ingredients except salmon steaks in a large saucepan, and bring to a boil. Add salmon and bring to boil again, then reduce heat and simmer about 4 minutes, or until salmon flakes easily. Serve salmon steaks on warm platter, sprinkling a little more chopped fresh dill over them. Makes 4 servings (220 calories per serving).

Note: May be served with the following:

Dill Sauce

½ cup cottage cheese	Salt to taste
3 tablespoons onion broth	Black pepper
1½ teaspoons snipped fresh dill	

Combine all ingredients in blender and process at low speed until creamy and smooth. Use as sauce for salmon steaks, also for other fish. (Yields 15 calories per tablespoon.)

Simple Canned Salmon (or Tuna)

2 cans (7¾ ounce) salmon (or tuna)	Black pepper
	1 teaspoon lemon juice
Salt	Capers or cut-up pickle

Remove salmon from cans, discarding large bones and draining off any oil. Sprinkle with seasonings and lemon juice, garnish with capers or pickle. Makes 4 servings (145 calories per serving).

Hot Herbed Canned Salmon (or Tuna)

1 can salmon (or tuna), about 8 ounces, broken into small flakes
2 eggs, beaten
1 tablespoon dried onion flakes (or instant minced onion)
1 tablespoon parsley flakes (or chopped parsley)

1 teaspoon prepared horseradish
1 teaspoon prepared mustard
1 teaspoon lemon juice
¼ teaspoon thyme
⅓ cup chicken bouillon
Lemon wedges

Drain salmon, then combine with all other ingredients. Cook over low heat in preheated no-stick skillet for about 10 minutes, stirring occasionally with wooden spatula to help heat through thoroughly. Serve with lemon wedges. Makes 4 servings (125 calories per serving).

Molded Salmon

1 can (7¾ ounce) salmon
1 teaspoon unflavored gelatin
½ cup cold water
1½ tablespoons lemon juice
1 teaspoon salad cheese (available in shaker-top jar)

1 teaspoon grated or instant minced onion
2 hard-cooked eggs, cut into wedges

Soften gelatin in water, add lemon juice and bring to boil, stirring until gelatin is dissolved. Cool.

Drain salmon and flake with fork, removing bones. Combine with salad cheese, minced onion, and gelatin mixture. Pour into 1 quart mold and chill until set. Unmold on platter and surround with wedges of hard-cooked egg. Makes 3 servings (185 calories per serving).

Sardine and Egg Salad

1 can (4¾ ounce) sar-
dines, drained

1 hard-cooked egg, minced
½ teaspoon prepared mustard

Place sardines into strainer under cold running water
to wash off oil. Transfer to small bowl and mash with
fork. Add minced egg and mustard. Continue mashing
until almost pastelike, or to whatever texture you prefer. Makes 2 servings (145 calories per serving).

Smoked Salmon Rolls

This recipe is not for water retainers

3 tablespoons cottage
cheese
2 teaspoons finely chopped
onion
½ teaspoon Worcestershire
sauce

4 slices lean smoked
salmon about 2½
to 5 inches,
2 ounces each
Mixed herbs

Combine the cottage cheese, onion and Worcestershire sauce. Spread ¼ of the mixture on a slice of
smoked salmon, sprinkle lightly with the mixed herbs,
and roll up slowly, fastening roll with toothpick. Make
3 more rolls in the same way. Makes 4 servings (110
calories per serving).

Jelled Salmon Loaf

12 ounces canned salmon,
drained, and flaked into
small pieces
1 tablespoon unflavored
gelatin
¼ cup very cold water
¾ cup boiling water
½ tablespoon lemon juice

1 tablespoon wine vinegar
¼ teaspoon seasoned salt
½ teaspoon instant minced
onion or flakes
½ teaspoon chopped parsley
or flakes
4 lemon wedges

Soften the gelatin in the cold water, then add the boiling water, lemon juice, vinegar, salt, onion, and parsley. Beat all ingredients together well, making sure gelatin is thoroughly dissolved. Chill until partially set, then whip mixture until fluffy light. Fold in the salmon to combine evenly. Place mixture in a loaf mold or pan, and chill until set. Unmold, and serve with lemon wedges. Makes 4 servings (125 calories per serving).

Baked Shad

1½ pounds fresh shad cleaned
Salt and pepper
1 teaspoon instant minced onion
2 teaspoons sweet pickle relish
1 tablespoon chopped parsley
2 teaspoons fresh lemon juice
1 teaspoon mixed herbs
½ teaspoon salt
Dash pepper

Sprinkle inside of fish with salt and pepper. Place skin side down on no-stick baking pan. Mix together remaining ingredients and place loosely in center of fish. Bake in preheated 350° oven 30 to 35 minutes, or until fish flakes easily with a fork. Makes 4 servings (300 calories per serving).

Shad Roe

2 small pair or 1 large pair fresh shad roe (½ pound)
Salt
Lemon pepper marinade (or black pepper)
Juice of ½ lemon

Wash shad roe gently, and carefully separate halves by removing membrane. Wipe bottom of no-stick skillet with paper towel with vegetable oil on it (just enough to coat the bottom of pan). Salt and pepper the roe, place in pan over medium flame, and squeeze half the lemon juice over it. Puncture top gently with fork holes.

In a few minutes turn the halves over in pan, using spatula or large spoon (avoiding breaking roe if possible), squeeze on rest of lemon, and sauté until a fork inserted in the center shows no red inside. Length of cooking time depends on thickness of roe. If very thick, a cover over the pan will help cook the inside which must not be permitted to dry out. Makes 2 servings (150 calories per serving).

Juicy Red Snapper

1½ pounds red snapper (halibut, striped bass, or bluefish may be substituted)
3 tablespoons onion, chopped
2 tablespoons vegetable bouillon
2 tablespoons canned pimiento, chopped
¾ teaspoon coriander seeds (optional)
2 tablespoons orange juice
1 tablespoon lime juice (unsweetened)
½ teaspoon salt
⅛ teaspoon lemon pepper marinade
Paprika
1 hard-cooked egg, chopped

Lightly brown onion in vegetable bouillon in no-stick skillet. Add pimiento and coriander and stir together for a minute or two. Add orange juice, lime juice, salt, and lemon pepper marinade.

Place fish in no-stick casserole, and pour the sauce over it. Bake, uncovered, in 400° preheated oven for 30 minutes, brushing fish with sauce 3 or 4 times while baking. Fish should be firm and flake easily with a fork, but do not overcook. Sprinkle paprika and chopped hard-cooked egg over top of fish before serving. Makes 4 servings (195 calories per serving).

Tuna (or Salmon) and Egg Caper Salad

1 can water-packed tuna
    fish (or regular tuna or
    canned salmon; place in
    strainer and run cold water
    through it to remove oil)
½ cup cottage cheese
½ envelope dry instant
    vegetable broth

1 teaspoon lemon juice
2 tablespoons water
2 hard-cooked eggs,
    chopped
12 capers
Paprika (optional)

Process cottage cheese, instant vegetable broth, lemon juice, and water in blender at low speed until smooth and creamy. Using fork, flake drained tuna and mix together with chopped eggs. Blend in sauce. Garnish each serving with 3 capers (and paprika if you like). Makes 4 servings (145 calories per serving).

Mama's Gefilte Fish

QWL *dieters eat only the fish*

3 pounds whitefish (or
    carp) and pike, cleaned,
    trimmed and ground at
    fish market
Fish scraps
2½ cups water
3 carrots, cut in ½-inch rounds

3 celery stalks, cut in ½-inch
    pieces
2 eggs
1 small onion, minced
2 drops artificial sweetener
¾ teaspoon salt
Black pepper to taste

When fish market grinds the fish, ask them to give you the head and scraps in a separate package. Cook the scraps in a saucepan with 2 cups of the water, some salt, carrots, and celery. Cover and simmer for 45 minutes until the vegetables are tender.

In chopping bowl, chop together until very fine the ground fish, eggs, onion, sweetener, and salt and pepper, gradually adding remaining ½ cup water. Shape (using wet hands) into ovals about 2½ inches long and 2 inches in diameter, being very careful not to crush tightly (we want them to be light and fluffy). Lower gently into vegetables, cover and simmer about 2 hours. Check the amount of water occasionally and if it boils away add a little more boiling water. Serve hot or cold with a little horseradish. Makes 6 servings (250 calories per QWL serving, fish only).

QWL Bouillabaise

10 ounces red snapper (cooked)
8 ounces shrimp (cooked)
8 ounces halibut (cooked)
6 ounces scallops (cooked) (or other lean fish combinations, such as cod, flounder, sea bass, lobster, etc., not to exceed ½ pound per serving)
1 cup chicken bouillon
1 cup instant vegetable broth
1½ cups clam juice

½ cup tomato juice
2 tablespoons lemon juice
1 clove garlic, crushed
1 bay leaf
2 tablespoons parsley flakes or chopped fresh parsley
2 tablespoons dried minced onion
1 tablespoon dried bell peppers (optional)
¼ teaspoon thyme
Dash saffron

Bring to boil bouillon and broth, lower heat, add clam juice, tomato juice, lemon juice, garlic, bay leaf, parsley, onion, peppers, thyme, and saffron. Simmer together 10 minutes.

Cut fish into 2-inch pieces and simmer in liquid until piping hot (3 or 4 minutes). Do not overcook. Remove bay leaf. Serve in deep bowls. Makes 4 servings (240 calories per serving).

Note: While tomato juice isn't usually included on the QWL Diet, there is so little per serving here that it is permitted.

Italian Fish Stew

½ pound raw shrimp, shelled, deveined and cut in small pieces	4 tablespoons vegetable bouillon
	1 clove garlic, crushed
6 ounces cod fillet (or flounder, sole, or any lean fish) cut in small pieces	1 medium onion, minced
	⅛ teaspoon red pepper
	3 cups water
	¾ cup dry red wine
6 ounces scallops, cut in small pieces	4 teaspoons tomato paste
	1 teaspoon salt (or more to taste)
6 ounces halibut, cut in small pieces	

Using a no-stick skillet, heat vegetable bouillon, and sauté garlic, onion, and red pepper in it until onion is tender and golden. Transfer to saucepan and add water and wine, stir, and bring to boil. Boil gently for 15 mintues, add tomato paste and salt and cook 5 minutes longer. Place shrimp, cod, scallops, and halibut in the liquid; bring to boil again, then simmer 10 minutes. Seafood should be just cooked through. Makes 4 servings (200 calories per serving).

Mom's Fish Loaf

For Teenage QWL dieters only, contains skim milk.

2 cups cooked lean fish, flaked	1½ teaspoons grated onion
	½ teaspoon seasoned salt
2 eggs, beaten	⅛ teaspoon Worcestershire sauce
1 cup skim milk	
½ cup cottage cheese	

Stir eggs, skim milk, and cottage cheese into flaked fish, then add other ingredients. Spoon into no-stick loaf pan and cover. Place covered pan on a rack in large saucepan (or in a steamer) just enough water to reach rack. Bring water to boil and let covered fish loaf steam over it for 1¼ hours. If water cooks away, add a little more.

When cooked, quickly run knife around edge of loaf to loosen it, place serving platter over fish and turn pan over. Remove pan and serve fish. Makes 4 servings (168 calories per serving).

Fish-Shrimp Combo

For Teenage QWL dieters only, contains buttermilk

1 pound cooked sole,
   flounder, or any lean fish
½ pound (about 14
   medium) cooked shrimp,
   shelled and deveined
1 tablespoon grated onion

½ teaspoon seasoned salt
¼ teaspoon imitation
   butter flavoring
¼ cup buttermilk
1½ teaspoons paprika

Break fish up with fork and cut shrimp into thin slices. Mix fish and shrimp together reserving about 16 slices of shrimp. Using fork, combine onion, salt, butter flavoring, and buttermilk with firsh. Spoon into no-stick casserole dish or 4 individual no-stick baking dishes, distributing reserved shrimp slices over top. Sprinkle liberally with paprika. Heat through in 425° preheated oven for 10 minutes. Makes 4 servings (140 calories per serving).

SHELLFISH

Shellfish Broil

3 cups cooked shellfish
   (may use crabmeat,
   shrimp, lobster, or minced
   clams—or a combination)
½ teaspoon garlic salt

1 tablespoon chili sauce
3 thin slices part skim
   mozzarella cheese
Paprika (optional)

Arrange seafood in shallow pan. Sprinkle lightly with garlic salt. Coat very thinly with chili sauce. Top with wafers of mozzarella cheese and place about 3 inches from broiler flame. Broil until hot and bubbly. Color with paprika, if desired. Serve immediately. Makes 4 servings (160 calories per serving).

Combination Shellfish Stew

QWL dieters eat only the shellfish

1 dozen littleneck clams in shell, unopened	4 canned, whole tomatoes, diced and drained
1 pound raw shelled shrimp, cleaned	⅛ teaspoon saffron powder
¾ pound scallops	1 teaspoon celery salt
3 tablespoons bouillon	¼ teaspoon red pepper
1 cup chopped onions	½ teaspoon poppy seeds
1 clove garlic, crushed	2 8-ounce bottles clam juice
	1 cup water

Rinse shrimp and scallops under cold water. Scrub clams thoroughly. In a deep heavy no-stick pan, heat the bouillon and sauté the onions and garlic until golden. Add tomatoes and all seasonings. Add clam juice and water and stir to combine well. Bring to a boil. Add clams, and boil 2 to 3 minutes until shells open; reduce heat to simmer. Add shrimp and scallops. Cook at medium heat, just below boiling, for about 8 minutes, or until shrimps and scallops are tender to the fork. Serve in soup bowls, sprinkling lightly with celery salt. Makes 4 servings (220 calories per QWL serving).

Cold Shellfish Salad

3 cups cooked shellfish (may use crab, shrimp, lobster, or minced clams, or a combination)	¼ teaspoon salt (or garlic salt, if preferred)
1 cup cottage cheese	3 sprigs fresh parsley, cut up
	Paprika

Process cottage cheese, salt, and parsley in blender at low speed until smooth and creamy. Arrange chilled seafood on platter and spoon sauce over it. Sprinkle paprika on top for color. Makes 4 servings (180 calories per serving).

Glazed Seafood

1½ pounds cooked shrimp, crab, lobster, scallops, or cold fish
1 envelope plain gelatin

1 cup cold water
1 packet instant chicken broth
1 tablespoon lemon juice

Place cooked seafood in serving bowl. Soften gelatin in 1 cup cold water. Add instant chicken broth and heat, stirring until gelatin is dissolved. Combine with lemon juice and pour over cooked shrimp, or crab, lobster, scallops, or cold fish. Place in refrigerator to jell. Makes 4 servings (150 calories per serving).

Baked Clams

2 dozen large clams
3 tablespoons chopped onion
1 teaspoon salt
Black pepper

3 teaspoons chopped parsley
½ teaspoon oregano
4 tablespoons onion broth

Scrub clams thoroughly. Pry open and sprinkle onion, salt and pepper over them. Combine parsley and oregano with onion broth, and distribute over the clams. Bake in shells in 375° preheated oven until edges of clams curl slightly. Makes 4 servings (100 calories per serving).

Steamed Clams

36 littleneck clams, un-opened, cleaned and scrubbed thoroughly
½ cup white cooking wine
1 tablespoon finely chopped parsley

1 teaspoon basil
1 teaspoon oregano
¼ teaspoon garlic powder
Lemon wedges

Place clams in a large saucepan with tight cover, with mixture of wine and all other ingredients except lemon wedges. Cover. Steam the clams until shells open (about 10 minutes). Remove clams and place in shells in a serving bowl. Strain liquid through a fine sieve, then pour the clear liquid over the clams. Serve with lemon wedges. Makes 4 servings (118 calories per serving).

Mamaroneck Clam Stew

2 small 10½-ounce cans whole baby clams, with liquid
3 chicken bouillon cubes
3 cups boiling water
2 tablespoons chopped chives

2 tablespoons chopped parsley
1½ tablespoons soy sauce
2 tablespoons dry white sherry

Dissolve bouillon cubes in boiling water. Add broth from clams and chopped chives; simmer for 3 minutes. Add rest of ingredients, heat 1 minute more until clams are piping hot, and serve. Makes 4 servings (110 calories per serving).

Clam Delight

For Stay-Slim Eating serve as dip on low-calorie crackers, melba toast, or as dip for celery, carrot sticks, cucumber slices, or raw cauliflower.

1 can minced claims, drained
½ cup cottage cheese
¼ teaspoon Worcestershire sauce
1 tablespoon chopped chives

Salt
Black pepper
2 hard-cooked eggs, sliced
Poppy seeds (or sesame seeds)

Process cottage cheese in blender (use smaller blender jar, if you have one), at medium speed until smooth like sour cream. Mix with clams, Worcestershire sauce, chives, salt and pepper. Serve on hard-cooked egg slices as main dish or as appetizer. Top with poppy seeds (or sesame seeds). Makes 2 servings (170 calories per serving).

Creamy Crab

For Stay-Slim eating this may be served as dip with carrot sticks, celery, or on cucumber rounds

1 cup cottage cheese
2 teaspoons lemon juice
1 teaspoon prepared Dijon mustard
½ teaspoon salt
⅛ teaspoon lemon pepper marinade
¼ teaspoon Worcestershire sauce

2 cans (about 8 ounces each) crabmeat (2 cups minced cooked shrimp may be substituted)
2 tablespoons chopped green pepper
Paprika or minced parsley

Process first 5 ingredients in blender at low speed until creamy. Remove tendons from crabmeat and add to blended cottage cheese with green pepper. Sprinkle with paprika or minced parsley. Makes 4 servings (180 calories per serving).

Marinated Crabmeat

1 pound fresh lump crab-meat (or 2 cans crab-meat, bones removed)
1 medium onion, chopped
1 cup lemon or lime juice

1 teaspoon salt
Black pepper
2 tablespoons minced parsley
Paprika

Combine onion, lemon or lime juice, salt, pepper and parsley. Pour over crab. Refrigerate overnight. Serve cold, sprinkled with paprika. Makes 4 servings (115 calories per serving).

Crabmeat "Quiche"

1 pound crabmeat, fresh, canned or frozen (thawed), tendons removed	8 ounces cottage cheese
	½ teaspoon salt
	Dash black pepper
4 eggs	

Beat eggs slightly. Separate crab, or keep in chunks if you prefer. Mix all ingredients together. Spoon into 4 small baking dishes, or 4 large seafood shells, and place about 4 inches from heat in preheated broiler. Broil until of custard consistency (about 10 minutes or less depending on size of eggs). May be baked in moderate oven, but takes longer. Makes 4 servings (250 calories per serving).

Lobsters Steamed in Wine

QWL dieters eat lobster meat only

4 1-pound live lobsters	8 sprigs parsley
3 cups water	1 bay leaf
2 cups dry white vermouth	1 tablespoon tarragon
1 carrot, sliced thin	3 teaspoons salt
1 large onion, sliced thin	5 whole peppercorns
1 rib celery, sliced thin	1 whole clove

Mix all ingredients except lobster in a large deep saucepan or steamer, and bring to a boil; lower heat and simmer for 15 minutes (alcohol cooks away). Stir once during cooking.

Wash lobsters under cold running water and place them in the boiling broth, cover, and steam for 20 minutes. Remove lobsters. Slit bottom of body of each lobster in half lengthwise with sharp knife, and remove dark vein running through, as well as all parts inside head except red roe in females and greenish liver. Crack claws with nutcracker. Continue boiling liquid in saucepan over high heat until most is cooked away. Strain, discard vegetables and use broth as sauce for lobsters. Makes 4 servings (110 calories per QWL serving).

Boiled Lobster with "Buttery" Sauce

4 1-pound lobsters
Boiling water to cover
1½ tablespoons salt
Juice of 1 lemon

½ teaspoon seasoned salt
½ teaspoon imitation
   butter flavoring

Select live lobsters. Plunge them into boiling salted water to cover. Bring to boil again, then simmer for 20 minutes. Take lobsters from water immediately.

Slit bottom of body in half lengthwise with sharp knife and remove dark vein running through as well as all parts in head except red roe in females and greenish liver. Crack the claws in a few places with nutcracker and serve hot or cold, accompanied by "buttery" sauce. Makes 4 servings (110 calories per serving).

"Buttery" sauce: Mix lemon, seasoned salt, and imitation butter flavoring together. Use sparingly with lobster, or other seafood.

Barbecued Lobster Tails or Lobster

8 medium lobster tail
  halves, or 4 1-pound
  lobsters
½ cup chicken bouillon

¼ teaspoon lemon pepper
   marinade
Lemon wedges

Lobster tails should be open, or lobsters split down the middle and claws cracked. Mix bouillon and lemon pepper marinade and brush well on open lobster meat. Grill lobster tails or lobsters over a low fire for about 20 minutes, brushing meat with seasoned bouillon every few minutes. Serve with lemon wedges. Makes 4 servings (120 calories per serving).

Lobster Tail Salad

4 frozen lobster tails	½ tablespoon parsley flakes
Water to cover in saucepan	½ tablespoon minced
1 teaspoon salt	onion, fresh or instant
2 tablespoons onion	½ teaspoon dry mustard
flavored instant broth	¼ teaspoon paprika
(liquid)	½ teaspoon celery salt
½ tablespoon wine vinegar	

Bring water with 1 teaspoon salt to boil. Drop in lobster tails and bring water to boil again; continue boiling 6 minutes. Remove lobster tails from saucepan, douse in cold water. Cutting away from shells, divide meat into bite-size chunks.

Combine all other ingredients, mix thoroughly, and spoon over chunks in serving bowl. Chill, tossing chunks frequently to coat all surfaces with sauce. After a final tossing, sprinkle on extra paprika, and serve. Makes 4 servings (110 calories per serving).

Steamed Mussels

32 mussels, thoroughly	1 tablespoon finely chopped
cleaned, scraped and	parsley
scrubbed, unopened	⅛ teaspoon thyme
½ cup white cooking wine	½ bay leaf
¼ cup water	Fresh lemon wedges
1 tablespoon finely chopped	
onion	

Place the cleaned, scrubbed mussels in a large saucepan with tight cover, in a mixture of the wine and all other ingredients except the lemon wedges. Cover. Steam slowly until shells open. Remove mussels in their shells, and place in long serving bowl. Strain the liquid through a fine sieve, then pour the clear liquid over the mussels. Serve with lemon wedges. Makes 4 servings (110 calories per serving).

Scallops Neapolitan

QWL dieters eat only the scallops

1½ pounds scallops
1 cup tomato juice
1 teaspoon garlic salt
3 tablespoons parsley, minced

¼ teaspoon oregano
¼ teaspoon paprika
1 large can bean sprouts
½ pound mushrooms, sliced

Marinate the scallops for 2 or 3 hours in a mixture of tomato juice, garlic salt, parsley, oregano, and paprika. Place scallops and sauce in shallow pan about 3 inches from heat in preheated broiler for 5 minutes. Turn scallops over and broil 5 minutes longer (if scallops are very small, cook shorter time; if very large, cook a little longer). Combine drained bean sprouts and mushrooms in saucepan, and heat well. Place on serving dish and pour scallops with sauce on top. May be sprinkled with a little grated Italian cheese. Makes 4 servings (145 calories per QWL serving, scallops only).

Scallops Hot or Chilled

QWL dieters eat the scallops alone or with cocktail sauce

1½ pounds small scallops
2 tablespoons lemon juice
1 small onion, quartered and separated
2 tablespoons minced parsley
1 stalk celery, cut up

½ teaspoon salt
Black pepper
½ teaspoon thyme
⅓ cup dry white wine
⅔ cup boiling water
Paprika, if desired

In skillet, heat together lemon juice, onion, parsley, celery, salt, pepper and thyme. Rinse scallops. Add with wine and boiling water to other ingredients. Bring to boil, lower heat and simmer 5 minutes. Remove scallops from broth and serve hot. (Discard broth.) Sprinkle with paprika if you like. Or refrigerate scallops and served chilled with small amount of catsup or cocktail sauce. Makes 4 servings (150 calories per QWL serving, scallops only).

Barbecued Scallops on Skewer

1½ pounds fresh or frozen (and defrosted) scallops, large enough pieces to hold when pierced
Barbecue sauce (see recipe for halibut steak sauce on page 104)
Lemon wedges

Place scallops on skewer, with space between each one. Brush well with barbecue sauce, covering all surfaces. Grill over very low fire, turning about every 3 minutes and brushing with sauce. After about 6 minutes on each side, check with fork to make sure scallops are cooked through (do not overcook). Serve with barbecue sauce and lemon wedges on side. (Onions, tomatoes, mushrooms, and green pepper may be alternated with scallops on skewers, for anyone not on QWL Diet.) Makes 4 servings (150 calories per serving, scallops only).

Cooked Fresh Shrimp

2 pounds fresh or frozen shrimp, peeled and cleaned
2 teaspoons seasoned salt
1 teaspoon paprika
2 stalks celery, cut up, including leaves
1 small onion, cut in eighths
Water

Place shrimp in saucepan and add water to cover; then add all other ingredients. Bring to boil, then simmer for 4 to 6 minutes, until shrimp are tender (depending on size of shrimp). Drain, discard everything but the shrimp. Chill. Serve with a little cocktail sauce, catsup, or lemon wedges. Makes 4 servings (125 calories per serving).

Scampi

QWL dieters eat shrimp without sauce. Others pour hot sauce over each serving

1½ pounds shelled raw shrimp, deveined (leave tails on)
1 teaspoon salt
4 garlic cloves, crushed
1 cup tomato juice

4 sprigs parsley, chopped
¼ teaspoon lemon pepper marinade
¼ teaspoon oregano
Paprika

Marinate shrimp for at least 2 hours in mixture of all other ingredients. Preheat broiler. Place marinated shrimp in shallow broiling pan, pour marinade mixture over them, and broil 2 to 3 inches from heat 5 minutes on each side (longer for jumbo shrimp). Makes 4 servings (160 calories per QWL serving, shrimp only).

Herbed Shrimp in Wine

QWL dieters eat only the shrimp

1 pound large raw shrimp, cleaned (do not remove tails)
1 small onion, cut in slices
2 tablespoons minced parsley
1 small carrot, sliced very thin

5 tablespoons lemon juice
¼ cup dry white wine
1 teaspoon oregano
½ teaspoon salt
Black pepper

Wash shrimp and pat dry. Combine remaining ingredients in saucepan, and add the shrimp. Cook, covered, over low heat until shrimp are done, about 8 minutes (depending on size of shrimp). Pour all into a bowl and refrigerate overnight. To serve, remove shrimp from marinade, drain, and serve as main course, with chopped hard-cooked egg added if desired. (May also be served as appetizer with toothpicks.) Makes 4 servings (110 calories per QWL serving, shrimp only).

Marinated Shrimp Salad

QWL dieters eat only the shrimp and egg

1 pound cooked and
    cleaned shrimp
2 tablespoons minced parsley
½ teaspoon dry mustard
Juice of ½ lemon
2 teaspoons grated onion

⅓ teaspoon Worcestershire
    sauce
½ teaspoon salt
Black pepper
¼ cup dry sherry
2 chopped hard-cooked eggs

Combine all ingredients except shrimp, wine, and egg. Simmer together for 3 minutes. Add shrimp and wine. Cool and refrigerate not less than 12 hours. Remove shrimp from marinade, drain, and serve very cold with chopped egg sprinkled over them. Makes 4 servings (140 calories per serving).

Ginger Shrimp

2 pounds uncooked shrimp
½ cup chopped parsley
3 tablespoons no-sugar
    soy sauce

Artificial sweetener equal
    to 1½ teaspoons sugar
1½ teaspoons powdered
    ginger
½ teaspoon allspice

Rinse, shell, and devein shrimp, then place in bowl. Mix other ingredients together and spread over shrimp. Let shrimp sit in sauce for at least 1 hour, then bake until tender in preheated 400° oven 12 to 15 minutes, depending upon size of shrimp. May be eaten hot or chilled. Makes 4 servings (145 calories per serving).

Creole Shrimp

QWL dieters eat only the shrimp

1½ pounds raw shrimp, shelled and deveined
3 tablespoons vegetable bouillon
½ cup onion, minced
1 clove garlic, crushed
1 teaspoon bell peppers
1 cup tomato sauce

2 fresh tomatoes, cut into eighths
½ teaspoon salt
⅛ teaspoon black pepper
Dash red pepper
⅛ teaspoon oregano
Pinch basil

Heat bouillon in large no-stick skillet, and brown onion and garlic in it. Add shrimp and sauté, stirring, for 3 minutes. Add peppers, tomato sauce, fresh tomatoes, and seasonings, cover, and simmer 15 minutes. Makes 4 servings (165 calories per QWL serving, shrimp only).

Swedish Shrimp

QWL dieters eat only the shrimp

1½ pounds cooked, shelled shrimp
½ cup white wine vinegar
4 sprigs fresh dill, cut up small
6 raw mushrooms, sliced

1 roast pimiento, cut in strips
½ teaspoon salt
Black pepper
8 cherry tomatoes, halved
1 rib celery, cut up small

Mix together vinegar, dill, mushrooms, pimiento, salt, pepper, tomatoes, and celery. Place shrimp in bowl and spoon vinegar sauce over them. Place shrimp in bowl and spoon vinegar sauce over them. Cover bowl, and refrigerate at least overnight before using. Before serving, drain off vinegar. Makes 4 servings (160 calories per QWL serving, shrimp only).

Curried Shrimp

20 large cooked shrimp
(reserve 1 cup cooking
water)
3 teaspoons minced onion
2 tablespoons beef broth
1/4 teaspoon (more or less to
taste) curry powder

1/8 teaspoon powdered
ginger
1 teaspoon dried bell pepper
1/2 teaspoon salt
2 teaspoons lemon juice
Dash red pepper

Shell and devein shrimp, setting aside 1 cup water in
which shrimp have been cooked. Sauté onion in beef
broth in no-stick pan until transparent and golden. Add
curry powder, ginger, peppers, and salt. Stir and simmer
10 minutes. Add lemon juice, red pepper, shrimp and
1 cup water in which shrimp have been cooked. Stir so
shrimp are completely coated. Taste, and if you prefer
more curry or salt, add it now. Cover, bring to boil,
and simmer 5 minutes longer. Makes 4 servings (95
calories per serving).

Shrimp in Sauce

16 cooked shrimp, cut in
thirds (or crabmeat,
fresh or canned)
1/2 cup cottage cheese
1/2 teaspoon seasoned salt
1/8 teaspoon black pepper
1/2 teaspoon paprika

2 drops pepper sauce
2 tablespoons catsup
3 eggs, (2 raw, 1 hard-
cooked and chopped)
1 tablespoon minced chives
(optional)

Process cottage cheese and 2 raw eggs in blender at
low speed until smooth. Transfer to top of double
boiler with salt, paprika, pepper sauce, and catsup.
Cook over hot water, stirring constantly, until thickened. Add shrimp and hard-cooked chopped egg to
sauce and spoon into casserole (or 4 individual casseroles). Bake in 350° oven until shrimp are heated
through, about 10 minutes. Sprinkle chives over each
portion. Makes 4 servings (160 calories per serving).

Skewered Shrimp

16 jumbo shrimp
1½ teaspoons garlic salt
½ cup lemon juice
5 drops pepper sauce
½ teaspoon Worcestershire sauce

5 tablespoons chopped parsley
1 hard-cooked egg, chopped (optional)

Clean, devein, and split shrimp, leaving tails on. Mix other ingredients together in bowl and marinate shrimp for 1 hour or more in this mixture (keep in refrigerator). Turn occasionally to soak all sides.

Thread four marinated shrimp lengthwise on each of four skewers and lay on preheated broiler tray, about 3 inches from heat. Broil, turning until cooked through (about 5 minutes on each side). Sprinkle a little chopped egg over each serving. Makes 4 servings (110 calories per serving).

Shrimp for Dipping

24 cooked shrimp (about 1 pound after cooking)
2 tablespoons fresh lemon juice
⅓ cup tomato juice
¼ teaspoon grated lemon rind

3 tablespoons finely chopped parsley
½ teaspoon prepared mustard (preferably Dijon)
½ teaspoon salt
2 drops hot pepper sauce

Combine thoroughly all ingredients except shrimp. Place shrimp in a deep bowl and pour marinade over them. Refrigerate at least 2 to 3 hours, turning over two or three times. Drain shrimp to serve, pouring liquid into a small serving bowl. Using toothpicks, dip individual shrimp into marinade instead of using cocktail sauce. Makes 4 servings (110 calories per serving).

Creamy Shrimp Casserole

For Teenage QWL dieters only, with nonfat dry milk

16 cooked shrimp, cut in thirds
2 eggs
¼ cup nonfat dry milk
¼ cup water
½ teaspoon seasoned salt
½ teaspoon paprika
2 drops pepper sauce
1½ tablespoons cider vinegar

Break the eggs into the top of a double boiler and beat slightly. Mix water and nonfat dry milk and add with all other ingredients except shrimp to the eggs. Cook over hot water, stirring constantly, until thickened. Place shrimp in small casserole and cover with hot sauce. Bake in 350° oven until shrimp are heated through (about 10 minutes). Makes 4 servings (130 calories per serving).

Shrimp and Chicken in Shells

4 ounces fine chopped chicken
2 cups cooked shrimp, cut up
¾ cup cottage cheese
¾ teaspoon no-sugar soy sauce
½ cup grated part skim "Swiss-type" cheese (such as Jarlsberg)
1 teaspoon minced parsley
1 teaspoon grated lemon peel
1 teaspoon dry instant chicken broth
Paprika

Mash chicken with 2 teaspoons of the cottage cheese and the soy sauce, to make a paste. Spread over bottoms of 4 coquille shells. Cover each with ½ cup shrimp. Mix balance of cottage cheese, parsley, grated cheese, and grated lemon peel, and spread over shrimp in each shell. Sprinkle dry chicken broth and paprika over tops. Bake in preheated 400° oven for 10 to 12 minutes, until piping hot. Makes 4 servings (150 calories per serving).

Shrimp "Quiche"

½ pound cooked shrimp,   1 teaspoon grated onion
   cut in quarters   or minced chives
4 eggs   ½ teaspoon salt
8 ounces cottage cheese   Dash black pepper

Preheat broiler. Beat eggs slightly and mix with all
other ingredients. Spoon into 4 small baking dishes or
4 large seafood shells. Broil about 4 inches from heat
until of custard consistency (about 10 minutes, more or
less, depending on size of eggs). May be baked in moderate oven, but takes longer. Makes 4 servings (185
calories per serving).

EGG

Egg Combinations
with Meat, or Fish, or Shellfish

1 large egg, well beaten   Pepper to taste
1 ounce leftover lean beef,   Mixed herbs to taste
   diced   Paprika
Salt to taste

Combine all ingredients, then cook in no-stick skillet,
stirring with wooden spatula until set as you like. Serve
and sprinkle top with a little paprika (or chopped parsley). Makes 1 serving (150 calories—80 for egg, 70 for
lean meat).

Variations

Meat—instead of lean beef, use leftover lean lamb or
other meat, total about same number of calories.

Smoked meats such as frankfurter, bologna, salami,
lean tongue (trim off all visible fat)—heat the smoked
meat first in no-stick skillet. Pat fat from meat with
paper towel, then dice. Wipe fat from skillet with

paper towel before further cooking. In addition to egg, 80 calories, figure about the following:

> salami, 1 ounce, 90 calories
> bologna, all beef, 1 ounce, 80 calories
> 1 frankfurter (medium), all-beef, 150 calories
> 1 ounce lean beef tongue, 70 calories
> 1 slice lean bacon, 50 calories

Chicken, turkey—use ¼ cup diced chicken or turkey, 2 teaspoons chicken bouillon (85 calories per serving).

Chicken livers—use 1 large chicken liver (40 calories per serving).

Fish—use leftover lean fish, or canned drained salmon, tuna, or sardines (wash off oil and pat dry with paper towel) in recipe, combining well beaten egg. Lean fish averages 20 to 25 calories per ounce. Canned fish and smoked salmon about 50 calories per ounce.

Seafood—use diced cooked shrimps, crabmeat, lobster, drained minced clams, combining with well beaten egg. Averages 20 to 25 calories per ounce. Celery salt makes a tasty seasoning, may also add a little catsup, or chili sauce or cocktail sauce in cooking.

Western Meat 'n Eggs

3 eggs	3 small stuffed olives
½ cup meat in small cubes or pieces (use leftover lean beef, lamb or veal)	chopped or slivered
	1 tablespoon chili sauce
	1 tablespoon water
1 teaspoon parsley flakes (or fresh minced parsley)	Imitation butter-flavored salt, or seasoned salt
1 teaspoon grated onion	Paprika

Combine eggs, meat and other ingredients in a bowl while heating no-stick skillet, including the special salt to taste. Stir with fork to combine all ingredients, but don't whip. Pour into pan and cook over low heat, stirring thickening mixture occasionally. When almost finished, cover pan, turn off heat, and let mixture set for 1 or 2 minutes, then divide into two servings, using wooden spatula. Sprinkle with paprika for extra color if desired.

(You may also use ham, bologna, tongue, frankfurters, or other lean smoked meat. If you do, heat first in the no-stick skillet, then pat meat and pan dry with a paper towel before combining with other ingredients and cooking.) Makes 2 servings (265 calories per serving).

Herbed Omelet

2 large eggs, yolks and whites separated
¼ teaspoon salt
¼ teaspoon mixed herbs
¼ teaspoon parsley flakes
¼ teaspoon onion flakes
1 tablespoon bouillon
Grated part skim cheese

Beat egg yolks with salt, herbs, parsley and onion flakes. Beat egg whites until stiff, then fold into yolks slowly. Put the bouillon in a no-stick skillet, and warm, then add the egg mixture and cook slowly over low heat for about 5 minutes. Place omelet under broiler for about 2 minutes until lightly browned, then sprinkle with a little grated cheese and remove carefully from pan. Makes 2 servings (85 calories per serving).

Variation: instead of grated cheese, use 1 cup diced chicken. Makes 2 servings (200 calories per serving).

Strawberry-Flavored Omelet

4 eggs
¼ teaspoon salt
¼ cup cottage cheese
2 teaspoons strawberry no-sugar flavoring (try other flavors, also)
1 teaspoon granulated no-sugar sweetener

Beat eggs with salt until foamy. Mash cottage cheese and flavoring together. Heat no-stick pan, then add eggs. Lift edges as eggs begin to cook to allow uncooked portion to run under and contact pan. When almost cooked but soft on top, spoon cottage cheese mixture over one side of eggs and fold other side over it. Sprinkle omelet with granulated sweetener. If de-

sired, place for 30 seconds right under broiler flame to
brown top a little. Makes 4 servings (98 calories per
serving).

Variation: add to eggs 1 tablespoon double-strength
chicken bouillon, 1 tablespoon cottage cheese, 1 teaspoon minced parsley, paprika to taste (84 calories per
serving).

Rosemary Coddled Eggs

2 large eggs
¼ teaspoon finely ground parsley (optional)
2 pinches finely ground rosemary

Place eggs in a small saucepan, cover with cold water.
Place over low heat and thus bring *slowly* to a boil. As
soon as water starts to boil, remove saucepan from heat
and leave eggs right in the hot water for 5 more minutes. Crack eggs open into dish, sprinkle sparingly with
parsley, and then a pinch of rosemary per egg (adding
a little salt if desired). The herb adds delicious subtle
flavor to the very tender coddled eggs. Makes 1 serving
(160 calories).

Scrambled Eggs Deluxe

2 eggs
⅓ cup cottage cheese
1 teaspoon grated onion

2 tablespoons chipped beef,
diced
1 tablespoon chopped pickle
(optional)

Beat all ingredients together and cook in no-stick
skillet, stirring with wooden spatula until done to your
taste (3 to 4 minutes). Sprinkle with paprika or nutmeg if desired. Makes 1 serving (290 calories).

Variations: *Caraway eggs*—add to eggs 1 tablespoon
cottage cheese, 1 teaspoon water, 1 teaspoon caraway or
poppy seeds, ⅛ teaspoon garlic salt, pepper (175
calories).

Sesame eggs—add to eggs 2 teaspoons sesame seeds,

½ teaspoon mixed herbs, salt and black pepper to taste (180 calories).

Caviar eggs (not for water-retainers)—add to eggs 3 tablespoons cottage cheese, 1 tablespoon salmon red roe caviar, or any black caviar (2 servings, 120 calories per serving).

Eggs 'n "bacon"—add to eggs 1 teaspoon imitation bacon bits, ¼ teaspoon salt, black pepper (160 calories).

Creamy scrambled eggs (for OWL TEEN dieters only)—add to eggs 4 tablespoons buttermilk, celery salt to taste, 1 teaspoon poppy seeds, paprika to taste (180 calories).

Poached Eggs in Chicken Broth

4 eggs
1 tablespoon vinegar
4 cups chicken broth from "instant" cubes or powder
¼ teaspoon lemon juice
½ bay leaf
⅛ teaspoon savory
Paprika

Poach eggs while broth is simmering. Open the eggs carefully so yolks don't break, into a bowl, then slip eggs gently into a shallow pan of boiling salted water containing the vinegar. Reduce heat to a simmer, cover pan, and simmer about 3 minutes or until you see whites set. Lift eggs out carefully with a perforated spoon, placing one in each bowl of broth.

A few minutes before eggs are poaching, combine lemon juice, savory and bay leaf in broth. Simmer until eggs are almost done, then remove bay leaf, and pour broth into 4 bowls. Add poached egg to each bowl, sprinkle on a little paprika, and serve immediately. Makes 4 servings (90 calories per serving).

Lemon Eggs and Seafood

2 eggs
1 tablespoon onion flakes
1 tablespoon parsley flakes
½ cup cooked lobster meat, crabmeat, or shrimp (or mixture of 2 or 3)
1 tablespoon chicken broth, double-strength
1 teaspoon lemon juice
¼ teaspoon salt
Pepper, herbs, spices to taste

In a bowl, combine all ingredients by whipping gently with a fork.

Pour into a heated no-stick skillet and stir frequently over low flame with a wooden spatula (or carefully with a fork) until cooked to the tender consistency you like. Makes 4 servings (85 calories per serving).

Egg-Clam Combination

4 hard-cooked eggs
¼ teaspoon lemon pepper marinade
¼ teaspoon salt

4 tablespoons cottage cheese
1 can minced clams, drained (reserve juice for drinking)
1 small dill pickle, chopped

Shell eggs, cut in quarters, add lemon pepper and salt, and chop 2 at a time in blender. Mix gently with cottage cheese and fold in clams and chopped pickle. Sprinkle with paprika, if desired. Makes 4 servings (140 calories per serving).

Crunchy Egg Salad

4 hard-cooked large eggs
½ cup cottage cheese
2 tablespoons water

½ envelope dry instant vegetable or beef broth
1½ teaspoons imitation bacon bits

Peel eggs, cut in quarters, and chop in blender for a few seconds. Combine cottage cheese, water, and instant broth in a small blender jar and process at low speed until smooth and creamy. Mix with chopped eggs and add bacon bits. Makes 4 servings (110 calories per serving).

Curried Stuffed Eggs

4 hard-cooked eggs
4 ounces cooked chicken
1 tablespoon chicken broth

¼ teaspoon curry powder
½ teaspoon white horseradish
Paprika

Cut eggs in halves lengthwise, carefully remove yolks. Process egg yolks, chicken, chicken broth, curry, and horseradish in blender at "chop" speed for a few seconds. Fill cavities in egg whites with this mixture, sprinkle each with paprika, and serve as a main dish or hors d'oeuvres. Makes 4 servings (125 calories per serving).

Shrimp Deviled Eggs

4 medium-sized hard-cooked
  eggs, chilled
2 tablespoons chopped,
  cooked shrimp
½ teaspoon chopped scallions
  or grated onion

1 teaspoon chicken or
  onion broth
Salt and pepper to taste
Paprika or chopped dill

Cut peeled eggs in halves lengthwise. Remove yolks carefully, reserving whites. Mash yolks with all other ingredients except last; fill cavities of egg whites with this mixture. Top each half with a sprinkle of paprika or chopped dill. Cover and chill until time to serve. Makes 2 servings (45 calories per egg half).

Basic Stuffed Eggs

4 large hard-cooked eggs,
  cold
1 teaspoon prepared mustard
  (preferably Dijon)

2 teaspoons chicken broth
⅛ teaspoon seasoned salt
Lemon pepper marinade
Paprika

Cut peeled eggs in halves lengthwise. Remove yolk carefully, reserving whites. Mash yolk with remaining ingredients except paprika, using fork. Place this mixture lightly into cavities of egg whites. Sprinkle with paprika; cover and chill until time to serve. Makes 4 servings (45 calories per stuffed half).

Poached Egg in Milk

For QWL TEEN dieters only, contains skim milk

8 tablespoons skim milk   Dash black pepper
4 eggs   Paprika (optional)
¼ teaspoon onion salt

Spoon 2 tablespoons skim milk into each of 4 custard cups. Break the eggs and gently slide from shell into the 4 cups. Sprinkle with salt and pepper and bake in preheated 325° oven until done to your liking, about 20 minutes. Top with paprika. Makes 4 servings (82 calories per serving).

COTTAGE CHEESE

Cottage cheese in all its variations is an excellent protein food, very important in successful QWL dieting. It can be a "life saver" as a snack, as a side dish, and as a main dish—delicious, satisfying, healthful. Enjoy the quick, easy cottage cheese recipes often, but never eat too-large portions at any time or else the calories and pounds will add up.

Herbed Cottage Cheese

1 cup cottage cheese   1 teaspoon skim milk,
1 teaspoon ground herb mix   if desired
(your favorite)   Salt
2 teaspoons parsley flakes   Paprika

Mix all ingredients well using salt and paprika to taste. Top with a little paprika for color. (As an hors d'oeuvre, spread small amounts on slices of hard-cooked eggs.) Makes 2 servings (125 calories per serving).

Caraway Cottage Cheese

2 hard-cooked eggs,
  chopped
1 cup cottage cheese
3 teaspoons caraway seeds
  (or poppy seeds)

¼ teaspoon seasoned salt
⅛ teaspoon Hungarian
  paprika

Mix first 4 ingredients together with fork. Serve cold
with a sprinkle of paprika over each serving. Makes 4
servings (100 calories per serving).

Cottage Cheese Broth Mix

16 ounces cottage cheese
2 packets onion broth (or
  chicken) instant mix
1 teaspoon onion flakes or
  grated onion

1 teaspoon parsley flakes or
  minced parsley
1 teaspoon sesame seeds

Mix well all ingredients except sesame seeds with a
fork or in blender. Chill. Sprinkle sesame seeds on each
serving. Makes 4 servings (135 calories per serving).

Cottage Cheese Flavor Blend

16 ounces cottage cheese
1 packet instant beef broth
  (or chicken or vegetable
  broth)
1 teaspoon lemon juice

1 teaspoon prepared
  horseradish
1 tablespoon finely chopped
  olives (green or black)
Paprika

Combine all ingredients well with fork or in a
blender. Chill. Sprinkle top of each serving with paprika
if desired. Makes 4 servings (130 calories per serving).

Curried Cottage Cheese

16 ounces cottage cheese
1 teaspoon curry powder
2 teaspoons chopped parsley

Combine cottage cheese, curry powder, and 1 teaspoon chopped parsley until thoroughly mixed with a fork. Sprinkle top with remaining parsley. Serve as is, or chilled. Makes 4 servings (125 calories per serving).

Jellied Cottage Cheese

16 ounces cottage cheese
2 tablespoons artificially sweetened jelly or jam, any flavor
Cinnamon

Mix the cottage cheese and jelly thoroughly with a fork. Sprinkle top with cinnamon. Chill before serving.

If sour cream consistency is preferred, process in blender at low speed for about 30 seconds. Makes 4 servings (125 calories per serving).

Variations: *Coffee cottage cheese*—process in blender, 16 ounces cottage cheese, 2 teaspoons coffee, artificial sweetener equal to 2 teaspoons sugar (more or less to taste), top with cinnamon. Makes 4 servings (120 calories per serving).

Orange cottage cheese—process in blender, 16 ounces cottage cheese, rind of a small orange, artificial sweetener equal to 2 teaspoons sugar more or less to taste). Makes 4 servings (130 calories per serving).

Cottage Cheese Orange Slices

8 ounces cottage cheese
1 egg
¼ teaspoon cinnamon
¼ teaspoon nutmeg
½ teaspoon orange extract
Artificial sweetener equal to 2 teaspoons sugar
Dash of salt

Combine all ingredients in a blender and process at low speed until thoroughly combined and smooth. Place in a loaf dish, and keep in freezer an hour or more. Serve in slices. Makes 4 servings (85 calories per serving).

Cheese Pimiento Slices

4 tablespoons creamed cottage cheese
1 tablespoon chopped pimiento
1 teaspoon pickle relish

Salt, pepper, mixed herbs—to taste
Paprika
2 large hard-cooked eggs, sliced

In blender or with fork, mix all ingredients except egg slices into a smooth paste. Spread paste on slices of hard-boiled egg. Sprinkle tops with paprika for color and serve as a luncheon dish (may also be used for hors d'oeuvres). Makes 2 servings (110 calories per serving).

Cottage Cheese and Caviar

½ cup creamed cottage cheese
1 tablespoon skim milk
1 tablespoon white fish roe caviar

1 chopped hard-cooked egg
Lemon juice

In blender (or by hand), combine cottage cheese and milk at low speed for a few seconds until thoroughly mixed. Divide into 2 servings, topping each with caviar and then chopped egg, and sprinkle on a little lemon juice. (Since the caviar has high salt content it should be avoided by individuals who tend to retain water, and eaten only sparingly by any dieter.) Makes 1 serving (230 calories).

Cottage Cheese with Salmon (or Tuna)

12 ounces cottage cheese
1 cup salmon well drained,
  or cooked fresh salmon,
  in small flakes (or tuna)
1 teaspoon lemon juice
½ teaspoon celery salt
1 teaspoon chopped onion
  or parsley
½ teaspoon rosemary
2 tablespoons chopped red
  pimiento

Combine all ingredients with a fork until well mixed, but do it lightly in order to keep salmon in flakes, and pimiento from becoming mashed. Makes 4 servings (160 calories per serving).

Cottage Cheese with Shrimp (or Crabmeat, or Lobster)

12 ounces cottage cheese
8 large cooked shrimp cut
  in ⅛-inch small slices
  (or 1 cup shredded crabmeat, or 1 cup diced
  lobster)
1 teaspoon lime or lemon juice
1 teaspoon minced onion or
  parsley
  (red pepper)
¼ teaspoon cayenne
1 teaspoon poppy seeds
  Allspice
4 lemon wedges

Mix all ingredients together lightly with a fork so shrimp slices are unbroken. Top each serving with a dusting of allspice and lemon wedge if desired. Makes 4 servings (110 calories per serving).

Cottage Cheese with Bologna

12 ounces cottage cheese
4 ounces all-beef bologna,
  diced into small bits
1 teaspoon chopped parsley
1 tablespoon chili sauce
¼ teaspoon dry mustard
4 teaspoons chopped green
  olives
Chili powder

Combine all ingredients with a fork, keeping mixture fluffy. Dust top of each serving lightly with chili powder if desired. Makes 4 servings (190 calories per serving).

Cottage Cheese and Bacon Bits

16 ounces cottage cheese
2 slices bacon, very well done, patted dry with paper towel, and crumbled into bits
1 teaspoon mixed herbs

With a fork, combine thoroughly the cottage cheese, crumbled bacon, and mixed herbs. Chill before serving. Makes 4 servings (140 calories per serving).

SAUCES AND DRESSINGS

Basic Spicy Sauce

½ cup cottage cheese   ½ teaspoon seasoned salt
2 tablespoons cider vinegar   Black pepper
½ teaspoon onion flakes
  (optional)

Process all ingredients together in blender at low speed until smooth and creamy (use small blender jar if you have one). Makes 1 cup (12 calories per tablespoon).

Variations: add poppy seeds, caraway seeds, sesame seeds, capers, chopped pickle, catsup, chili sauce, imitation bacon bits, and so on.

Excellent as substitute for: mayonnaise ... cream sauce ... sour cream ... and other high calorie sauces.

Delicious as dip for bits of meat, poultry, shrimp, crabmeat, lobster, scallops, fish ... whatever foods are permitted on QWL Diet.

Basic Variety Sauce

½ cup cottage cheese
2 tablespoons water
½ envelope instant chicken, beef, or vegetable broth

Process all ingredients together in blender at low speed until smooth and creamy (use small blender jar if you have one). Makes 1 cup (13 calories per tablespoon).

Variations: You may use vinegar instead of water ... you may add poppy seeds, caraway seeds, capers, chopped pickle, catsup, chili sauce, onion flakes, parsley flakes, garlic, other herbs and spices for variety.

Excellent as substitute for: mayonnaise ... cream sauce ... sour cream ... and other high calorie sauces.

Delicious as dip for bits of meat, shrimp, crabmeat, lobster, scallops, poultry, and so on, whatever foods are permitted on QWL Diet.

Spicy Sauce for Beef

1½ teaspoons garlic salt
1 tablespoon Worcestershire sauce
⅛ teaspoon pepper sauce
⅓ cup chili sauce

Mix all ingredients together. Spread over steaks or roasts before placing in oven or on grill. May also be used (sparingly) instead of catsup. Makes ⅓ cup (10 calories per tablespoon).

Western Coffee Meat Sauce

May be used sparingly on meats where extra flavor and juiciness, along with spiciness, is desired

1 cup black coffee, extra-strong
½ cup Worcestershire sauce
1 cup catsup
2 tablespoons lemon juice
Artificial sweetening equal to 1 tablespoon sugar
1 teaspoon seasoned salt
⅛ teaspoon pepper sauce

In a saucepan, mix and stir all ingredients well. Bring almost to boiling point, then simmer for ½ hour, stirring several times. Spoon sparingly on meats before or after cooking, refrigerating excess, and reheating when used again. Makes 2 cups (6 calories per tablespoon).

Lamb Mint Sauce

½ cup white wine vinegar
½ cup fresh mint
1½ cups water
¼ teaspoon powdered
  ginger

¼ cup lemon juice
½ teaspoon salt
Artificial sweetener equal to
  2 teaspoons sugar
  (or more, to taste)

Combine vinegar, ¼ cup mint, and 1 cup water in saucepan. Bring to boil, then simmer for about 20 minutes (about ½ of liquid should be cooked away). Put through strainer. Add ½ cup water, ginger, lemon juice, salt, and sweetener. Refrigerate. Add rest of mint leaves when cool. Use sparingly with lamb. Makes 2 cups (1½ calories per tablespoon).

Horseradish-Curry Sauce

2 tablespoons prepared
  horseradish
2 teaspoons prepared
  mustard
3 tablespoons chili sauce
½ teaspoon garlic salt

½ teaspoon curry powder
Juice of 1 lemon
½ teaspoon grated lemon
  rind
Dash cayenne pepper
White pepper to taste

Drain horseradish. Stir all ingredients together and keep refrigerated. Use very sparingly to flavor cold meats. Makes ½ cup (5 calories per teaspoon).

Meat-Poultry-Fish Herb Garnish

1 teaspoon fresh herbs, chopped, or ½ teaspoon dried
 herbs (see below)
1 teaspoon lemon juice

Mix lemon juice with one of the following and use as
garnish for boiled or broiled meats, poultry, or fish.

 1 teaspoon mint, chopped chives, chopped scallions,
 chopped dill
 or
 ½ teaspoon tarragon, thyme, marjoram, oregano, mixed
 herbs

Use sparingly, calories negligible.

Herb Vinegar

1 cup cider vinegar
½ cup fresh tarragon, basil, or dill (or combinations of all
 three)
or
¼ cup same herbs, dried

Combine vinegar and herbs in covered jar. Shake together well to intermix flavors thoroughly. Keep in a
warm place for at least a week, shaking well now and
then. Then strain twice through cheesecloth.

Use for marinating meats, or brush on fish before
broiling or baking, or as salad dressing; also in the
Inches-Off Diet and Stay-Slim Eating. Makes 1½ cups
(5 calories per tablespoon).

Mayonnaise-Type Dressing

½ cup cottage cheese
1 egg, beaten
¼ teaspoon seasoned salt
Dash freshly ground
 black pepper

⅛ teaspoon dry mustard
1 tablespoon tarragon wine
 vinegar

Place all ingredients together in blender and process at low speed until well mixed and creamy. Use as substitute for mayonnaise. Makes ¾ cup (17 calories per tablespoon).

Blender Mustard Sauce

⅓ cup cider vinegar	1 tablespoon paprika
1 egg	2 tablespoons prepared
Artificial sweetener equal to	mustard
1 teaspoon sugar	

Process all ingredients together in blender at high speed until smooth and creamy. Cook over low heat in saucepan, stirring constantly until thickened.

Use sparingly as cold sauce with meats, poultry, fish eggs. Also spread lightly over meats, poultry, or fish, before broiling. Makes ½ cup (15 calories per tablespoon).

Vinaigrette Sauce

May also be used on Inches-Off Diet, for salads, vegetables, etc., and for Stay-Slim Eating

2 cloves garlic, crushed	4 tablespoons water
½ cup tarragon vinegar	1 teaspoon salt
¼ teaspoon paprika	1 teaspoon mixed herbs
½ teaspoon liquid artificial	(dill, rosemary, thyme)
sweetener	

Shake all ingredients together in a covered refrigerator container. Will keep in refrigerator indefinitely. Use on cold fish, lamb, chicken, etc., for unusual flavor. Makes ¾ cup (3 calories per tablespoon).

Tangy Marinade Barbecue Sauce

Use for QWL diet, or Inches-Off Diet, also for
Stay-Slim Eating

½ cup chili sauce
1 teaspoon prepared mustard
½ teaspoon salt
Dash pepper sauce
1 teaspoon lemon juice

Artificial sweetener equal
  to ½ teaspoon sugar
Dash chili powder
½ cup water

Shake all ingredients together thoroughly in a jar.
Marinate meats in sauce for at least 2 hours, and baste
with remaining sauce while cooking (good for outdoor
barbecues, too). Makes 1 cup (20 calories per tablespoon).

Seafood Cocktail Sauce

1 cup chili sauce
1 teaspoon prepared horseradish
1 teaspoon Worcestershire
  sauce
½ teaspoon prepared
  mustard

¼ teaspoon seasoned salt
½ teaspoon finely chopped
  onion
3 drops bottled hot
  pepper sauce
1 teaspoon lemon juice

Mix ingredients well, and chill. Keep in tightly covered bowl or bottle for use sparingly with QWL servings. Makes 1½ cups (12 calories per tablespoon).

Creamy Seafood Sauce

Use on hot or cold shellfish and fish

½ cup cottage cheese
2 tablespoons clam juice

Dash black pepper
Paprika

Process first three ingredients together in blender at
low speed (use small blender jar if you have one) for a

few seconds until creamy. Spoon over shellfish or fish.
Top with a sprinkle of paprika. Makes 1 cup (4 calories
per teaspoon).

Sauce for Basting Poultry

½ cup vinegar
½ cup prepared mustard
1½ tablespoons Worcester-
    shire sauce
Artificial sweetener equal
    to ½ cup sugar

¼ teaspoon pepper sauce
⅛ teaspoon basil
⅓ cup light white wine

Beat all ingredients together and use to baste poultry
(chicken, turkey, Rock Cornish hens) during roasting,
broiling, or on spit. Makes 1⅓ cups (8 calories per
tablespoon).

DESSERTS

The QWL dessert recipes here are delicious, satisfying, low in calories, and conform to speedy QWL
reducing. The number of desserts possible with QWL
permitted protein ingredients is necessarily limited. If
you prefer, just skip dessert at any or every meal, and
you'll lose weight even quicker.

Gelatin Fluff

1 ⅜-ounce packet raspberry
    (or cherry) low-calorie
    gelatin

1 cup boiling water
1 cup cold water
2 egg whites

Dissolve gelatin in boiling water in a bowl; add cold
water. Chill until partly jelled. Beat until frothy with
egg beater or electric mixer. Beat egg whites in another
bowl until almost stiff. Fold into partly jelled gelatin

until evenly distributed. Spoon into 4 dessert glasses and chill 2 to 3 hours until firm. Makes 4 servings (18 calories per serving).

Cottage Gelatin Dessert

½ cup serving artificially sweetened gelatin dessert (no more than 15 calories)	½ teaspoon granulated sugar substitute
1 tablespoon cottage cheese	2 dashes vanilla extract
	Nutmeg

Prepare gelatin dessert according to package directions. With a fork, combine cottage cheese with sugar substitute and vanilla. Spoon mixture over gelatin dessert. Sprinkle top of cheese with nutmeg. Makes 1 serving (35 calories).

Orange Gelatin Ices

1 package artificially sweetened orange gelatin dessert	1 teaspoon orange juice
1 cup cold water	1 teaspoon grated orange rind
1 cup boiling water	Cinnamon (optional)

Mix the gelatin in the boiling water in a bowl until completely dissolved. Add cold water, orange juice, and rind, stirring until completely combined. Place bowl in refrigerator until mixture is slightly thickened. Process thickened mixture in blender at moderate speed until foamy (about 2 minutes). Pour at once into 4 individual serving dishes, set them in freezer until frozen, usually 3 or more hours. Serve with a sprinkling of cinnamon on top if desired. Makes 4 servings (12 calories per serving).

Deluxe Coffee Jell

1 envelope unflavored
gelatin
4 heaping teaspoons in-
stant coffee (regular or
no-caffeine)
⅛ teaspoon salt
1¾ cups water

Artificial sweetener equal to
6 teaspoons sugar (more
or less to taste)
2 teaspoons non-dairy
creamer
Nutmeg

Mix together gelatin, instant coffee, salt, in a saucepan. Add ½ cup of the water, place over low heat, stirring until all ingredients are dissolved. Remove from
heat, add remaining water, sweetener, creamer, stirring
well until all ingredients are thoroughly dissolved and
combined. Pour into a bowl or 4 serving dishes. Chill
until firm. Serve with sprinkle of nutmeg on top if desired. Makes 4 servings (16 calories per serving).

Creamy Gelatin Dessert

4 half-cup servings artificially sweetened gelatin dessert,
your choice of flavors
4 ounces cottage cheese
Cinnamon (optional)

Prepare the gelatin dessert according to package directions. When gelatin is slightly thickened, not set,
add the cottage cheese and process with a rotary beater
until thoroughly combined. Chill until set. Sprinkle
with cinnamon, if desired. Makes 4 servings (45 calories
per serving).

Vanilla Gelatin Dessert

1 envelope lemon flavor artificially sweetened gelatin
dessert (32 calories)

2 cups boiling water
½ teaspoon vanilla extract
Nutmeg

Sprinkle gelatin slowly into the boiling water, and stir to dissolve completely. Stir in the vanilla extract. Pour into 4 dessert dishes. Chill until firm. Sprinkle a little nutmeg on top when serving. Makes 4 servings (9 calories per serving).

Orange-Juice Gelatin Dessert

1 envelope unflavored
   gelatin (30 calories)
½ cup cold water
1¼ cups boiling water
¼ cup granulated artificial
   sweetener
½ teaspoon salt

2 tablespoons no-sugar
   orange juice
1 tablespoon lemon juice
½ teaspoon orange extract
⅛ teaspoon vanilla extract
Grated orange peel

Combine gelatin slowly with the cold water to soften. Add hot water, sweetener, and salt, and stir until fully dissolved. Add orange juice, lemon juice, orange extract, and vanilla, and stir well. Pour into 4 dessert dishes. Chill until firm. Sprinkle top lightly with grated orange peel when serving. Makes 4 servings (15 calories per serving).

Lemon-Juice Gelatin Dessert

1 envelope unflavored
   gelatin (30 calories)
½ cup cold water
1¼ cups boiling water
⅓ cup granulated artificial
   sweetener

⅛ teaspoon salt
2 tablespoons lemon juice
½ teaspoon lemon extract
⅛ teaspoon vanilla extract
Grated lemon peel

Sprinkle gelatin slowly over the cold water to soften. Add hot water, sweetener and salt, and stir until fully dissolved. Add lemon juice, lemon extract, and vanilla, and stir well. Pour into 4 dessert dishes. Chill until firm. Sprinkle top lightly with grated lemon peel when serving. Makes 4 servings (20 calories per serving).

Gelatin Dessert with Creamy Topping

Prepare artificially sweetened gelatin dessert in your favorite flavor (no more than 15 calories per ½ cup serving) according to package directions; or made with unflavored gelatin and artificially sweetened flavored syrup. Top with:

QWL Creamy Topping

1 white of egg	½ teaspoon instant coffee
Pinch of salt	⅛ teaspoon vanilla extract
⅓ cup granulated sugar substitute	

Beat white of egg, with salt added, until stiff. Very slowly add sugar and coffee, and beat until mixture stands in stiff peaks. Fold in vanilla. Spoon on top of gelatin dessert. Makes 1 serving (40 calories, topping only).

Topping for Gelatin Desserts

2 egg whites	3 tablespoons artificial sweetener flavoring (your choice of flavors)
2 teaspoons granulated artificial sweetener	
¼ teaspoon cream of tartar	1 teaspoon unflavored gelatin

Mix all ingredients together in top of double boiler over boiling water (do not let top saucepan touch the water). Beat mixture together with electric beater until it is stiff and forms peaks (about 5 minutes). (10 calories per tablespoon.)

Cinnamon Pudding

3 tablespoons cottage cheese, small curd	½ teaspoon granulated artificial sweetener
½ teaspoon cinnamon	⅛ teaspoon vanilla extract

Mix ingredients together with fork, and serve. Top with a sprinkling of a little more cinnamon or grated orange rind. Makes 1 serving (60 calories).

Maple Coffee Dessert

1 enveloped unflavored
   gelatin (30 calories)
¼ cup artificially sweetened
   "maple" pancake syrup
   (10 calories)

2 cups very hot black coffee
   Nutmeg or cinnamon

Sprinkle gelatin slowly into syrup to soften. Add very hot coffee and stir until combined thoroughly with syrup and gelatin. Divide into 4 serving dessert dishes, and chill. Just before serving, top with sprinkle of nutmeg or cinnamon. Makes 4 servings (15 calories per serving).

Cottage Jam Blend

3 tablespoons cottage cheese
1 teaspoon orange or other flavor low-calorie jam, no more than 13 calories per teaspoon
Nutmeg or orange rind

Combine cottage cheese and jam thoroughly with a fork or in a blender. Mound on serving dish, and sprinkle top with nutmeg or orange rind. Makes 1 serving (60 calories per serving).

Cottage Cheese Pudding

2 cups cottage cheese,
   small curd
3 eggs, well beaten
½ teaspoon vanilla
½ teaspoon orange extract

Artificial sweetener to equal
   2 tablespoons sugar
¼ teaspoon cinnamon
⅛ teaspoon salt

Combine all the ingredients gently, and spread in a shallow, no-stick baking dish. Sprinkle top with a little nutmeg (even tastier if nutmeg is fresh-scraped on a small grater).

Bake in 325° oven (preheated) for about ¾ hour (test by inserting knife in pudding, done when knife comes out clean). Makes 8 servings (90 calories per serving).

Refreshment Ice

16 ounces no-sugar flavored soda (your choice of flavors)
2 teaspoons lemon juice

Combine soda and lemon juice, pour into ice tray (preferably with individual ice cube cups). Freeze until solid cubes, then use as desired any time you want quick, sweet refreshment.

You can make your own flavor combinations by mixing 2 or more sodas together, such as orange soda and ginger ale, then freezing. Makes 2 servings (calories negligible).

"Like Ice Cream"

For QWL TEEN dieters only, contains milk

1 tablespoon unflavored gelatin
2 tablespoons cold skim milk
1½ cups skim milk to be heated
3 ounces no-sugar flavoring syrup, your choice of flavors

⅛ teaspoon salt
1½ cups nonfat dry milk
1 tablespoon orange juice
1 teaspoon grated orange rind
¾ cup water

Soften gelatin in 2 tablespoons cold skim milk with a fork. Heat the 1½ cups skim milk, flavoring, and salt in a saucepan almost to boiling point (don't boil), then add to gelatin mixture and stir until all ingredients are dissolved and combined. Chill in refrigerator until slightly thickened.

While mixture is chilling, combine 1½ cups dry milk with orange juice, rind, and ¾ cup water, then beat in electric mixer until stiff (5 minutes or longer). Now fold into slightly thickened mixture from refrigerator, combine thoroughly, and spread in ice trays. Leave until frozen firm. Makes 4 servings (82 calories per serving).

"Like Frozen Custard"

For QWL TEEN dieters only, contains milk

1 tablespoon unflavored gelatin

2 ounces cold water

2 cups skim milk

2 eggs

Artificial sweetener equal to 2 teaspoons sugar (more or less to taste)

½ teaspoon vanilla extract

½ teaspoon orange extract

Sprinkle gelatin in the cold water in a saucepan to soften. Heat skim milk to boiling point (don't boil), and combine with gelatin mixture, eggs, and sweetener; stir until gelatin is dissolved. Keep stirring over low flame until mixture thickens, then stir in the vanilla and orange flavorings. Pour entire mixture into ice tray, place in refrigerator. Stir every half hour until mixture is fairly set and ready to eat like frozen custard. Makes 4 servings (87 calories per serving).

Egg Custard

For TEEN QWL dieters only, contains skim milk

2 eggs, lightly beaten

1 teaspoon granulated artificial sweetener

2 cups skim milk

1 teaspoon vanilla

Nutmeg

Beat sweetener into eggs. Add skim milk and vanilla slowly and mix thoroughly. Divide into 4 custard cups.

Sprinkle nutmeg on each. Place cups in a pan of hot water in preheated 325° oven and bake about 1 hour. A knife inserted into custard should come out clean. Makes 4 servings (82 calories per serving).

Coffee "Parfait"

For QWL TEEN dieters only, contains skim milk

1½ envelopes unflavored gelatin	Pinch of salt
⅛ cup cold water	1 cup strong coffee
1 cup heated skim milk	½ teaspoon vanilla
2 medium eggs, separated	Liquid artificial sweetening equal to ⅓ cup sugar

Soften gelatin in cold water. Add to hot skim milk and stir to dissolve gelatin. Beat egg yolks, pour into top of double boiler, add coffee and salt. Cook over boiling water 5 minutes. Remove from heat and stir gelatin into mixture. Cool while you beat egg whites 1 minute, add sweetener, and continue beating until egg whites form stiff peaks. Add vanilla. Fold into gelatin mixture and spoon into 4-cup mold or 4 individual molds. Chill until firm. Makes 4 servings (67 calories per serving).

Coffee Froth

For QWL TEEN dieters only, contains milk

¼ cup nonfat dry milk	3 tablespoons no-sugar coffee syrup (try other flavors too)
½ cup water	
⅓ cup crushed ice	

Process all ingredients together at medium speed in blender. Serve with straw and spoon. Makes 1 serving (35 calories).

Coffee Nog

For QWL TEEN dieters only, contains skim milk

4 cups chilled black coffee (regular or no-caffeine)
4 eggs
4 ounces nonfat dry milk

Artificial sweetener equal to 8 teaspoons sugar (more or less, to taste)
½ teaspoon vanilla extract
Nutmeg

Pour the coffee into blender container. Add eggs and other ingredients except nutmeg. Process at moderate speed until mixture is thickened and fluffy (about 2 minutes). Serve with nutmeg sprinkled on top. Makes 4 servings (90 calories per serving).

Mock Whipped Cream

For QWL TEEN dieters only, contains skim milk

4 ounces evaporated skim milk
Artificial sweetener equal to 1 teaspoon sugar

½ teaspoon vanilla extract
1 tablespoon lemon juice
¼ teaspoon powdered unflavored gelatin

Chill evaporated skim milk until nearly frozen. Pour into small deep mixing bowl and beat with electric mixer until almost stiff. Add other ingredients and continue whipping until stiff. Delicious topping for black coffee, with low-calorie sodas, or on gelatin desserts. Use immediately, or rewhip for each subsequent use. Sprinkle nutmeg or cinnamon on top if you like. Makes about 1½ cups (5 calories per tablespoon).

Variations: *Almond Cream*—same recipe but use ½ teaspoon almond extract instead of vanilla. *Rum Cream* —use ½ teaspoon rum extract instead of vanilla. *Coffee Cream*—substitute 1 teaspoon instant coffee instead of vanilla. *Ginger Cream*—substitute powdered ginger to your taste instead of vanilla. *Orange Cream*—substitute ½ teaspoon orange extract instead of vanilla. *Lemon Cream*—substitute ½ teaspoon lemon extract instead of vanilla.

Nutmeg Dessert Topping

For QWL TEEN dieters only, contains milk

¼ cup ice water
¼ cup nonfat dry milk

Artificial sweetener equal
to 2 teaspoons sugar
(more or less, to taste)
¼ teaspoon nutmeg

Combine all ingredients in electric mixer bowl. Beat at high speed until mixture is consistency of whipped cream. Use as dessert topping, also on beverages if desired. Makes 1 serving (6 calories per tablespoon).

BEVERAGES

Coffee-Egg Bracer

2 cups strong black coffee
Yolk of 1 egg
2 pinches of cinnamon

1 pinch of paprika
1 pinch ground ginger
¼ teaspoon lemon juice

Place all ingredients in a blender and process at low speed until completely combined. Chill. Stir briskly before serving. Makes 2 servings (35 calories per serving).

Western Ranch Coffee

½ cup ground coffee,
    any grind to suit type
    of coffee-maker
1 small egg, well beaten

½ cup cold water
Salt, a dash
1 quart cold water

Mix well the ground coffee, beaten egg, ½ cup cold water, and salt. Place in coffee-maker along with 1 quart cold water and cook according to general instructions for the coffee-maker.

For those robust individuals who like strong coffee,

with or without added artificial sweetener. Makes 4 servings (22 calories per serving).

Creamy Cooler

8 ounces no-sugar carbonated beverage (your choice of flavors)
1 teaspoon nonfat dry milk or non-dairy coffee creamer
Nutmeg or cinnamon

To a glass of soda in blender container, add the milk powder, a dash of nutmeg or cinnamon, and several ice cubes. Process at medium speed until thoroughly blended. Serve in a chilled glass with an added sprinkle of nutmeg or cinnamon on top. Makes 1 serving (15 calories).

Cinnamon Coffee

1 jar (2 ounce) freeze-dried coffee (regular or decaffeinated)	Artificial sweetener (granulated) equivalent to ¾ cup sugar
1 tablespoon ground cinnamon	2 teaspoons dried orange peel

Mix these dry ingredients together thoroughly and pack in tightly covered jar. To serve, for each cup of spiced coffee, pour ¾ cup hot water over 1 tablespoon of the mixture; stir until dissolved. (17 calories per serving.)

Spiced Coffee

4 cups strong black coffee	1 dozen cloves
1 teaspoon powered nutmeg	Artificial sweetener
1 teaspoon powdered cinnamon	

Brew (or use instant) strong black coffee until finished. To the pot add nutmeg, cinnamon and cloves. Stir well, then simmer, don't let boil, for 5 to 10 mintues. Pour into cups, and serve along with artificial sweetener for use according to individual taste.

For iced spiced coffee, prepare the hot mixture as directed, then chill and serve in glasses, each containing ice cubes. Makes 4 servings (calories negligible).

Fruited Iced Coffee

4 cups strong black coffee	¼ teaspoon vanilla extract
¼ teaspoon orange extract	¼ teaspoon ground nutmeg
¼ teaspoon lemon extract	Cinnamon

Mix coffee with all ingredients except cinnamon. Chill. Stir again. Pour into 4 tall glasses containing ice cubes. Sprinkle each serving with a little cinnamon.

May also be served hot. Have artificial sweetener available for those who may want it. Makes 4 servings (10 calories per serving).

Lemony Spiced Tea

Also delicious for Inches-Off Dieters and Stay-Slim Eaters

1 quart spiced tea brewed according to package directions from any brand of "Spiced tea" available in bags or loose tea
4 thin slices lemon
Artificial sweetener

Brew the hot spiced tea, pour into 4 cups, place 1 lemon slice in each cup on top of liquid. Provide granulated or liquid artificial sweetener for use according to individual taste.

For iced tea, brew hot, then chill, and serve in tall, thin glasses preferably, filled with ice cubes. Makes 4 servings (20 calories per serving).

Variations: *Orange Spiced Tea*—use thin slice orange instead of lemon. *Cinnamon Spiced Tea*—in addition to thin lemon slice, stir each drink with a cinnamon stick and leave it in cup or glass when serving. *Cloved Spiced Tea*—insert 4 cloves in lemon or orange slice, and place atop tea in each cup or glass. *Pineapple Spiced Tea*—stir each drink with a pineapple spear and leave it in cup or glass when serving (QWL dieters don't eat the pineapple, others will).

Cloved Iced Tea

1 quart boiling water	½ lime (or lemon)
4 teaspoons tea in metal ball	8 cloves
or 4 tea bags	Artificial sweetener

To boiling water in heavy pitcher or other container, add tea, entire squeezed ½ lime (including peel) and cloves. Let stand for about an hour until cooled. Remove squeezed tea bags or tea ball. Chill in refrigerator. Each individual may add artificial sweetener to taste, if desired. (Will keep several days in refrigerator.) Makes 4 servings (4 calories per serving).

Minty Lemon Cooler

For QWL TEEN dieters only, contains skim milk
QWL adult dieters leave out the milk

16 ounces no-sugar	4 sprigs of mint
lemon-type soda	4 thin lemon slices
16 ounces skim milk	

Combine cold soda and milk, mixing well. Pour into 4 tall glasses, drop a sprig of mint in each glass and top with lemon slice. For an extra refreshing touch, chill glasses beforehand in refrigerator, or for a few minutes in freezer. Makes 4 servings (45 calories per serving).

Tempting Cooler

For QWL TEEN dieters only, contains skim milk;
also for Stay-Slim Eaters

6 ounces skim milk
Artificial sweetened flavored syrup (according to bottle
   directions)
3 ice cubes

Combine in blender and mix at "stir" speed (or
"low" speed) for 1 minute. Makes 1 serving (75
calories).

Milk Refresher

For QWL TEEN dieters only, contains milk

Crushed ice   1 teaspoon no-sugar flavored
8 ounces skim milk   syrup (more or less to taste,
Sprig of mint (optional)   your favorite flavors)

Fill glass halfway with crushed ice, pour in milk and
add flavoring, stirring briskly until contents are well
combined and very cold. Float sprig of mint on top, if
available. Makes 1 serving (92 calories).

Caribbean Eggnog Delight

For QWL TEEN dieters only, contains milk

6 ounces skim milk   ⅛ teaspoon vanilla extract
1 egg, yolk and white   ⅛ teaspoon rum extract
   separated   2 ice cubes
No-sugar sweetener equal to   Nutmeg
   1 teaspoon sugar (more
   or less to taste)

Combine skim milk, beaten egg yolk, sweetener,
vanilla and rum extracts, ice cubes, and dash of nutmeg, in blender container. Process until fully mixed and

thickened. Meanwhile, beat the egg white separately until a bit stiff, then gently fold egg white into the mixture. Serve in chilled glass with a little more nutmeg sprinkled on top. Makes 1 serving (150 calories per serving).

Thick Coffee Milk Shake

For QWL TEEN dieters only, contains milk

12 ounces cold water	No-sugar sweetener equal to
2 teaspoons instant coffee (regular or no-caffeine)	3 teaspoons sugar (more or less to taste)
¼ cup nonfat dry milk	4 ice cubes

Place all ingredients in blender container, and process at high speed until fully combined and thickened (1 or 2 minutes). Makes 2 servings (25 calories per serving).

Buttermilk Treat

For QWL TEEN dieters only

1 pint buttermilk	¼ teaspoon cinnamon
1 teaspoon vanilla extract	Artificial sweetener equal
¼ teaspoon nutmeg	to ¼ cup sugar

Mix all ingredients well. Chill, then stir again. Serve in small glasses and sprinkle a little more cinnamon or nutmeg on each serving. Makes 4 servings (50 calories per serving).

Guidelist of Herbs and
Spices For Seasoning
a Variety of Foods

HERBS AND SPICES are particularly helpful in varying recipes for the Quick Weight Loss Diet (also for the Inches-Off Diet, and for Stay-Slim Eating). Such seasoning won't add any calories to a dish, but it enhances the flavor.

To help you use these additives creatively, here are some basic guidelines. Until you learn the character and strength of the seasonings, use very small amounts. Then be guided by your own likes and dislikes. You'll note that many of the herbs are suggested for more than one type of food. This listing provides a general guide rather than a strict rule.

MEAT

Allspice	Dill	Pepper
Basil	Garlic	Rosemary
Bay Leaves	Marjoram	Sage
Cayenne (Red	Mint	Salt
Pepper)	Mustard	Savory
Celery Salt	Onion	Tarragon
Chili	Oregano	Thyme
Cloves	Paprika	Tumeric
Curry	Parsley	

POULTRY

Basil	Marjoram	Rosemary
Bay Leaves	Mint	Saffron
Cayenne	Mustard	Sage
Celery Salt	Onion	Salt
Chervil	Oregano	Savory
Coriander	Paprika	Tarragon
Curry	Parsley	Thyme
Garlic	Pepper	
Ginger	Poultry Seasoning	

FISH / SHELLFISH

Allspice	Fennel	
Bay Leaves	Garlic	Rosemary
Cayenne	Mace	Sage
Celery Salt	Marjoram	Salt
Celery Seed	Mint	Savory
Chervil	Onion	Thyme
Curry	Paprika	
Dill	Parsley	

EGGS / SALADS / VEGETABLES

Bay Leaves	Garlic	Sage
Cayenne	Onion	Salt
Celery Salt	Oregano	Tarragon
Chervil	Paprika	Thyme
Coriander	Parsley	
Dill	Pepper	

Useful in many recipes for a large variety of foods, to add flavor and texture: Caraway Seeds—Poppy Seeds—Sesame Seeds.

Quick Weight
Loss Menus

HERE ARE TWO WEEKS of typical menus on the Quick
Weight Loss Diet. You'll find the recipes listed in the
index by page numbers. You may follow the menus
exactly, then repeat until you're down to your ideal
weight. Or, choose other recipes to make up your own
satisfying daily QWL menus according to your likes
and available foods.

Substitute as you wish, but don't exceed the size of
servings given in the recipes, averaging 4 ounces for
meat, 5 ounces of poultry, 6 ounces of fish or shellfish.
It's just common sense that the less you eat, the quicker
you'll lose those unwanted pounds and inches of fat
and flab.

With QWL menus along these lines, you'll lose
pounds rapidly, week after week. You may also substitute for a recipe the basic food itself, such as plain lean
hamburger, broiled steak or fish, boiled eggs, or plain
cottage cheese. Or use your own combinations of the
basic permitted QWL foods and seasonings.

You don't have to eat every course listed in the
menus. If you eat only the main course and beverage at
each meal, as many newly-slim QWL dieters do, you'll
lose weight even more quickly.

As explained previously, you don't count calories on
the Quick Weight Loss Diet. However, if you wish to
—as a double check that you're not taking portions that
are too large (and therefore are overeating in respect to
losing weight), then check the counts given with each

recipe. Furthermore, these calorie counts are necessary when you use QWL recipes for Stay-Slim Eating, as you will.

Reminder: don't forget your daily vitamin-mineral pill.

Quick Weight Loss Menus

MONDAY

Breakfast
Strawberry-flavored omelet
Coffee, tea, or other QWL beverage (you are not to use cream, milk, or sugar, while on the QWL Diet)
Snack
Curry soup
Lunch
Onion broth
Poached fish with herbed egg
Gelatin fluff
Coffee, tea, or other QWL beverage
Snack
Creamy cooler
Dinner
Jellied beef bouillon
Beef Japanese style
Caraway cottage cheese
Pickle relish
Maple coffee dessert
Coffee, tea, or other QWL beverage
Snack
Cinnamon pudding

TUESDAY

Breakfast
Herbed cottage cheese
Coffee, tea, or other QWL beverage
Snack
Chicken liver canapé

Lunch
    Jellied clam consommé
    Quick beef minute steak
    Pickle slice
    Coffee gelatin dessert
    Coffee, tea, or other QWL beverage
Snack
    Lemony spiced tea
Dinner
    Chopped liver balls
    Tasty chicken breasts
    Seasoned cottage cheese
    Orange gelatin ices
    Coffee, tea, or other QWL beverage
Snack
    Refreshment ice

WEDNESDAY

Breakfast
    Rosemary coddled eggs
    Coffee, tea, or other QWL beverage
Snack
    Tasty cheese balls
Lunch
    Snowball onion-clam soup
    Fish in "see-through bag"
    Chili sauce
    Deluxe coffee jell
    Coffee, tea, or other QWL beverage
Snack
    Cottage cheese pudding
Dinner
    Meat-bits bouillon
    Thymed leg of lamb
    Artificially sweetened mint jelly
    Vanilla gelatin dessert
    Coffee, tea, or other QWL beverage
Snack
    Cottage jam

THURSDAY

Breakfast
Orange cottage cheese
Coffee, tea, or other QWL beverage
Snack
Refreshment ice
Lunch
Shrimp-bits bouillon
Shellfish broil
Pickle relish
Lemon juice gelatin dessert
Coffee, tea, or other QWL beverage
Snack
Seasoned liver canapé
Dinner
Jellied chicken/turkey bouillon
Simple broiled chicken
Olives
Gelatin dessert with creamy topping
Coffee, tea, or other QWL beverage
Snack
Coffee-egg bracer

FRIDAY

Breakfast
Herbed omelet
Artificially sweetened jelly
Coffee, tea, or other QWL beverage
Snack
Cottage cheese orange slice
Lunch
Jellied egg bouillon
Chili-beefburger
Pickle slice
Creamy gelatin dessert
Coffee, tea, or other QWL beverage
Snack
Cottage cheese-sardine balls
Dinner
Fish-bits bouillon

Poached salmon steaks
Pickle relish
Orange juice gelatin dessert
Coffee, tea, or other QWL beverage
Snack
Refreshment ice

SATURDAY

Breakfast
Jellied cottage cheese
Coffee, tea, or other QWL beverage
Snack
Curried stuffed egg
Lunch
Jellied meat and bouillon
Herbed lamb kabobs
Artificially sweetened mint jelly
Cottage cheese pudding
Coffee, tea, or other QWL beverage
Snack
Chopped liver balls
Dinner
Chicken-bits bouillon
Broiler-barbecued chicken
Herbed cottage cheese
Maple coffee dessert
Coffee, tea, or other QWL beverage
Snack
Gelatin fluff with creamy topping

SUNDAY

Breakfast
Scrambled eggs deluxe
Artificially sweetened strawberry preserves
Coffee, tea, or other QWL beverage
Snack
Hard-cooked egg
Dinner
Beef bouillon

Open-baked ham
Curried cottage cheese
Orange gelatin ices
Coffee, tea, or other QWL beverage
Snack
Seasoned liver canapé
Supper
Consommé with caviar
Cold shellfish salad
Pickle relish or cocktail sauce
Gelatin fluff
Coffee, tea, or other QWL beverage
Snack
Pink cottage cheese

MONDAY

Breakfast
Scrambled eggs with chicken livers
Artificially sweetened jam
Coffee, tea, or other QWL beverage
Snack
Herbed cottage cheese
Lunch
Dilled clam soup
Barbecued halibut steak
Pickle relish
Refreshment ice
Coffee, tea, or other QWL beverage
Snack
Cottage cheese-sardine balls
Dinner
Meat-bits bouillon
Lamb chop broil
Artificially sweetened mint jelly
Orange gelatin ices
Coffee, tea, or other QWL beverage
Snack
Crunchy egg salad

TUESDAY

Breakfast
Cottage cheese bouillon
Artificially sweetened jelly
Coffee, tea, or other QWL beverage
Snack
Chicken-bits bouillon
Lunch
Mamaroneck clam stew
Maple coffee dessert
Coffee, tea, or other QWL beverage
Snack
Egg-clam combination
Dinner
Jellied egged bouillon
Panfried veal loin chop
Pickle relish
Cinnamon pudding
Coffee, tea, or other QWL beverage
Snack
Refreshment ice

WEDNESDAY

Breakfast
Western meat 'n eggs
Coffee, tea, or other QWL beverage
Snack
Herbed cottage cheese
Lunch
Clam-shrimp-onion soup
Jelled cod
Pickle relish
Lemon juice gelatin dessert
Snack
Chef's bouillon
Dinner
Egg drop soup
Baked chicken parmesan
Artificially sweetened lemon jelly

Refreshment ice
Coffee, tea, or other QWL beverage
Snack
Vanilla gelatin dessert

THURSDAY

Breakfast
Herbed cottage cheese
Artificially sweetened strawberry jam
Coffee, tea, or other QWL beverage
Snack
Hard-cooked egg
Lunch
Curry soup
Beef steak panbroiled
Pickle slice
Orange juice gelatin dessert
Coffee, tea, or other QWL beverage
Snack
Chopped liver balls
Dinner
Fish-bits bouillon
Parsleyed fish broil
Cottage cheese with chives
Gelatin dessert with creamy topping
Coffee, tea, or other QWL beverage
Snack
Refreshment ice

FRIDAY

Breakfast
Poached eggs in chicken broth
Artificially sweetened jelly
Coffee, tea, or other QWL beverage
Snack
Caraway cottage cheese
Lunch
Jellied beef broth
Vealburgers

Pickle relish
Deluxe coffee jell
Coffee, tea, or other QWL beverage
Snack
Cottage cheese-sardine balls
Dinner
Snowball onion-clam soup
Baked shad
Herbed cottage cheese
Orange gelatin ices
Coffee, tea, or other QWL beverage
Snack
Jellied chicken bouillon

SATURDAY

Breakfast
Cottage cheese with salmon
Artificially sweetened lemon jelly
Coffee, tea, or other QWL beverage
Snack
Jellied egged bouillon
Lunch
Fish-bits bouillon
Sole birds
Pickle relish
Gelatin fluff
Coffee, tea,, or other QWL beverage
Snack
Seasoned liver canapé
Dinner
Jellied beef bouillon
Beef tenderloin
Herbed cottage cheese
Pickle slice
Maple coffee dessert
Coffee, tea, or other QWL beverage
Snack
Cinnamon pudding

SUNDAY

Breakfast
Herbed omelet
Artificially sweetened pineapple preserves
Coffee, tea, or other QWL beverage
Snack
Cottage cheese flavor blend
Dinner
Curry soup
Roast turkey
Artificially sweetened raspberry jelly
Olives
Orange gelatin ices
Coffee, tea, or other QWL beverage
Snack
Chopped liver balls
Supper
Snowball onion-clam soup
Barbecued lobster tails
Pickle relish
Lemon juice gelatin dessert
Coffee, tea, or other QWL beverage
Snack
Cinnamon pudding

The Doctor's Quick
Inches-Off Diet

The Doctor's Quick Inches-Off Diet, used by millions
of women and men, was created both to slim you and
then take extra inches off "problem spots" on your
body. With this diet, you slim where you need it most.
(For full description and detailed instructions on how
this diet works, see the book, *The Doctor's Quick
Inches-Off Diet.*)

Almost the opposite of the Quick Weight Loss Diet,
your eating here concentrates on low protein (not no
protein) foods. Once you're down to your desired
weight, Inches-Off dieting acts to slim and trim more
inches off heavy hips, abdomen, legs, arms, shoulders,
wherever you are excessively bulky (your personal pri-
mary "muscle masses").

Many dieters have reduced very successfully by using
the Quick Weight Loss Diet one week, enjoying meats,
poultry, fish, eggs, and other high protein foods. The
next week they switch to Inches-Off dieting, concentrating on vegetables, fruits, and other low protein foods.
Alternating week after week, this provides a change of
foods for those who, after a week on meats and such,
wail, "I must have some vegetables and fruits or I'll
perish!" Or those on Inches-Off who live on vegetables,
fruits, for a while, then complain, "I'll die if I don't get
some meat!"

This alternating system works wonderfully for some,
and that's great with us since *your* successful reducing
is what concerns us most. Basically, the Quick Weight

Loss Diet gives you speediest weight loss, but the Inches-Off (I-O) Diet will also take off pounds in a hurry.

However, once down to your desired weight, you must stay on the Inches-Off Diet for six weeks to trim off those reluctant extra inches from your heavy problem spots. Then you have a medical checkup, and back on the Inches-Off Diet another six weeks if you want to trim your bulky areas even more.

You'll see a marvelous change as you slim down oversize hips, thighs, or whatever is your personal figure problem. An ecstatic lady writes: "How can I thank you for your Quick Inches-Off Diet? I'm 27 years old, and for the first time in my life (as far back as I remember) I'm at a decent weight and size . . . I was a gross 190 pounds and wearing a size 20 dress . . . I'm now 136 and wearing size 13, my goal is 119 and size 9 . . . and I'm positive I'll achieve it . . . It's a delight to get on the scale and see pounds drop off every morning."

Pattern your daily eating, using the I-O recipes, along the lines of the sample slimming Inches-Off menus given later. You can choose an appetizer, a main dish of a salad or vegetable plate combining various vegetable recipes of your own choosing (or raw or plain cooked vegetables if you prefer), dessert and beverage. You may have snacks between meals, as in the sample menus. Also, as in any eating, if you divide the same 3-meal food total into 6 spaced smaller meals instead, you'll lose pounds and inches even quicker.

With such menus, you'll slim and trim swiftly. If you're not losing rapidly enough, cut down on the number and size of servings—just having a vegetable combination plate and beverage, for instance, for lunch or dinner. Check your weight each morning, then regulate your daily intake of Inches-Off foods to lose pounds and inches in a hurry—as so many have done with thrilling success, getting down to their personal minimum dimensions (for instance, we can't promise everyone pencil-thin legs, but many have trimmed off as much as 4 extra inches from thighs, 6 to 10 inches from waist, buttocks and hips, and so on).

Judge your daily calorie intake, to stay at ideal weight

while trimming off *extra* inches from bulky spots, according to the "Ideal Weight and Calorie Chart" and "Stay-Slim Calorie Tables" on later pages in this book. *You eat permitted Inches-Off foods only* (as in every Inches-Off recipe). When you weigh yourself daily upon arising, and if you're edging *over* your ideal weight, cut out some servings, or cut down on portions. If you go *under* your ideal weight, increase the size of portions, or add some servings—or a little butter, bread, cookies, wine, or whatever you desire from the list of Inches-Off permitted foods.

Basic Permitted Inches-Off Foods

1. VEGETABLES—you may eat practically all vegetables, from artichokes to zucchini, but *not* (because of high calorie content) avocadoes, beans (green and wax beans are okay), peas, or potatoes, especially sweet potatoes. If you do eat peas and potatoes, limit yourself to very small servings, at least half the usual servings of other vegetables, no more than a half-cup.

2. VEGETABLE JUICES—all single or mixed vegetable juices.

3. FRUITS—fresh, frozen, and canned fruits; when canned, select "low calorie," "diet," "artificially sweetened," for quicker slimming.

4. FRUIT JUICES—drink no-sugar-added juices for fewer calories, and in small quantities for quicker weight loss.

5. FRUIT SPREADS, JAMS, JELLIES, PRESERVES, MARMALADE, "FRUIT BUTTER"— for speedier reducing choose only "low calorie," "diet," and "artificially sweetened" types.

6. SOUPS—vegetable and fruit soups of all kinds, all clear soups, broth, bouillon, consommé, any soups without bits of meats, poultry, fish, egg, other protein foods (clear meat and chicken types, okay).

7. CONDIMENTS—catsup, chili sauce, pickles and pickle combinations, relishes, low calorie salad dressing, low calorie "mayonnaise substitute" or 1 teaspoon mayonnaise, tomato sauce, but no sauces containing any bits of meats, poultry, fish, cheese, or other high protein foods.

8. SEASONINGS—salt, pepper, herbs, and spices to your taste; avoid oversalting, especially if you have a tendency to retain water and are prone to swelling ankles and legs.

9. CEREALS—small (half-cup) portions of any cold or hot cereals except those with extra protein added, or sugar-coated or sugar-added types (because of higher calories).

10. BREAD, ROLLS, CRACKERS, COOKIES—small portions, no more than 1 slice extra-thin bread, or a very small roll, or 2 crackers or cookies per meal or snack—but none with extra protein added.

11. FLOUR, MACARONI, SPAGHETTI, RICE, POPCORN—small portions (half-cup or less) because of high calorie content, but none with extra protein added. No egg noodles.

12. BEVERAGES—coffee, tea (non-dairy creamer or a dash of cream permitted), artificially sweetened sodas, and small quantities of alcoholic beverages (wine, whiskies, beer, brandy, cordials). No milk (a dash or spoonful of buttermilk permitted in recipes).

13. MISCELLANEOUS—use only in very small quantities because of high calories, no more than a dash of cream, a dab of butter, a scant teaspoon of sugar or honey, ⅓ cup of pudding occasionally (if you take a usual or large portion of high-calorie items and decide it's a "small" portion, you're only fooling yourself):

Butter, Margarine, Vegetable Oils, Cream, Non-Dairy Creamers, Honey, Molasses, "Diet" Puddings, Tapioca, Sugar, Sugar Syrups. (Don't use any varieties of these foods labeled "contains protein.")

14. VITAMIN-MINERAL PILL DAILY, "high potency" types if you are over age 40.

Before going on this or any diet, get your doctor's approval.

Inches-Off Dieting Tips

Avoid high calorie foods such as spaghetti, macaroni, rice, butter, bread, cookies, and others listed among "permitted" Inches-Off foods. Such items are "permitted" because they're very low in protein, *but they are not recommended for reducing quickly.* Therefore they are included only rarely in Inches-Off recipes, and then only in very small amounts. Once you're down to ideal weight, and eating Inches-Off foods primarily to trim your problem spots further, you can add some of these items, *but eliminate them completely if you're gaining weight.*

As with everything in life, you must apply your own good sense. You'll achieve the slim, attractive figure you want—through sensible Inches-Off dieting as instructed, and with the fine, low calorie recipes provided. *But "you can't have your cake and slim down too!"* You must change the ways of eating that made you fat, lest you exceed your daily ideal weight maintenance intake according to the "Ideal Weight and Calorie Chart" on later pages.

By avoiding high calorie, high fat foods, you'll not only trim down quicker, but also you'll combat many ills including heart disease (as proved further in recent findings of the Inter-Society Commission for Heart Disease Resources). It's all part of the basic life-saving concept of this *different* cookbook—*to change your old ways of cooking and eating,* for healthier living for yourself, your family, and guests.

Drink at least 10 glasses (8 ounces) or cups of liquid daily, including water, coffee, tea, and artificially sweetened carbonated drinks.

Snacks of low calorie foods permitted on the Inches-Off Diet may be eaten between meals. Raw vegetables such as carrot sticks, cauliflower buds, celery, green pepper, radishes are excellent. Small pieces or portions of fruits are satisfying. Clear soups will fill you without adding significantly to your total daily calorie intake.

Keep portions quite small until you're down to your desired weight, and have trimmed off the inches as wanted. Then you'll stay at your desired weight with Stay-Slim Eating, checking your daily calorie intake simply and easily, as described in detail later.

Concentrating on vegetables is a big help on the Inches-Off Diet for quick, beautiful results. Green salads (without high calorie dressings) and vegetables are so low in calories that you can eat sizable portions and still lose pounds and inches swiftly. True vegetarians, who eat nothing but vegetables, are slim all over and stay at ideal weight or a little under, *further proof that low protein Inches-Off dieting will reduce your weight and heavy problem spots.*

Keep washed lettuce in a damp towel in the refrigerator, along with watercress, tomatoes, and other low calorie items for the "instant salad" recipes here. No matter what others in the family are eating, you can always enjoy a quick salad to help keep slimming and trimming.

Vary vegetable recipes and flavors to your taste by adding your favorites—such as chopped celery, fresh green pepper, chives, lemon juice, scallions, diced carrots, spices, and other permitted items.

Check Stay-Slim and QWL tips, many of them helpful in Inches-Off dieting. *Remember, all Inches-Off recipes are excellent too for Stay-Slim eating.*

HORS D'OEUVRES

*These recipes may be used with many different
raw vegetables*

As you will note, these hors d'oeuvres—like all recipes in this book—are low calorie and delicious, proving again that no recipe has to be rich and greasy to be good. All these hors d'oeuvres also make tasty, satisfying snacks between meals if you *must* have something. As always, eat moderate portions, don't load up or you'll be loading on calories and pounds. Of course, plain raw vegetables provide a limitless number of hors d'oeuvres and snacks—radishes, olives, pickles, cauliflower buds, cherry tomatoes, and so on.

Celeriac Tidbits

Celeriac, cut into 3-inch
   long, ¼-inch thin "sticks"
   (or celery, or carrots)
Diet mayonnaise-type dressing

1 teaspoon lemon juice
Paprika or mixed herb
   seasoning

Arrange celeriac sticks in serving dish. Mix lemon juice and paprika or mixed herb seasoning with mayonnaise-type dressing. Spoon sparingly over celeriac, leaving ends of sticks free of sauce, to be picked up with the fingers. Chill and serve as hors d'oeuvres. (8 calories per "stick" with dressing.)

Cucumber Snack

1 medium cucumber	Pepper
1 lemon, juice	Celery salt, or chopped
½ teaspoon grated onion	chives, or fresh dill
Salt (or seasoned salt)	

Scrub cucumber thoroughly, cut off ends, and slice very thin. Mix lemon juice, onion, salt and pepper, combine with cucumber. Sprinkle celery salt, chopped chives, or fresh dill on top. Chill before serving. Makes 2 servings (22 calories per serving).

Marinated Mushrooms

12 raw mushrooms (1-inch diameter)
¼ cup vinaigrette sauce (see recipe in Inches-Off Dressings)
Chopped fresh dill or parsley

Wash mushrooms and arrange in shallow serving bowl or dish. Soak in vinaigrette sauce; sprinkle with dill or parsley. Refrigerate 2 or more hours before using, turning mushrooms occasionally in sauce. Serve with a toothpick thrust into each mushroom. (5 calories per mushroom, 62 calories entire recipe.)

Vegetable Snacks

2 cups chicken broth	3 Belgian endive, split
Herb seasoning (to taste)	lengthwise
Pepper (to taste)	2 leeks, split lengthwise
3 ribs celery, cut into 2-inch lengths	

Season broth to taste with herb seasoning and pepper. Simmer vegetables in broth until tender but still crisp.

Pour off broth and serve as a delicious clear soup.

Chill the vegetables and serve with salt, pepper, and herb seasoning to taste. (110 calories entire recipe.)

SOUPS

Soups, such as in the recipes here (not the creamy, high calorie, high fat recipes given too often in other cookbooks), are especially helpful in slimming and trimming beautifully. A good low-calorie cup (or bowl) of soup is refreshing, invigorating, and filling—a perfect, satisfying aid for quick reducing.

A serving of soup under 50 calories makes an ideal course as part of a meal, and as a robust snack between meals. A higher calorie soup such as the recipe for barley soup, 170 calories per serving, should serve as practically a meal in itself, not between meals.

Thick Blender Soup

½ cup French-cut green beans, cooked
1 can green asparagus, with juice
2 sprigs parsley, cut up
⅛ teaspoon paprika
½ teaspoon onion flakes
¼ teaspoon seasoned salt
Pepper to taste
½ can bean sprouts, drained
1 small can mushrooms, drained

Process all ingredients except last two in blender at low speed. Pour into saucepan, add bean sprouts and mushrooms, and heat thoroughly before serving. Add more seasoning if desired. Makes 4 servings (40 calories per serving).

Barley Soup

Served with 1 slice of toast, will make a full meal

½ cup barley
1 quart water
3 ounces minced onion
½ cup grated carrots

1 rib celery, cut fine
2 tablespoons oatmeal
Salt (to taste)
Pepper (to taste)

Boil barley in water with onion 1 hour. Add carrots, celery, oatmeal, salt and pepper; simmer 1 hour longer. Makes 4 servings (170 calories per serving).

Simple Beet Soup (Borscht)

For Stay-Slim eating, add a sliced hard-cooked egg to each piping-hot serving

4 cups low-calorie borscht
(beet soup) from bottle
(or packets mixed
with water)
8-ounce can small beets,
includes juice, beets diced

1-ounce package dehydrated
soup greens, or 2 table-
spoons chopped fresh parsley
Artificial sweetener equal to
4 teaspoons sugar
Salt and pepper to taste

Combine all ingredients, bring to boiling point, then simmer for 25 minutes. Each person uses salt and pepper to taste. Individuals may also add 1 teaspoon cream, or 2 teaspoons non-dairy creamer, to serving if desired. Makes 4 servings (45 calories per serving, without cream or creamer).

Cabbage Soup

Served with 1 slice of toast will make a full meal

1 quart chicken or beef
broth
8 cups shredded cabbage
1 teaspoon granulated
artificial sweetener

½ teaspoon salt
1 small can tomato paste
1 teaspoon lemon juice

Shred cabbage and add to broth in large saucepan. Add sweetener, salt and tomato paste, stir and simmer 1 hour. Add lemon juice and serve hot. Makes 4 servings (98 calories per serving).

Cauliflower Soup

1 cauliflower (about 1½ pounds)	1 teaspoon rosemary
3½ cups water	⅛ teaspoon pepper
1 teaspoon seasoned salt	1 can (10½-ounce) condensed tomato soup
2 bay leaves	Salt and pepper
⅓ cup minced onion	4 sprigs watercress

Separate cauliflower flowerets, discarding stem, and cook in water in partially covered saucepan with salt, bay leaves, onion, rosemary, and pepper until cauliflower is tender (about 15 minutes). Add tomato soup, salt, and pepper. Serve with a sprig of watercress floating on each portion. Makes 4 servings (77 calories per serving).

"Creamed" Cauliflower Soup

1 large cauliflower head, broken into small pieces	2 cups boiling water
2 packets instant chicken broth	Chopped pimiento

Stir instant chicken broth in hot water until dissolved. Add cauliflower pieces and simmer until just tender. Process in blender at low speed until liquid. Reheat, then serve. Float chopped pimiento on top for color. Makes 4 servings (25 calories per serving).

Blender Cucumber Soup

2 medium cucumbers,
  peeled and cut in thirds
3 chicken bouillon cubes
3 cups boiling water
½ teaspoon onion flakes
  (or 1 teaspoon grated
  onion)

½ cup water mixed with
  2 tablespoons non-dairy
  creamer
1 teaspoon chopped fresh dill
Black pepper
Chopped chives

Process cut-up cucumbers in blender at low speed. Dissolve bouillon cubes in boiling water. Add blended cucumbers and onion to bouillon and simmer for 8 minutes. Remove from heat, chill, and just before serving mix in cold water-creamer mixture, dill, and pepper. Float chopped chives on top of each ice-cold serving. Makes 4 servings (25 calories per serving).

Chicken-Vegetable Soup

2 cups chicken consommé
2 cups tomato-vegetable
  juice
Chopped parsley

Chopped chives
1 can mixed vegetables
  (16 ounces)

To consommé or bouillon add the same amount of tomato-vegetable juice. Add chopped parsley or chives or broth. Heat thoroughly, stirring occasionally. Makes 4 servings (42 calories per serving).

Escarole-Spinach Soup

1 can escarole-in-chicken-broth (19½ ounces)
½ pound fresh spinach, cooked, or package of frozen spinach (not creamed)
Seasonings

Use canned "escarole-in-chicken-broth," removing any fat from top (or use 3 cups clear chicken broth if the canned escarole soup is not available). Add cooked or frozen spinach and simmer until spinach and soup are hot, seasoning with salt, pepper, herbs and spices as desired. Makes 4 servings (23 calories per serving).

Creamy Mushroom Soup

1 pound fresh mushrooms	2 tablespoons non-dairy
3 tablespoons chopped onion	creamer mixed in ½ cup
4 cups clear chicken broth	water
2 tablespoons flour	Black pepper
	3 sprigs parsley, chopped

Wipe mushrooms with a damp towel and cut into thin slices; use stems as well as caps. In a large no-stick pan, sauté onions and mushroom slices in 2 tablespoons of the chicken broth, until onions are soft and mushrooms cooked through (about 6 minutes). Remove from heat, blend in flour, return to heat and add rest of broth, stirring. Simmer gently 15 minutes. Add the creamer-water mixture and dash of black pepper. Heat until almost boiling. Sprinkle each serving with parsley. Makes 6 servings (40 calories per serving).

Onion Soup

1¼ cups sliced onions	Salt to taste
1 teaspoon butter	⅛ teaspoon black pepper
1 quart beef bouillon	⅛ teaspoon herb seasoning

Sauté onions lightly in butter. Drain off butter thoroughly. Combine onions in pot with bouillon, salt, black pepper, and herb seasoning. Bring to boil. Then simmer 30 minutes. Pour into 4 individual earthenware soup bowls or casseroles. Serve grated Parmesan cheese separately, but sprinkle only lightly on soup, if at all. Makes 4 servings (40 calories per serving).

Chinese Onion Soup

2 chicken bouillon cubes
2 cups boiling water
1 large onion, minced

1 can bean sprouts
1 small can water chestnuts, sliced thin

Dissolve bouillon cubes in boiling water. Lightly brown onion with 1 tablespoon bouillon in a no-stick pan. Drain bean sprouts thoroughly and add to onions, continuing browning. Combine this mixture, sliced water chestnuts, and bouillon, bring just to the boiling point, and serve. Makes 4 servings (75 calories per serving).

Quick Pea Soup

2 envelopes instant chicken broth
2 cups boiling water
2 packages frozen peas

½ teaspoon onion flakes
1 teaspoon chopped parsley
Chopped pimiento

Stir instant broth into hot water until dissolved. Cook frozen peas according to directions on package, using broth instead of water. Add onion flakes. Process at low speed in blender until pulverized. Add parsley and remainder of bouillon, bring to boiling point. Serve in 4 soup bowls. Float chopped pimiento on top for added flavor and color. Makes 4 servings (90 calories per serving).

Spanish Cold Soup

3 medium onions, quartered
8 medium tomatoes, peeled, quartered
2 tablespoons red wine
½ teaspoon garlic salt (or more, to taste)
Black pepper
1 tablespoon paprika

1 tablespoon olive oil
10 ripe olives, sliced
1 large cucumber, peeled, diced
2 tablespoons chopped parsley

Process half the onions, tomatoes, wine, salt, and pepper in blender at medium speed until smooth. Pour into saucepan and repeat with other half of the onions, tomatoes, wine and salt. Add paprika and oil, simmer all together 10 minutes. Add olives and cucumber, sprinkle parsley over the top, and chill. Serve cold. Makes 6 servings (105 calories per serving).

Basic Hearty Beef-Tomato Soup

1 can condensed tomato soup	1 teaspoon grated onion
1 can condensed beef broth	Salt to taste
½ cup orange juice	Parsley (optional)
1 cup water	

Heat all ingredients together just to boiling point, stirring occasionally. When serving, float a little minced parsley on top if you like. Makes 4 servings (70 calories per serving).

Variations: Following a basic recipe like this, you can make many different recipes, combinations of tomato juice or canned condensed soup, along with other ingredients. To the basic tomato soup, you might add chicken, beef, onion, or vegetable broth . . . a small amount of cooked rice, sliced mushrooms, dehydrated vegetables, spinach, or other fresh, frozen or canned vegetables . . . lemon juice . . . chopped cucumbers, chives, onion, celery, parsley, herbs, and so on. You might float a few toast squares on top, or a spoonful of sour cream (beware of high calorie ingredients always). A tablespoon of vermouth plus a teaspoon of grated lemon rind add unusual flavor to heated canned tomato soup.

Our Favorite Vegetable Soup

¼ medium head of cabbage, shredded
4 ribs celery, cut up small
1 green pepper, diced
1 package frozen French-style green beans
1½ cups tomato juice
2 chicken or beef bouillon cubes

4 cups water
1 bay leaf (remove when vegetables are cooked)
1 can mushrooms (butter, if any, removed), drained
1 can water chestnuts, drained, sliced

Cook together until vegetables are tender, cabbage, celery, pepper, green beans, tomato juice, bouillon cubes, water, and bay leaf (about 20 minutes). Remove bay leaf. Drain, reserving liquid. Process cooked vegetables in blender at medium speed until pulverized. Add to liquid, mixing thoroughly, mushrooms and water chestnuts. Serve piping hot, with lemon slices or watercress as garnish, if you like. Makes 4 servings (100 calories per serving).

Chinese Vegetable Soup

2 envelopes instant chicken broth
2 cups boiling water
1 cup green beans, cooked and cut in thirds
¼ cup canned bamboo shoots, drained, chopped

1 can water chestnuts, drained, sliced
½ cup cooked peas
½ red pepper, diced
1 tablespoon lemon juice
Black pepper

Dissolve instant broth in boiling water. Add remaining ingredients and simmer 10 minutes. Serve piping hot. Makes 4 servings (60 calories per serving).

Watercress Pepper Pot

4 chicken bouillon cubes
  (or 4 packets instant
  chicken broth)
4 cups boiling water

1 bunch watercress, washed
  and thick stems removed
¼ red pepper, diced

Dissolve bouillon cubes in hot water. Process watercress and 1 cup of the bouillon in blender very briefly. Pour into remainder of bouillon and heat. Sprinkle diced red pepper (or parsley if you prefer) into each serving. Makes 4 servings (15 calories per serving).

VEGETABLES

Every delicious vegetable recipe here is, in effect, a slimming recipe, low in calories. These are truly "gourmet" recipes created to enhance the fine natural flavors of the foods, not to overwhelm them with butter, cream, cornstarch, flour, sugar, and other rich ingredients used in so many vegetable recipes in other cookbooks. Even though some such rich ingredients are among permitted Inches-Off items, they're not loaded into our recipes since our one overriding purpose always is to slim and trim you quickly, pleasantly, healthfully.

Two, three, or four low-calorie vegetable recipes on a plate make an excellent main dish, whereas you won't lose pounds and inches with fatty, high-calorie vegetable casseroles. Even eating naturally low-calorie vegetables, rich additives can fatten instead of slimming you—"overweight happens when you take the butter with the sweet."

For example, a typical vegetable recipe in another cookbook includes eggs, whole milk, and buttered croutons, totaling *over 300 calories per serving*. Compare this with our recipe for delicious "Whipped Vegetable Medley"—*only 42 calories per serving*.

Once you're down to ideal weight, and want to trim your bulky problem spots further, you eat only vegetables and other permitted Inches-Off foods, and you regulate your total daily intake to stay at ideal weight. You check your weight on the scale each morning upon arising. Then you cut down or add to the amount of Inches-Off foods you eat daily so that you stay at ideal weight—while the *kinds* of foods you're eating will help reduce your problem spots as wanted.

Eggplant with Zucchini

2 medium eggplants
2 large zucchini
4 large onions, sliced
2 green peppers, cut in strips (seeds removed)
2 tomatoes, cut in eighths
1 can mushrooms, drained, butter (if any) removed
2 tablespoons minced parsley
1½ teaspoons garlic salt
½ teaspoon oregano
½ teaspoon paprika

Cut eggplants into ½-inch slices (do not peel). Scrub zucchini, remove ends, and cut into ½-inch slices (do not peel). Cook onions and peppers together in no-stick skillet until nearly soft (about 10 minutes); turn up heat and brown. Remove. Cook eggplant, zucchini, tomatoes, mushrooms, and parsley together, with seasonings, until just tender. Add onions and peppers, mix, and serve hot or cold. Add more seasoning, if desired. Makes 4 servings (110 calories per serving).

Stuffed Eggplant Italian Style

2 medium eggplants
1 pound fresh mushrooms, sliced, (or 2 6-ounce cans mushrooms, drained, butter, if any, removed)
1 medium onion, chopped
2 teaspoons chopped parsley
2 medium tomatoes, cut in eighths
1 teaspoon garlic salt
½ teaspoon oregano
Paprika

Wash eggplants and bake in 350° oven until tender to the touch (about 20 minutes). Remove from oven, cut in halves lengthwise, and carefully remove pulp, reserving shells. Combine pulp with all other ingredients except paprika, and simmer gently on top of stove until tomatoes and mushrooms are soft. Heap mixture into eggplant shells and return to oven for 5 minutes. Sprinkle paprika over tops before serving (try nutmeg if you're adventurous). Makes 4 servings (80 calories per serving).

Rice and Mushroom Casserole

¼ pound mushrooms, sliced
1 beef bouillon cube
(or envelope)
1¼ cups boiling water
½ cup uncooked long
grain rice

½ cup chopped onions
1 teaspoon margarine
½ teaspoon black pepper
½ teaspoon salt
⅛ teaspoon thyme
¾ cup chopped celery

In 1½ quart casserole dissolve bouillon cube (or powder) in boiling water. Sauté rice and onions in hot margarine in no-stick skillet over moderate heat for 5 minutes until golden brown. Add rice, seasonings, and celery to bouillon in casserole dish, and bake covered for 45 minutes in 350° oven. Uncover, add sliced mushrooms, and bake 15 minutes longer. Serve immediately. Makes 4 servings (120 calories per serving).

Casserole of Vegetables

4 teaspoons vegetable margarine
½ cup breadcrumbs
8 scallions, including green
stalks, minced
1 cucumber, pared and sliced

4 tablespoons celery, chopped
4 ripe tomatoes, sliced
½ teaspoon salt
½ teaspoon sugar
Lemon pepper marinade
Oregano (optional)

Melt 2 tablespoons of the margarine and mix with fork into dry breadcrumbs. In small skillet, brown scallions slowly in remaining 2 teaspoons margarine until tender. Gently combine cucumber, celery, and toma-

toes, and place in layers in a casserole, sprinkling each
layer with cooked scallions, sugar, lemon pepper marinade, and (optional) oregano. Bake in preheated 375°
oven 20 minutes. Distribute buttered breadcrumbs over
the top and bake 10 minutes more or until vegetables
are tender. Makes 4 servings (120 calories per serving).

Stewed Vegetable Medley

May be served with ¼ cup rice for each portion.
(Add 46 calories per serving.)

1 teaspoon vegetable mar- garine	1 large onion, sliced thin
3 cups cabbage, shredded fine	4 tomatoes, peeled and diced
6 ribs celery, sliced thin	1 teaspoon seasoned salt
½ green pepper, sliced thin	½ teaspoon paprika
	Black pepper to taste

Heat margarine in bottom of saucepan and add all
other ingredients. Stir with fork, cover, bring just to
boiling. Lower heat and simmer 8 to 10 minutes, or until vegetables are tender. Makes 4 servings (74 calories
per serving).

Whipped Vegetable Medley

1 package frozen chopped broccoli	¼ teaspoon fine mixed herbs
1 package frozen brussels sprouts	Salt
½ cup finely chopped scallions	Pepper

Cook broccoli and brussels sprouts in saucepan according to directions until tender; drain. Add scallions,
and chop all vegetables together very fine, adding herbs,
and salt and pepper to taste. Heat over low flame, taking care not to burn. If you want the vegetable medley
extra fine, whip by hand or chop in electric blender.
Makes 4 servings (42 calories per serving).

Broiled Eggplant

2 large firm eggplants,
  with skin
Paprika
1 teaspoon parsley flakes
¾ teaspoon garlic salt

½ teaspoon oregano
⅛ teaspoon lemon pepper
  marinade
3 tablespoons tomato juice

Wash eggplant, remove ends, and cut lengthwise into ¾-inch slices. Mix seasonings together and rub well into both sides of eggplant slices. Cover bottom of large shallow broiler pan with tomato juice and set eggplant slices in it. Broil 4 inches from heat in preheated broiler until first side is very brown. Turn with spatula, and broil other side until tender and brown (about 10 minutes). If not cooked through, lower heat and broil a little longer. Makes 4 servings (40 calories per serving).

Eggplant Mélange

1 medium eggplant, peeled
  and cubed
1 cup chopped onion
½ tablespoon olive oil
2 strips green pepper, cut up

1 cup chopped tomatoes
  (fresh or canned)
½ teaspoon salt
¼ teaspoon ground pepper
¼ teaspoon oregano

Sauté onions in oil. Add green pepper and eggplant; sauté, stirring frequently. Combine tomatoes, salt, pepper, and oregano with above. Cook covered for 30 minutes. Add a little water if liquid cooks away. Makes 4 servings (60 calories per serving).

Lemoned Asparagus

2 dozen medium asparagus
  stalks
Water
1 teaspoon salt
1 tablespoon diet margarine,
  melted

2 tablespoons lemon juice
Seasoned salt to taste
Paprika

Cut off any tough ends from asparagus stalks, and wash thoroughly. In deep saucepan with a close-fitting cover, place about 2 inches of water, add 1 teaspoon salt, bring to boil. Tie asparagus in a bunch, stand with tips at top in boiling water. Cover, boil rapidly for 15 to 20 minutes until tender (steam will cook the tips). Drain, untie, and place asparagus on warmed serving plate. Spoon on mixture of melted margarine, lemon juice, and seasoned salt. Sprinkle on paprika to taste. Makes 4 servings, 6 stalks each (40 calories).

Herbed Artichokes

4 artichokes	8 tablespoons vinaigrette sauce
1 dried bay leaf	(see recipe among sauces)
¼ teaspoon tarragon	

Cut off all but ¼ inch of bottom stems of artichokes, and remove some of the outer leaves if tough (discard stems and tough leaves). Wash thoroughly with cold water, then let stand in salted cold water for 15 minutes. Simmer in salted water to which you have added bay leaf and tarragon, for 20 to 30 minutes, or until tender; test bottom of artichoke for softness, and if leaf pulls out easily, artichoke is done.

Drain artichokes upside down. Serve with 2 tablespoons vinaigrette sauce in each of 4 side dishes. Eat by pulling off each leaf, dipping into sauce, and scraping off the soft meat between the teeth. When leaves are gone, remove spiny part, and eat meaty center with fork and knife. Makes 4 servings (70 calories per serving).

Green Beans with Mushrooms

1 (9-ounce) package frozen green beans
Chicken bouillon, double-strength
6 medium mushrooms, sliced thin

Prepare frozen beans according to package directions, substituting chicken bouillon for water. Remove from heat while beans are still very crisp; drain. Fold in sliced mushrooms, return to heat and cook over low flame, turning over with fork, 3 or 4 minutes until mushrooms are tender. Makes 2 servings (56 calories per serving).

Frenched Green Beans

1¼ pounds fresh green beans
½ teaspoon garlic salt
½ teaspoon butter-flavored salt
¼ teaspoon black pepper
3 tablespoons diced roasted pimiento
2 sprigs parsley, cut up small

Wash green beans, cut off and discard ends, then French them (cut into long thin strips, putting through special gadget for that purpose). Place in saucepan, just cover with water and cook over medium heat until barely tender (do not overcook). Drain, mix in pimiento and seasonings, cover and heat for 1 minute longer. Serve immediately with parsley sprinkled over top. (Try substituting ¼ teaspoon ground nutmeg for parsley.) Makes 4 servings (20 calories per serving).

Honeyed Beets

3 cups beets, grated
6 tablespoons water
½ teaspoon salt
1½ teaspoons honey
Nutmeg (optional)

Cook grated beets in salted water in covered saucepan ¼ hour. Drain. Spoon honey over cooked beets, stir, and sprinkle with nutmeg if you like. Makes 4 servings (60 calories per serving).

Onioned Beets

3 cups raw beets, peeled and diced
¾ cup onion, chopped
½ cup boiling water
1 envelope instant beef broth

Place beets and onions in a 1 quart casserole. Add boiling water and sprinkle instant beef broth on top. Cover and bake 1¼ hours in 375° preheated oven. Stir once or twice and add more boiling water if more liquid is needed during baking. Makes 4 servings (64 calories per serving).

Pickled Beets

2 cups cooked (or canned) beets, sliced (reserve liquid)
½ cup beet liquid
½ cup cider vinegar
½ teaspoon liquid no-sugar sweetener

1 teaspoon mixed pickling spices
½ teaspoon salt
¼ teaspoon red food coloring (optional)

Bring all ingredients to boil in a saucepan. Remove beets and pack them in a sterilized pint jar. Bring liquid to boil again, pour over beets until jar is filled to ¼ inch from top. Seal, allow to cool, and store in refrigerator. Makes 4 servings (44 calories per serving).

Shredded Cabbage

6 cups cabbage, finely shredded
Water to cover
½ teaspoon sugar
¾ teaspoon dry mustard

½ teaspoon salt
1½ teaspoons butter
1½ teaspoons lemon juice

Cook cabbage in saucepan in water to cover. Combine sugar, mustard, salt, and butter in separate pan and cook gently, stirring, until smooth. Add lemon juice to this sauce.

Drain cooked cabbage, place in serving bowl, and pour hot sauce over it. Mix together with fork. Makes 4 servings (86 calories per serving).

Simple Carrots

1 pound carrots, scraped and cut into ½-inch circles	½ teaspoon sugar
	Water to cover
1 teaspoon salt	⅛ teaspoon black pepper

Place carrots in saucepan with salt and sugar in water to cover. Bring to boil, then simmer 20 to 30 minutes, cooking time depending on the tenderness you prefer. Drain before serving and sprinkle with pepper. Makes 4 servings (22 calories per serving).

Variation: Bouillon Carrots—Cook carrots in chicken or beef bouillon instead of water. Add salt and pepper to taste.

Baked Carrots

1 packet instant chicken broth	1 teaspoon butter-flavored salt
1 cup very hot water	½ cup dry skim milk
1 bunch very small carrots	Black pepper

Dissolve chicken broth in hot water. Wash and scrape the carrots, leaving them whole. Sprinkle them with butter-flavored salt. Heat 2 tablespoons of the broth in a large no-stick skillet, and brown carrots in it, turning them as necessary. Remove the carrots from skillet, and coat them with dry skim milk powder mixed with a dash of pepper (roll them in it). Place coated carrots in no-stick baking pan and pour remaining broth over them. Bake in preheated 325° oven for 1 hour, or until carrots are tender. Makes 4 servings (42 calories per serving).

Herbed Cauliflower

1 medium cauliflower head	Paprika
Salt	1 tablespoon margarine
1 teaspoon mixed herb seasoning	

Separate cauliflower into flowerets, trim stems, and boil in lightly salted water to cover until tender, but not soft. Drain. Spread florets, tops up, on serving platter. Dot with margarine and sprinkle generously with seasonings. Makes 4 servings (40 calories per serving).

Italian Cauliflower

1 small head cauliflower	2 teaspoons flour
1 teaspoon salt	1 teaspoon garlic salt
Water to cover	⅛ teaspoon black pepper
6 tablespoons grated onion	1 can (1 pound) tomatoes
2 tablespoons chicken bouillon	

Wash cauliflower and break into flowerets; trim stems, and cook with 1 teaspoon of the salt in water to cover, until tender.

Sauté onion in bouillon in large no-stick skillet until golden. Stir in flour and add garlic salt, pepper, and tomatoes. Cook together, stirring often, until thick, about 10 minutes. Drain cauliflower, arrange on serving dish, and pour the tomato sauce over it. Makes 4 servings (51 calories per serving).

Celery Chinese Style

2 bunches green celery	¼ cup no-sugar soy sauce
2 cubes chicken or beef bouillon	1 sprig parsley, chopped
¼ cup water	¼ cup water chestnuts, drained, sliced

Wash and trim celery, removing leaves. Cut rib stalks into ½-inch pieces. Bring water to boil in saucepan, stirring in bouillon cubes until dissolved. Add soy sauce and bring to boil. Add celery, water chestnuts, and chopped parsley and sauté gently, stirring occasionally, until celery is cooked to your taste, preferably fairly crunchy. Serve hot. Makes 6 servings (40 calories per portion).

Celery Quarters with Mushrooms

2 bunches green celery
1 can (4 ounce) sliced mush-
    rooms (butter, if any,
    lifted off top)
5 small white onions,
    cut in thin rings

1 chicken bouillon cube
1 cup boiling water
¼ teaspoon salt
Pepper
1 tablespoon cornstarch

Wash celery and cut whole bunches crosswise about 7 inches from bottom. Split each bunch lengthwise into 4 quarters. Place them in a large skillet. Add mushrooms (save juice) and onion rings. Dissolve bouillon cube in boiling water with salt and pepper, and pour over celery.

Bring to boil, reduce heat, and simmer for 15 minutes until celery is tender but still crisp. Stir cornstarch into mushroom liquid and cook, still stirring, until thickened and clear. Pour over hot celery to serve. Makes 8 servings (38 calories per serving).

Snappy Cucumbers

3 medium cucumbers
Seasoned salt
⅔ cup cider vinegar
2 teaspoons granulated
    artificial sweetener
1 teaspoon vegetable oil

1 tablespoon fresh lemon
    juice
1 tablespoon water
¼ teaspoon paprika
1 teaspoon caraway seeds
1 teaspoon poppy seeds

Wash cucumbers well, then slice as thinly as you can, leaving skin on. Dust slices lightly with seasoned salt and let stand in dish on kitchen counter for about 1 hour. Meanwhile, in a bowl containing the cider vinegar, mix all the other ingredients well. Place the cucumber slices in the marinade, mixing so that all surfaces are covered. Chill thoroughly before serving. Makes 4 servings (34 calories per serving).

Chopped Escarole

2½ pounds escarole
1 clove garlic, chopped
1 teaspoon butter-flavored salt

½ teaspoon lemon pepper
marinade
Water to cover

Trim escarole and wash carefully. Place in large saucepan, sprinkle with seasonings, cover with water, and boil for 20 to 30 minutes, until tender. Drain in colander and squeeze out water. Chop. Sprinkle more butter-flavored salt and pepper over it if you wish. Makes 4 servings (35 calories per serving).

Escarole Italian Style

2½ pounds escarole
1 teaspoon butter-flavored salt
¼ cup beef or chicken bouillon

½ teaspoon garlic powder
3 sprigs fresh parsley, cut up small with scissors
Fresh ground pepper
Paprika (optional)

Separate and wash escarole thoroughly, tearing off outer leaves and any browning edges. Break leaves in half. Combine with other ingredients except paprika in saucepan and cook over medium heat for 20 minutes, stirring with fork occasionally. Sprinkle paprika over top when serving if desired. Makes 4 servings (35 calories per serving).

Baked Endive

8 stalks endive, cut in halves lengthwise
3 tablespoons lemon juice
Artificial sweetener equal to 1 teaspoon sugar

1 teaspoon butter-flavored salt
½ teaspoon black pepper
½ cup chicken broth
Nutmeg (optional)

Place halves of endive in a shallow baking pan or casserole and sprinkle lemon juice over them. Mix rest of ingredients together and pour over endive. Bake, covered, in 350° oven for 35 minutes. Remove cover and continue baking 10 minutes longer. If you like, sprinkle a little nutmeg on top when serving. Makes 4 servings (28 calories per serving).

Braised Endive

12 large Belgian endive	Juice of 1 lemon
1 teaspoon salt	½ cup water
½ teaspoon granulated artificial sweetener	1 tablespoon butter, melted

Place endive in saucepan and add salt, sweetener, lemon juice, and water. Steam covered about 40 minutes, until endive are tender. Drain well.

Arrange endive in shallow pan and brush tops with melted butter. Broil until brown. Makes 4 servings (46 calories per serving).

Braised Lettuce with Carrots

4 small heads of lettuce (or equivalent)	4 tablespoons finely chopped carrots
Water to cover	1 cup beef bouillon, double-strength
1 teaspoon salt	Paprika
2 tablespoons finely chopped onion	
2 tablespoons finely chopped parsley	

Place washed lettuce in saucepan and pour in enough boiling water to cover, stirring in salt. Cover pan and simmer for 1 to 2 minutes. Drain thoroughly in colander. Cut heads in half and place in skillet, cut sides down. Mix onion, parsley, and carrots with beef broth and add to lettuce. Cover and simmer over low heat for 10 minutes. Place in serving bowl, pour the remaining liquid over lettuce, sprinkle lightly with paprika if desired, and serve. Makes 4 servings (60 calories per serving).

Buttered Mushroom Caps

1 pound fresh mushrooms
1 teaspoon melted butter
¾ teaspoon seasoned salt

Juice of 1 lemon
Seasoned pepper

Wash mushrooms quickly, breaking off stems (set stems aside to use in another recipe). Distribute mushroom caps, bottom side up, in shallow baking pan. Mix other ingredients together and brush over mushrooms. Broil near heat 6 to 10 minutes on each side (depending on size of mushrooms). Makes 4 servings (32 calories per serving).

Lemoned Mushrooms

24 medium size fresh
mushrooms
1 tablespoon margarine,
melted

Juice of 1 lemon
¼ teaspoon oregano
Salt
Lemon pepper marinade

Wash mushrooms quickly and trim off bottoms of stems. Scrape stems with knife if necessary. Place in broiler pan, sprinkle with melted margarine, lemon juice, and seasonings. Broil near heat for 6 minutes, turn over with large spoon and broil 6 minutes longer until golden brown. Makes 4 servings (55 calories per serving).

Sautéed Green Peppers

3 large green peppers, cut
in eighths and seeds
removed
¼ cup tomato juice
2 tomatoes, quartered
¾ teaspoon garlic salt (or
seasoned salt with garlic in it)

2 tablespoons minced
parsley
¼ teaspoon oregano
1 can mushrooms, drained,
butter (if any) removed

Combine pepper eighths, tomato juice, tomato quarters, garlic salt, minced parsley, and oregano in a covered skillet. Cook over low heat, stirring occasionally, until peppers and tomatoes are cooked through (15 to 20 minutes). Add mushrooms and continue cooking for 2 minutes. Serve hot or cold. Makes 4 servings (50 calories per serving).

Variation: May be served hot over 1 cup cooked rice for whole recipe. (Add 46 calories per serving.)

Creamy Spinach

2 packages frozen spinach	Black pepper
3 tablespoons minced onion	1 tablespoon non-dairy
2 tablespoons chicken bouillon	creamer
⅛ teaspoon grated nutmeg	½ cup water
1 teaspoon salt	1 tablespoon flour

Thaw the spinach. Brown the onions in bouillon in a no-stick skillet. Add the spinach, and sprinkle with nutmeg, salt and pepper. Mix with fork. Cook gently, covered, for 5 minutes, stirring once or twice. If liquid has accumulated, drain it off. Mix water and non-dairy creamer, and whip in flour, using fork; add to spinach. Stir, and cook over low heat, until slightly thickened (about 5 minutes). Makes 4 servings (60 calories per serving).

Spinach with Mushrooms

2 packages frozen chopped spinach	12 medium mushrooms, cooked, sliced
Chicken broth	Mixed herbs
1 tablespoon instant minced onion	Salt

Prepare frozen spinach, substituting chicken broth and minced onion for water called for in package directions. When cooked, mix in sliced mushrooms, using a fork, and heat together for 3 to 4 minutes. Add salt and herbs to taste. Makes 4 servings (45 calories per serving).

Sweet Acorn Squash

1 acorn squash
½ teaspoon light brown sugar for each half
Salt

Bake whole acorn squash on cookie sheet or in shallow pan in moderate oven until tender to the touch (¾ hour or more depending on size). Remove from oven, cut in half lengthwise, scoop out seeds, sprinkle brown sugar and salt in each half. Return squash halves to oven for 5 minutes or brown under broiler. Makes 2 servings (47 calories per serving).

Acorn Squash Rings

2 acorn squash, medium size
2 tablespoons granulated artificial sweetener
Salt
1½ cups low-calorie applesauce
Nutmeg

Bake acorn squash in shallow no-stick pan until almost tender (¾ to 1 hour, according to size). Remove from pan, slice into ¾-inch rings sidewise, removing seeds. Return to pan, sprinkle with artificial sweetener and salt. Bake 5 to 10 minutes longer, until tender. Heat applesauce. Serve squash rings with applesauce in holes. Sprinkle with nutmeg. Makes 4 servings (52 calories per serving).

Italian Tomatoes Mélange

3 tablespoons chicken bouillon, double-strength
1 cup chopped onion
1 cup chopped pepper
¼ cup chopped parsley
¼ teaspoon oregano
¼ teaspoon poppy seeds
1 (16-ounce) can Italian peeled tomatoes
Salt and coarse pepper to taste

In a saucepan combine all ingredients except tomatoes, salt and pepper. Stir well, cook until onions start to soften. Add tomatoes, stir. Simmer 5 to 10 minutes over very low heat. Taste, then add salt and pepper as needed. Makes 4 servings (62 calories per serving).

Herbed Grilled Tomatoes

4 medium tomatoes
1 tablespoon finely chopped parsley
¼ teaspoon tarragon
¼ teasoon salt
⅛ teaspoon black pepper
Artificial sweetener equal to ½ teaspoon sugar

Cut tomatoes in half across. Mix all other ingredients thoroughly, and sprinkle mixture over cut surfaces of tomatoes in a broiler pan. Place pan about 5 inches from heat, and broil about 10 minutes, or until tomatoes are tender to the fork. Makes 4 servings as side dish (30 calories per serving).

French-Style Zucchini

4 large zucchini, sliced
4 tomatoes, peeled and diced
1 teaspoon granulated no-sugar sweetener
1½ teaspoons garlic salt
¼ teaspoon thyme
⅛ teaspoon basil
Pepper

Mix all ingredients together in a saucepan and simmer slowly until zucchini is just tender (30 to 40 minutes). Makes 4 servings (82 calories per serving).

Italian Zucchini with Onion

8 medium zucchini, cut in thin slices
1 large onion, minced
1 clove garlic, crushed
4 tablespoons chicken bouillon
2 medium tomatoes, cut in small pieces
1 green pepper, minced
1 teaspoon seasoned salt
¼ teaspoon oregano
Black pepper

Brown onion with garlic in bouillon, using large no-stick skillet (about 5 minutes). Add zucchini slices, and cook over meduim heat until zucchini slices are golden, turning occasionally with spatula (about 8 minutes). Add tomatoes, green pepper, salt, oregano, and black pepper to the zucchini, cover, and simmer 20 minutes, stirring once or twice. Makes 4 servings (70 calories per serving).

Zucchini Treat

4 large or 6 small zucchini (or yellow crookneck squash)

¼ teaspoon salt

2 medium onions, sliced

4 egg tomatoes, or 3 medium tomatoes, sliced

Black pepper

Scrub zucchini, cut off ends, and split in halves lengthwise. Arrange in baking dish, open side up, and sprinkle with salt. Distribute sliced onions over zucchini halves; salt. Place slices of tomatoes over onions; sprinkle with salt and pepper. Bake in 350° preheated oven until vegetables are tender. Makes 4 servings (75 calories per serving).

Squash Vinaigrette

4 large yellow crookneck squash, scrubbed thoroughly

1 teaspoon butter-flavored salt

Pepper

2 teaspoons chicken bouillon

2 drops liquid no-sugar sweetener

5 tablespoons wine vinegar

1 tablespoon sweet basil, chopped

3 sprigs parsley, chopped (or 1 teaspoon parsley flakes)

½ roasted pimiento, chopped (optional)

Snip ends off and cut squash into slices lengthwise, about ¼ inch thick. Sprinkle with butter-flavored salt and pepper. Brush bottom of large no-stick pan with bouillon, and brown squash slightly on both sides, turning with spatula. Cover pan and cook gently 5 minutes. Add liquid sweetener and vinegar, cook all together 3 minutes more, sprinkle with basil, parsley, and pimiento, and serve. Makes 4 servings (50 calories per serving).

SALADS

Salads are a very important mainstay food for swift, effective Inches-Off reducing. Recipes here are delicious, low calorie, satisfying, filling—help yourself to generous servings, good health, and delightful slimming.

Garden Vegetable Salad

½ head lettuce, torn into bite-size pieces	1 small onion, diced (optional)
½ green pepper, thinly sliced	Escarole may be added if desired
1 cucumber, diced	Pimiento may be added if desired
2 ribs celery, diced	
1 tomato, sliced, then slices cut in half	1 tablespoon mayonnaise
6 red radishes, sliced thin	1 tablespoon chili sauce
	¼ cup water

Combine all vegetables in a bowl and chill. Process the mayonnaise, chili sauce and water in blender, and combine well with vegetables until they are covered with dressing. Or, you may use any low-calorie dressing you prefer. Makes 2 servings (120 calories per serving).

Variety Vegetable Salad

Assorted salad greens equal to 2 small heads lettuce (or 1 large)

1 package (10 ounce) frozen (cooked) or canned asparagus spears, drained

1 package (10 ounce) frozen (cooked) or canned baby carrots, drained

1 package (10 ounce frozen (cooked) or canned green beans, drained

12 large radishes, cut in thin slices

½ cup chopped parsley

Seasoned salt

Low-calorie dressing, your choice

Spread a large platter with the salad greens of your choice. Arrange asparagus spears around platter pointing from inside to edge. Arrange two mounds in center of platter, of carrots and green beans. Spread radish slices around platter on asparagus spears. Sprinkle parsley on top of radish slices, carrots, and green beans. Serve with seasoned salt and low-calorie dressing on side for individual use. Makes 6 servings (50 calories per serving).

Bibb Lettuce Salad

1 clove garlic

4 heads Bibb lettuce, broken into bite-size pieces

1 bunch watercress, stems trimmed

8 leaves celery cabbage, broken into bite-size pieces

12 cherry tomatoes

Dressing

1 teaspoon dry mustard

1 teaspoon vegetable oil

2 tablespoons wine vinegar

1 teaspoon salt

½ teaspoon oregano

1 teaspoon tarragon

1 teaspoon minced chives

1 teaspoon minced parsley

Rub salad bowl with garlic. Place chilled greens in bowl. Mash mustard into oil until smooth and combine in screw-top jar with rest of dressing ingredients. Shake vigorously and pour over greens at serving time. Toss well and serve immediately. Makes 4 servings (67 calories per serving).

Green Salad

2 Belgian endive, cut in ¾-inch circles	8 sprigs watercress
1 small head Boston lettuce	Celery cabbage, to taste
½ small head Romaine lettuce	1 teaspoon salt
8 escarole leaves	1 clove garlic
½ large head Iceberg lettuce	3 tablespoons low-calorie dressing

Use any combination of the above greens. Wash, and dry thoroughly. Tear into bite-size pieces. Sprinkle 1 teaspoon salt into rough wooden salad bowl. Rub clove of garlic on salt until dissolved. Put greens in the bowl, add low-calorie dressing, and toss to combine all flavors. Add a few slices of raw mushrooms if desired. Use immediately. Makes 4 servings (45 calories per serving).

Summer Salad with Red Onions

1 head Boston lettuce	2 sprigs parsley, minced
1 head Romaine lettuce	1 teaspoon vegetable oil
1 medium cucumber, sliced very thin (skin on)	1 teaspoon seasoned salt
1 medium red onion, cut in very thin rings	Pepper to taste
2 small zucchini, sliced very thin (skin on)	2 tablespoons wine vinegar
2 raw mushrooms, sliced through tops and stems	8 red radishes, trimmed, cut into rosettes, and crisped in ice water

Wash vegetables, and keep very cold before using, for crispness. Cut lettuce into salad bowl in 1-inch strips. Add other vegetables. Beat together vegetable oil, salt, pepper, and vinegar, pour over salad and toss lightly but thoroughly. Top with whole radishes. Serve immediately. Makes 4 servings (72 calories per serving).

Seasoned Coleslaw

2 cups cabbage, shredded
½ cup fresh green pepper, diced
4 radishes, sliced thin
3 tablespoons scallions, chopped
½ roasted pimiento, diced

3 tablespoons vinegar
¾ teaspoon liquid artificial sweetener
½ teaspoon seasoned salt
¼ teaspoon celery seeds
10 capers
Black pepper

Toss all ingredients together in a salad bowl and serve chilled. Makes 4 servings (29 calories per serving).

Buttermilk Coleslaw

3 cups shredded cabbage (about 1 small head)
½ teaspoon dry mustard
1½ teaspoons lemon juice
¾ cup buttermilk
1 teaspoon sour cream
1 teaspoon mayonnaise

1 small onion, minced
½ teaspoon salt
Black pepper
Paprika
1 teaspoon caraway seeds, if desired

Beat together dry mustard, lemon juice, buttermilk, sour cream and mayonnaise. Add onion, salt, pepper and a dash of paprika. Sprinkle in caraway seeds if desired. Mix into shredded cabbage with fork and spoon. Refrigerate at least 4 hours before serving. Makes 4 servings (55 calories per serving).

Spiced Celery Root Salad

1 pound celery root (celeriac)
2½ tablespoons vinegar
2 tablespoons Dijon mustard

1 tablespoon polyunsaturated oil
½ teaspoon salt
Dash red pepper

Trim celery root and cook in boiling salted water for 5 or 6 minutes. Drain and cool. When chilled, thinly slice against grain into lengths. Beat mustard, vinegar, oil, and seasonings together. Just before serving beat dressing again and spoon over lengths of celery root, turning the latter to absorb the dressing. Makes 4 servings (65 calories per serving).

Bean Sprout Salad

1 can (16 ounce) bean sprouts, rinsed and drained
2 tablespoons low-calorie French dressing
6 small pimiento-stuffed olives, sliced
1 teaspoon wine vinegar
1 teaspoon lemon juice
1 teaspoon no-sugar soy sauce

2 tablespoons chopped onion
2 tablespoons chopped green pepper
¼ cup chopped celery
¼ cup chopped sweet pickle
Lettuce, medium head
2 medium tomatoes
Salt
Dash of pepper

Mix first ten ingredients well with a fork. Chill in refrigerator about ½ hour, then toss lightly. Prepare 4 plates with beds of lettuce, top with portions of the salad mixture, and add tomatoes, cut in narrow wedges. Sprinkle with salt and pepper to taste. Makes 4 servings (90 calories per serving).

Endive and Artichoke Salad

4 large or 6 small whole Belgian endive, chilled
12 artichoke hearts in brine, drained
1 roast pimiento, cut in strips

1½ tablespoons vegetable oil
1 tablespoon tarragon vinegar
Black pepper
½ teaspoon garlic salt
Capers

Wash and dry endive, cut off ends, cut in bite-size pieces, either crosswise or lengthwise, into salad bowl. Drain and quarter hearts of artichoke and add to endive, together with pimiento strips. Pour oil over top of salad and toss well to coat all surfaces. Add vinegar, pepper, garlic salt and capers, toss again and serve immediately (do not add dressing until just before serving). Makes 4 servings (52 calories per serving).

Cucumber Salad

2 large or 3 medium cucumbers, chopped fine (or very thinly sliced)	½ teaspoon caraway seeds
	¾ teaspoon salt
	⅛ teaspoon black pepper
2 tablespoons chopped onion	4 tablespoons sour cream
1 tablespoon tarragon vinegar	

Mix chopped onion, vinegar, caraway seeds, salt and pepper with sour cream. Toss with chopped cucumber and set in refrigerator for at least 4 hours before serving. Makes 4 servings (52 calories per serving).

Cucumber-Tomato Surprise

4 medium tomatoes	Artificial sweetener equal to 1 teaspoon sugar
2 small-to-medium cucumbers	
¼ cup wine vinegar	Small onion, chopped (optional)
1 tablespoon dill, preferably fresh	Salt, pepper, to taste
½ teaspoon mixed herbs	Lettuce
½ teaspoon tarragon	

Cut tops off tomatoes, removing pulp and placing in bowl; chop pulp. Set tomato shells aside in refrigerator. Cut cucumbers into very thin slices and add to chopped tomato pulp. Combine all remaining ingredients except lettuce in a cup, stir well, and pour over cucumbers and chopped tomato. Stir with a fork to combine well.

Marinate for an hour or more in refrigerator. Salt and pepper tomato shells to taste, and place on lettuce on individual serving plates. Drain marinated mixture and spoon into tomato shells, spooning any excess on lettuce around the tomato shells. Top with a little chopped parsley if desired. Makes 4 servings (50 calories per serving).

Sesame Tomato Salad

Medium head lettuce in leaves
4 medium size tomatoes
2 tablespoons sesame seeds
1 tablespoon minced onion
1 tablespoon minced parsley
Wine vinegar
Seasoned salt

Spread lettuce leaves on a salad plate, and top with tomatoes cut in slices, quarters, or eighths, as you prefer. On the tomatoes, sprinkle the sesame seeds, onion, parsley, and a little wine vinegar. Add seasoned salt to your taste. Serve on open platter, or toss in a bowl before serving. Makes 4 servings (45 calories per serving).

Apple Cabbage Slaw

3 cups shredded green cabbage
¼ cup low-calorie dressing, your choice
2 tablespoons chopped sweet pickles
¼ cup juice from sweet pickles
1 medium apple, cut in thin slices
¼ teaspoon salt

Toss all ingredients gently but well. Chill and serve. Makes 4 servings (40 calories per serving).

Tossed Greens with Grapefruit

2 medium grapefruit, peeled and sectioned (or 2 cans unsweetened drained grapefruit sections)
1 small head Iceberg lettuce, broken into bite-size pieces
1 bunch watercress, trimmed
1 cup fresh spinach, well washed and drained
3 scallions, with tops, sliced
6 radishes, sliced
½ cucumber, sliced thin, with or without peel
1 tablespoon fresh lemon juice
⅓ cup low-calorie French dressing
Black pepper

Cut all but 6 grapefruit sections in half and place in salad bowl. Add bite-size pieces of greens, scallions, radishes and cucumber slices. Mix lemon juice with low-calorie dressing and pour over salad. Sprinkle on black pepper and toss. Add salt if necessary. Garnish with 6 remaining grapefruit sections. Serve immediately. Makes 4 servings (108 calories per serving).

Grapefruit Shells Salad

1 medium head lettuce, divided into leaves
2 large grapefruit, halved
4 tangerines, segmented
2 medium apples, diced
1 cup small white seedless grapes

Juice of 1 lemon
1 tablespoon finely chopped fresh mint leaves (optional)
Granulated artificial sweetener (optional)

Arrange lettuce leaves on 4 serving plates, in a ring around uncovered center of plate. Carefully remove sections from grapefruit, and place in a bowl; remove all membrane dividers and any pits from shells. Cut rims of shells in a decorative zigzag pattern if desired. Add tangerine segments, diced apples, grapes, and lemon juice to grapefruit sections in bowl, and mix well but gently. Place grapefruit shells in center of plates, fill shells with fruit mixture, arranging any excess on the encircling lettuce leaves. Sprinkle tops of filled grapefruit with chopped mint leaves. Sprinkle with sweetener if desired. Makes 4 servings (175 calories per serving).

Onion-Fruit Salad

1 medium head lettuce
1 large cucumber, cut in long thin spears
2 large oranges
2 medium pears

2 medium apples
1 medium sweet onion, in thin slices
1 lemon, quartered wedges
Low-calorie dressing

Arrange washed lettuce leaves on a large platter. Place cucumber spears at angles from center outward to divide platter into 3 triangular segments. Slice oranges thinly and layer in one segment. Cut pears in thin spears and arrange in second segment. Cut apples in thin spears and pile in remaining segment. Spread onion slices over top of all loosely. Serve immediately with lemon wedges and low-calorie dressing. Makes 4 servings (135 calories per serving).

SALAD DRESSINGS

Low-calorie bottled dressings of your choice are permitted; however, make sure that so-called "low-calorie" or "diet" dressings are no more than about 5 calories per teaspoon (check labels carefully). Use dressings sparingly, for crisper, fresher-tasting servings.

Basic Salad Dressing

1 cup water	¾ teaspoon salt
1 tablespoon cornstarch	¾ teaspoon paprika
1 clove garlic, crushed	Lemon pepper marinade,
¼ cup wine vinegar	to taste
1 tablespoon vegetable oil	

Mix a little water into cornstarch until smooth, then add rest of water a little at a time. Heat slowly to boiling point, stirring, and continue cooking for 5 minutes. Place in small deep bowl and cool. Add rest of ingredients and beat with rotary beater. Keep in covered jar in refrigerator, and shake well before using. Makes 1½ cups (8 calories per tablespoon).

Spicy All-Purpose Sauce

1 teaspoon dry mustard	1 teaspoon capers
2 tablespoons white wine vinegar	1 teaspoon parsley, chopped fine
1 tablespoon chopped sweet pickle	1 teaspoon salt
1 tablespoon fresh green pepper (chopped)	Dash white pepper
	4 tablespoons water

Mash mustard in vinegar until thoroughly mixed. Combine with other ingredients in covered jar, shake well, and refrigerate for use on salads and other cold foods. Shake before each use. Heat if desired for use on hot foods (2 calories per tablespoon).

Dill Salad Dressing

Can also be used sparingly on QWL Diet,
on fish and seafood

¼ cup tarragon vinegar (or cider vinegar)

1 spray fresh dill (or more to taste)

1 drop liquid artificial sweetener (or more to taste)

½ teaspoon salt

Pour vinegar into small jar. Snip dill into tiny bits and add to vinegar with sweetener and salt. Chill. Shake before using. Makes ¼ cup (5 calories per tablespoon).

Fresh Lemon Dressing

1 teaspoon dry mustard
Artificial sweetener equal to
    ½ teaspoon sugar
Juice of 2 lemons

Pinch of seasoned salt
Dash black pepper
1 teaspoon paprika

Shake all ingredients together vigorously in a covered jar until well blended. Refrigerate when not in use (12 calories per tablespoon).

Variety Dressing

½ cup tomato juice
½ teaspoon dry mustard
½ teaspoon salt
¼ teaspoon black pepper
¼ teaspoon paprika

1 tablespoon grated onion
2 tablespoons minced parsley
2 teaspoons chopped green pepper
Dash cayenne

Place all ingredients in a jar and shake together vigorously until thoroughly blended. Cover and refrigerate when not in use (4 calories per tablespoon).

Vinaigrette Sauce

2 tablespoons white wine vinegar
1 tablespoon water
½ teaspoon vegetable oil

Dashes of salt, pepper, thyme
1 tablespoon finely chopped shallots (or onions)

Mix all ingredients thoroughly, and chill in refrigerator. Stir or shake well before using (9 calories per tablespoon).

Multi-Purpose Tomato Sauce

1 garlic clove, finely chopped
1 large onion, finely chopped
1 tablespoon olive oil
1 can tomato paste (6 ounce)
1 large can peeled Italian tomatoes (2 pound 13 ounce)

1 teaspoon salt (or more to taste)
½ teaspoon black pepper
1 teaspoon dried basil
1 bay leaf
½ teaspoon oregano
¼ teaspoon thyme

In large no-stick pan, sauté garlic and onion in oil until onion is golden. Add all but last 2 ingredients, boil, then simmer over low flame for 25 minutes. Mix in oregano and thyme, and remove from heat. Pour into quart jar, refrigerate; gently reheat when used on hot vegetables, or on small servings of macaroni, spaghetti, or rice (4 calories per tablespoon).

Grapefruit Dressing for Greens

¼ cup unsweetened grapefruit juice
¼ cup unsweetened lemon juice
Liquid artificial sweetener equal to ⅛ cup sugar

1 teaspoon dry mustard
½ teaspoon salt
⅛ teaspoon pepper

Shake all ingredients together in closed jar. Chill well before using, for all kinds of green salads (4 calories per tablespoon).

Herb Garnish for Vegetables

1 teaspoon fresh herbs, chopped, or ½ teaspoon dried
  herbs
1 teaspoon lemon or lime juice

Mix lemon or lime juice with one of the following
and use as garnish for vegetables such as artichokes,
squash, carrots, zucchini, eggplant, asparagus, green
beans, etc.—also as further variations of hors d'oeuvres
and snacks when chilled.

1 teaspoon mint	1 teaspoon chopped dill
1 teaspoon chopped chives	1 teaspoon minced parsley
1 teaspoon chopped scallions	

or

½ teaspoon chervil	½ teaspoon thyme
½ teaspoon coriander	½ teaspoon oregano
½ teaspoon dill	½ teaspoon mixed herbs

(Calories negligible.)

VEGETABLE RELISHES

*These delicious, low-calorie relishes may be used as side
dishes any time, with many different Inches-Off and
Stay-Slim servings*

Deluxe Eggplant Relish

1 large eggplant	Pepper
1 large tomato	Vinegar
1 medium onion, sliced thin	Granulated artificial
½ roasted pimiento, diced	sweetener
Salt	

Boil eggplant until soft, about 10 to 15 minutes,
drain, chop fine with the tomato, onion and pimiento.

Add salt and pepper to taste, 2 dashes of vinegar, and a pinch of sweetener. Combine well with entire mixture. Chill and serve as a relish or side dish. Keep in covered container in refrigerator for future servings (4 calories per tablespoon).

Special Eggplant Relish

1 medium eggplant	1 teaspoon salt
1 large onion	Black pepper
2 large tomatoes	Garlic powder
1 green pepper, seeded	½ teaspoon granulated
12 pimiento stuffed olives, sliced	artificial sweetener

Wash eggplant, bake in 375° oven until soft, about 45 minutes. Cool, then peel and chop in bowl. Chop onion, tomatoes, and pepper, and add with sliced olives to chopped eggplant. Add salt, pinch of pepper, pinch of garlic powder, and sweetener. Mix all ingredients together well with a fork. Chill before serving. Will keep for a week or longer in a tightly covered container in refrigerator (6 calories per tablespoon).

Mushroom Relish

Use small servings with lunch or dinner where desired, as a salad side dish or salad dressing

Combine in large bowl:

1 pound raw mushrooms, washed, trimmed and sliced sideways with stems on, slices about ⅛ inch thick	2 carrots, raw, very thinly sliced
	8 ribs raw celery, thinly sliced
	¾ cup thinly sliced pimientos

Combine well and place mixture in 2 sterilized 1-quart jars.

Combine in saucepan:

2 cups cider vinegar	¼ teaspoon basil leaves
¼ cup tarragon vinegar	2 tablespoons dried or fresh
1¾ cups water	minced parsley
⅛ cup vegetable oil	10 whole coriander,
2 tablespoons dried or fresh	if available
minced onion	2 teaspoons salt
1 teaspoon garlic salt	2 pinches ground black
1½ teaspoons dried oregano	pepper
leaves	

Bring ingredients to boil in saucepan. Simmer 5 minutes. Pour this hot marinade over mushroom mixture in jars. Cover jars tightly; refrigerate; don't use for 2 days. Lasts 2 weeks or more. Keep refrigerated. (Experiment with other raw vegetables added to mixture, such as green beans and cauliflower.) (3 calories per tablespoon.)

Chili Mushroom Relish

2 pounds mushrooms, washed	1 teaspoon salt
1 quart cider vinegar	¼ cup chili sauce
1 lemon sliced	⅓ cup allspice

Boil together all ingredients except mushrooms. Add mushrooms (if large, slice sidewise) and bring to second boil. Pack into sterilized jars and refrigerate. May be used for up to 3 weeks (2 calories per tablespoon).

Red Pepper Relish

12 large red peppers	2½ teaspoons tarragon
1 garlic clove, chopped or	vinegar
crushed	2 teaspoons parsley, chopped
1 teaspoon seasoned salt	Black pepper to taste
(or more, to taste)	

Scrub red peppers, dry them, and place in preheated broiler 6 inches from heat source. Turn every few minutes to brown all over for about 20 minutes, or until tender. Remove from broiler, allow to cool and peel off outer skin. Remove seeds, and cut peppers into eighths. Place in deep bowl. Meanwhile, combine other ingredients to make marinade. Sprinkle over peppers in bowl, toss, and refrigerate at least 4 hours. Serve cold; use as side dish, relish or snack (25 calories per ½ cup).

Pickled Zucchini

3½ to 4 pounds zucchini	1 quart cider vinegar
4 large onions	2 teaspoons celery seed
Liquid artificial sweetener equal to 2 cups sugar	2 teaspoons mustard seed
¼ cup salt	1 teaspoon tumeric

Sterilize 2 quart or 4 pint jars. Cut zucchini into ¼-inch slices. Thinly slice onions. Combine sweetener, salt, vinegar, celery seed, mustard seed and tumeric in large saucepan. Bring to boil, and remove from heat. Add sliced zucchini and onions. Bring again to boil, then simmer 4 minutes. Spoon into hot jars and seal immediately (3 calories per tablespoon).

FRUITS AND DESSERTS

Fruit recipes serve well as side dishes with lunch and dinner, or use several fruit recipes combined on a plate as your main dish, as a breakfast dish, as snacks, or as desserts.

Desserts, as well as snacks, may be eliminated entirely from your Inches-Off dieting if you wish to lose pounds more quickly—until you're down to your desired weight.

Baked Apples A L'Orange

4 medium baking apples	4 teaspoons granulated artificial sweetener
2 cups hot water	
4 tablespoons raisins	4 teaspoons artificially sweetened marmalade

Core apples, and cut away peel 1 inch from tops and bottoms. Arrange in baking dish with water; fill each apple core with raisins. Sprinkle 1 teaspoon sweetener over each apple. Bake in 400° preheated oven ½ hour, basting twice. Spread 1 teaspoon marmalade over top of each apple. Continue baking until tender. Makes 4 servings (102 calories per serving).

Variations: 1. Prepare apples as above, but without raisins. Heat (don't boil) 10 ounces low-calorie citrus flavored soda and pour over apples. Baste with soda while baking. Sprinkle with cinnamon or nutmeg before serving (80 calories per serving).

2. Prepare apples as above. Sprinkle each with a little artificial sweetener and cinnamon, and wrap each apple in aluminum foil. Bake until tender (80 calories per serving).

Apple Tapioca Pudding

4 medium apples, pared and sliced thinly	Artificial sweetener to taste, equal to about ⅓ cup sugar
5 teaspoons tapioca	1 tablespoon lemon juice
½ cup cold water	2 teaspoons grated lemon
3 cups boiling water	rind

Mix tapioca in cold water. Soak 5 minutes, then add boiling water. Cook in double boiler over boiling water for 30 minutes, stirring occasionally. Add sweetener, stirring until dissolved. Add lemon juice and lemon rind (optional), stir in gently. Pour mixture over sliced apples in baking dish, and bake until apples are soft. Makes 6 servings (75 calories per serving).

Cranberry Applesauce

2 pounds cooking apples, peeled and quartered	⅛ teaspoon salt
4 cups raw cranberries	Liquid artificial sweetener equal to 2 cups sugar
1 cup water	

Cook all ingredients in a large covered saucepan until
berries pop and apples are tender (15 to 20 minutes).
Crush with fork, and chill. Makes 8 servings (85 calories per serving).

Variations: Double-Flavored Applesauce—Cook apples in saucepan in ¼ cup water, add 2 tablespoons
no-sugar flavoring (strawberry, cherry, or grape), and process in blender until of desired consistency. Makes 6
servings (70 calories per serving).

Simple Sweetened Applesauce—Cook apples in ¼
cup water, mash through sieve. Add sweetener equal to
½ cup sugar, also 1 tablespoon lemon juice. Makes 6
servings (70 calories per serving).

Lemon-Orange Applesauce—Cook apples in ¼ cup
water, with 2 ¼-inch slices lemon, ⅛ teaspoon salt, and
artificial sweetener equal to 6 teaspoons sugar. Remove
from heat when soft, and break up with a fork. Add
and stir in 2 tablespoons grated orange rind, and more
sweetener if desired. Makes 6 servings (70 calories per
serving).

Spiced Cantaloupe

2 cantaloupes	2 cloves
⅔ cup unsweetened	1 small cinnamon stick
pineapple juice	2 teaspoons crystallized ginger
¼ cup white wine vinegar	Grated nutmeg
¼ cup brown sugar	

Remove shell from cantaloupes and discard seeds.
Cut melon into bite-sized pieces and place in bowl.

Mix remaining ingredients together in saucepan,
bring to boil, and simmer for 10 minutes. Pour over
cantaloupe and place bowl in refrigerator overnight to
marinate. Serve cold with a little nutmeg sprinkled over
each portion. Makes 4 servings (120 calories per serving).

Cloved Stewed Apricots

12 small fresh apricots
Water to just cover
Artificial sweetener equal to
    3 tablespoons sugar (more
    or less, to taste)

2 cloves
Juice of ¼ lemon

Wash apricots and cook in water in covered saucepan together with other ingredients. Bring to boil, then simmer for 10 minutes, or until done to the tenderness you prefer. Discard cloves. Serve with juice, hot or chilled. Makes 4 servings (35 calories per serving).

Vanilla Fruit Cup

1 pint fresh strawberries,
    sliced
1 cantaloupe, cut up into
    balls (or honeydew melon)
20 seedless grapes, halved
½ cup orange juice

1 tablespoon sugar
1 teaspoon vanilla extract
Dash salt
4 sprigs of fresh mint

Gently mix sliced strawberries, cantaloupe balls, and grape halves in a bowl. Combine orange juice, sugar, vanilla and salt, and pour over fruit. Chill until serving time. Garnish each portion with a sprig of mint. Makes 4 servings (98 calories per serving).

Rice-Fruit Medley

1 cup raw rice
2 tablespoons dried currants
⅓ cup dried apricots, minced
¼ cup seedless raisins

1 teaspoon margarine
1 teaspoon salt
2½ cups boiling water
Nutmeg

Mix all ingredients together with a fork in a 1-quart casserole. Cover and bake in preheated 350° oven 1 hour. Rice should be fluffy and all liquid absorbed. If necessary, bake a little longer. Sprinkle a little nutmeg on top before serving. Makes 4 servings (193 calories per serving).

Apple Petals on Grapefruit

2 halves grapefruit, seeds removed
½ red apple, cut in thin wedges

6 white seedless grapes
Granulated no-sugar sweetener (optional)

Remove cores of grapefruit halves, and loosen each section with grapefruit knife. Insert a thin wedge of apple between every 2 sections and arrange 3 grapes in the center of each half forming a flower design. Sprinkle sweetener over all if desired. Makes 2 servings (82 calories per serving).

Crystal Grapefruit

2 fresh grapefruit
2 egg whites
Granulated artificial sweetener

Divide grapefruit into sections and set on paper towels to dry. Beat egg whites until frothy, almost to soft peak stage. Coat each grapefruit section with beaten egg white, then dip in sweetener. Dry on wire rack to crystallize. Chill until serving time. Makes 4 servings (80 calories per serving).

Variation: Oranged Grapefruit—on cored grapefruit halves, place a teaspoon of artificially sweetened orange marmalade in each center, and sprinkle on artificial sweetener if desired. (57 calories each ½-grapefruit serving.)

Fruit-Flavored Broiled Grapefruit

1 grapefruit, halved
2 tablespoons no-sugar flavoring, your choice (cherry, raspberry, strawberry, etc.)
Sprig of mint

Remove seeds and center core from grapefruit halves. Spoon 1 tablespoon flavoring over each half. Broil in preheated broiler 3 inches from heat for 10 minutes. Garnish with mint leaves. Makes 2 servings (50 calories per serving).

Variation: Simple Broiled Grapefruit—brush liquid artificial sweetener to taste on grapefruit half, and broil 3 inches from heat source until heated through. (55 calories per ½-grapefruit serving.)

Mango Delight

Serve as a main dish, side dish, dessert, or on lettuce as salad

2 large nearly ripe mangoes	4 ounces orange juice
2 small bananas	3 mint leaves, minced (or
30 seedless white grapes	sprinkle of nutmeg)
Juice of ½ lemon	

Peel and cut mangoes and bananas in bite-size pieces into serving bowl. Add grapes (cut in halves, if you like) and orange juice, and sprinkle lemon juice over all. Top each serving with a sprinkle of minced mint leaves, or nutmeg if you prefer it. Makes 4 servings (150 calories per serving).

Cranberry-Apple-Orange Compote

3 medium apples, peeled and sliced	2 cups orange segments
2½ cups fresh cranberries, well washed	1 cup granulated artificial sweetener

Place apple slices, cranberries, and orange sections in alternate layers in casserole or baking dish. Combine sweetener with ¼ cup water, bring to boil, and pour over the fruit. Cover and bake in 350° oven 1 hour. Makes 8 servings (70 calories per serving).

Orange-Cranberry Dessert

2 cups fresh cranberries
1 orange, with peel

Liquid artificial sweetener
equal to 1 cup sugar
2 tablespoons lemon juice

Wash cranberries. Quarter orange and discard seeds. Put both together through a food chopper, using fine blade. Stir in the liquid sweetener and lemon juice thoroughly, and chill. Makes 4 servings (44 calories per serving).

Wined Orange Slices

4 seedless oranges
4 tablespoons dry white wine
(Chablis, Sauterne, etc.)
½ teaspoon ground rosemary

Salt
1 teaspoon granulated
artificial sweetener

Peel the oranges and clean off white tissue as well as possible. Cut oranges horizontally into slices about ⅜-inch thick, and spread slices fanwise in a shallow baking dish. Sprinkle on the wine, rosemary, a few light dashes of salt and the sweetener—evenly. Decorate with border of fresh mint leaves if available. Seal in dish with a plastic bag and tie, or plastic wrap. Place in refrigerator for about ½ hour. Remove plastic covering, and serve with a serving fork, either as a first course, side dish, or dessert. Makes 4 servings (95 calories per serving).

Broiled Peaches

1 can (10 ounce) no-sugar peach halves
¼ teaspoon brown sugar for each peach half
¼ teaspoon vanilla extract

Sprinkle brown sugar and small amount of juice from peaches into each peach half. Place in shallow pan under preheated broiler for 2 or 3 minutes (depending on size of peaches). Serve hot or cold, first sprinkling each half with vanilla extract. Makes 4 servings (25 calories per serving).

Peach-Plum Compote

4 fresh peaches	1½ cups water (or more,
4 fresh plums	to cover)
2 thin slices lemon	6 teaspoons granulated
1 clove	artificial sweetener

Wash and quarter peaches, discarding pits. Wash and halve plums, discarding pits. Place fruit in saucepan with lemon slices and clove. Cover with water and sweetener, bring to boil. Turn heat down and simmer gently until tender. Serve hot or chilled. Makes 4 servings (70 calories per serving).

Poached Pears

4 firm ripe Bosc pears	1 clove
with stems	1 stick cinnamon
1 cup water	½ cup granulated artificial
½ cup dry red wine	sweetener
1 slice lemon	

Cook all ingredients except pears together in saucepan for 5 minutes. Peel whole pears leaving on stems and removing star at bottom. Place pears in the syrup and gently cook together for 10 or 15 minutes or until tender (test with fork). Chill and serve in juice. Makes 4 servings (130 calories per serving).

Home-Style Pineapple Sherbet

1 cup no-sugar pineapple	1½ tablespoons granulated
juice	artificial sweetener
1 cup no-sugar apple juice	4 maraschino cherries
1 tablespoon lemon juice	
1 teaspoon grated lime	
(or lemon) peel	

In a bowl combine all ingredients except cherries. Stir to mix well until sweetener is completely dissolved. Pour mixture into an ice-cube tray from which separator has been removed. Freeze at least a half day before serving.

Just before serving, use an ice scraper (or edge of strong tablespoon) to scrape off frozen mixture and fill 4 prerefrigerated sherbet glasses. Top each serving with a cherry and serve immediately. Makes 4 servings (67 calories per serving).

Prune Pudding

1 cup stewed pitted prunes; reserve juice
Water to make 1 cup
1 tablespoon cornstarch
2 tablespoons cold water
1 tablespoon granulated artificial sweetener
1 tablespoon lemon juice

Press prunes through sieve, or process briefly in blender. Add water to make 1 cup and transfer to top of double boiler. Stir cornstarch into 2 tablespoons cold water until smooth. Combine with puréed prunes, also adding prune juice. Cook all together over boiling water 30 minutes, until thickened, stirring often. Add sweetener and lemon juice. Serve hot or chilled. Makes 4 servings (150 calories per serving).

Quick Rice Dessert

2 cups cooked white rice
Cinnamon to taste
Granulated artificial sweetener, to taste

To the just-cooked or leftover rice, add liberal sprinkles of cinnamon and sweetener, mixing gently with a fork. A tablespoon of skim milk per serving may be added to moisten rice, if desired. Sprinkle more cinnamon on each serving. Makes 4 servings (93 calories per serving).

Rhubarb Delight

1½ pounds rhubarb, peeled
    and cut into 1-inch pieces
½ cup water
½ teaspoon ginger
½ teaspoon cinnamon

¼ teaspoon ground cloves
½ cup vinegar
Artificial sweetener (liquid)
    equal to 2 cups sugar

Place all ingredients into covered large saucepan and cook gently for 20 to 25 minutes, until rhubarb is tender. Chill. Makes 8 servings (11 calories per serving).

Liqueur Strawberries

4 cups strawberries
2 teaspoons granulated
    artificial sweetener
1 tablespoon lemon juice

1 tablespoon orange juice
2 teaspoons orange or
    other sweet liqueur

Wash, drain and hull strawberries, then spread out in shallow bowl. Distribute sweetener over berries. Mix lemon juice and orange juice with liqueur, and spoon mixture over berries. Mix and tumble gently with fork, to coat all surfaces. Place in refrigerator for an hour or more, turning berries once after about 30 minutes. Serve cold. Makes 4 servings (83 calories per serving).

Strawberry-Rhubarb Sauce

1 pound rhubarb, peeled and
    cut into ½-inch pieces
1 tablespoon grated
    orange rind
1 teaspoon grated lemon rind
Artificial sweetener (liquid)
    equal to 1 cup sugar

½ cup orange juice
1 tablespoon lemon juice
1 pint fresh strawberries,
    cleaned and hulled
Artificial sweetener
(granulated) equal to ½
    cup sugar

Combine first six ingredients in covered saucepan and cook gently until rhubarb is just tender (about 10 minutes). Cool.

Sprinkle the granulated sweetener over chilled straw-berries, and mix with rhubarb when serving. Makes 8 servings (25 calories each).

Cinnamon Toast

Can be used as a simple dessert, or for breakfast, with a main dish, or as a snack

4 pieces thin-sliced white bread
Cinnamon
Granulated artificial sweetener

Toast bread slightly in toaster. Arrange on broiler pan. Sprinkle cinnamon and sweetener over toasted bread and place in broiler 30 seconds to heat through. You can spread with no-sugar jelly, if desired. Makes 4 servings (60 calories per serving).

BEVERAGES

In addition to these Inches-Off recipes, enjoy as much as you want of refreshing, filling artificially sweet-ened carbonated beverages. Choose any flavors you pre-fer, in sodas of no more than 1 calorie per ounce—check labels carefully; while sugar is "permitted" among Inches-Off foods, it is not recommended since high-calorie content interferes with quickest reducing.

Citrus Iced Drink

1 cup water
Granulated artificial sweetener
  equal to ⅓ cup sugar
¼ cup mint leaves,
  cut up small

⅔ cup lemon juice
  (unsweetened)
2 cups orange juice
  (unsweetened)
1 quart no-calorie ginger ale

Boil together water, sweetener, and mint. Strain liquid and allow to cool. Add orange and lemon juice.

When ready to serve, add ginger ale and ice cubes or crushed ice. Add more sweetener if desired. Makes 8 servings (36 calories per serving).

Cranberry-Orange Drink

2½ cups low-calorie
    cranberry juice
Granulated sugar substitute
    equal to ¾ cup sugar
4 cloves
1 stick cinnamon

⅓ cup lemon juice
    (unsweetened)
½ cup orange juice
    (unsweetened)
⅛ teaspoon salt

Boil together and simmer 5 minutes cranberry juice, cloves, cinnamon and sweetening. Allow to cool. Add lemon, orange and salt. Serve chilled. Makes 6 servings (36 calories per serving).

Variation: Cranberry-Citrus Drink—combine 3 cups low-calorie cranberry juice with juice of 1 lemon, juice of 2 oranges, a dash of salt, and artificial sweetener to taste. Makes 4 servings (68 calories per serving).

Grape Sparkle

1 cup grape juice,
    no sugar added
⅓ cup granulated artificial
    sweetener

2 cups citrus-flavored no-
    sugar carbonated drink
2 cups club soda
Ice cubes

Stir together grape juice and sweetener in 2 quart pitcher. Chill. At serving time, add other ingredients. Makes 10 half-cup servings (19 calories per serving).

Lemon (or Orange) Cooler

4 tablespoons fresh lemon
    juice (or 4 ounces fresh
    orange juice)
Granulated artificial sweetener
    equal to ¼ cup sugar

1½ cups water or
    club soda
2 slices lemon (or orange)

Combine first three ingredients, stir, pour over crushed ice. Make cut in one side of each slice of lemon (or orange), fit over sides of glasses as garnish. Makes 2 servings (10 calories per serving of lemon cooler; 25 calories per serving of orange cooler).

Fruit Punch

4 cups orange juice
¾ cup lemon juice
1½ cups artificially sweetened apricot juice (12 ounces)
Granulated artificial sweetener equal to ½ cup sugar
1 quart bottle no-calorie ginger ale or citrus soda

Mix all ingredients but ginger ale, and chill. Serve in punch bowl over ice, add ginger ale. Decorate by adding fresh strawberries, lemon slices, orange slices, if desired. Makes 16 punch servings, ½ cup (40 calories per serving without fruit slices).

Tangy "Cocktail"

2 cups sauerkraut juice
Juice of 1 lemon
½ teaspoon caraway seed
1 raw apple, grated
Dash of salt

Shake ingredients together and chill before serving. Makes 4 servings (38 calories per serving).

Spiced Tea Refresher

Rind from 1 orange, grated
1 cup water
5 whole allspice
3 whole cloves
Granulated artificial sweetener equal to ½ cup sugar
1½ cups orange juice
⅓ cup lime juice
1½ cups cold tea
Orange or lime slices and fresh mint garnish

Boil together orange rind, water, allspice and cloves for 20 minutes. Strain, then add rest of ingredients.

Stir well. Serve over crushed ice, garnished with orange or lime slice and fresh mint. Makes 4 servings (45 calories per serving).

Minted Gin or Vodka Refresher

12 mint leaves and 4
    separate sprigs of mint
4 thin lemon slices
4 ounces gin or vodka,
    as preferred

4 bottled cherries, washed
    under water
No-calorie lemon soda
    as needed

Using 4 tall, thin, chilled glasses, drop 3 mint leaves and a lemon slice in each, and crush with a muddler. Add 1 ounce gin or vodka to each glass, and several ice cubes. Fill glass with no-calorie lemon soda, stir. Drop a cherry and sprig of mint in each glass. Provide straws. Makes 4 servings (89 calories per serving).

White Wine Spritzer

8 ounces dry white wine
    (dry Sauterne, Chablis,
    or other)
2 tablespoons brandy
Artificial sweetener (liquid)
    equal to 4 teaspoons sugar

Club soda as needed
4 bottled cherries, washed
    with water
4 thin lemon slices

In shaker, combine and stir the wine, brandy, and sweetener. Divide evenly in 4 chilled, tall glasses, with ice cubes in each glass. Add chilled club soda to near top. Stir. Add a cherry and slice of lemon to each glass. Serve with wide straw for each. Makes 4 servings (80 calories per serving).

Quick Inches-Off Menus

IN ORDER TO LOSE POUNDS and inches rapidly on the Inches-Off Diet, as so many others have, limit your servings to the amounts given in the recipes, and eat only the permitted foods. If you'd like to reduce still more quickly, make your portions even smaller, and avoid completely the higher calorie foods such as breads and cereals, concentrating primarily on vegetables.

It's difficult to state what is a "small," "medium," or "large" fruit (such as an apple), or a vegetable (such as an eggplant), or some other items. All calories in the charts and servings here are figured as "medium" size unless listed otherwise. Judge for yourself, realizing that if you eat a large apple, for instance, and pretend that it's a small or medium apple, you'll only be fooling yourself since you won't lose pounds and inches as swiftly as you should.

Of course, you don't always have to use the menus and recipes here; at times you may prefer simple sliced tomatoes instead of a fancier recipe, or plain cooked spinach instead of a recipe such as "spinach delight."

Just follow the basic Inches-Off rules correctly (as in these menus), and you'll soon find happily that a vegetarian is not only "a salad citizen," but also a beautifully slim and trim one, with a figure to be admired and envied.

MONDAY

Breakfast
 Spiced cantaloupe
 1 slice extra-thin toast with artificially sweetened jelly
 Coffee, tea, or other I-O beverage (coffee or tea may
  be taken with a dash of cream or non-dairy
  creamer, and artificial sweetener, if desired).

Snack
 Wined orange slices

Lunch
 Simple beet soup
 Garden vegetable salad with basic salad dressing
 Orange-cranberry dessert
 Coffee, tea, or other I-O beverage

Snack
 Strawberry-rhubarb sauce

Dinner
 Thick blender soup
 Stewed vegetable medley
 Green salad with dill salad dressing
 Quick rice dessert
 Coffee, tea, or other I-O beverage

Snack
 Cloved stewed apricots

TUESDAY

Breakfast
 Apple petals on grapefruit
 2 slices melba toast with artificially sweetened preserves
 Coffee, tea, or other I-O beverage

Snack
 Apple or orange

Lunch
 Cauliflower soup
 Variety vegetable salad with fresh lemon dressing
 Apple tapioca pudding
 Coffee, tea, or other I-O beverage

Snack
 Cucumber snack

Dinner

Cabbage soup

Vegetable plate of baked carrots, braised endive, lemoned mushrooms

Poached pears

Coffee, tea, or other I-O beverage

Snack

Citrus iced drink

WEDNESDAY

Breakfast

Spiced cantaloupe

1 slice extra-thin toast with artificially sweetened preserves

Coffee, tea, or other I-O beverage

Snack

Cranberry-orange drink

Lunch

Chinese onion soup

Summer salad with red onions, with spicy all-purpose sauce

Orange-cranberry dessert

Coffee, tea, or other I-O beverage

Snack

Grape sparkle

Dinner

"Creamed" cauliflower soup

Vegetable plate of green beans with mushrooms, whipped vegetable medley, eggplant mélange

Quick rice dessert

Coffee, tea, or other I-O beverage

Snack

Fruit punch

THURSDAY

Breakfast

Simple broiled grapefruit

2 rye wafers with artificially sweetened jam

Coffee, tea, or other I-O beverage

Snack
   Cranberry applesauce
Lunch
   Blender cucumber soup
   Tossed greens with grapefruit with spicy all-purpose
      sauce
   Home-style pineapple sherbet
   Coffee, tea, or other I-O beverage
Snack
   Lemon cooler
Dinner
   Basic hearty beef-tomato soup
   Vegetable plate of stewed vegetable medley, sweet
      acorn squash, onioned beets
   Cloved stewed apricots
   Coffee, tea, or other I-O beverage
Snack
   Artificially sweetened soda with lemon slice

FRIDAY

Breakfast
   Crystal grapefruit
   1 slice extra-thin toast with artificially sweetened jelly
   Coffee, tea, or other I-O beverage
Snack
   Orange cooler
Lunch
   Creamy mushroom soup
   Endive and artichoke salad with basic salad dressing
   2 rye wafers with artificially sweetened jelly
   Broiled peaches
   Coffee, tea, or other I-O beverage
Snack
   Broiled peaches
Dinner
   Cauliflower soup
   Vegetable plate of Frenched green beans, buttermilk
      coleslaw, herbed artichoke
   Poached pear
   Coffee, tea, or other I-O beverage

Snack
  Celeriac snacks

SATURDAY

Breakfast
  Crystal grapefruit
  1 slice extra-thin toast with artificially sweetened preserves
  Coffee, tea, or other I-O beverage
Snack
  Mango delight
Lunch
  Escarole-spinach soup
  Bibb lettuce salad
  Sliced tomato with variety dressing
  Strawberry-rhubarb sauce
  Coffee, tea, or other I-O beverage
Snack
  Tangy cocktail
Dinner
  Spanish cold soup
  Vegetable plate of baked endive, broiled eggplant, Italian zucchini with onion
  Quick rice pudding
  Coffee, tea, or other I-O beverage
Snack
  Spiced tea refresher

SUNDAY

Breakfast
  Fruit-flavored broiled grapefruit
  1 slice cinnamon toast
  Coffee, tea, or other I-O beverage
Snack
  Rice-fruit medley
Dinner
  Onion soup
  Vegetable plate of escarole Italian style, sautéed green peppers, creamy spinach

2 rye wafers with artificially sweetened jam
Home-style pineapple sherbet
Coffee, tea, or other I-O beverage
Snack
Mushroom snacks
Supper
Creamy mushroom soup
Bean sprout salad with vinaigrette sauce
Vanilla fruit cup
Coffee, tea, or other I-O beverage
Snack
Cranberry-orange drink

MONDAY

Breakfast
Half cantaloupe
Unsweetened dry cereal with dashes of cream
Coffee, tea, or other I-O beverage
Snack
Grape sparkle
Lunch
Clear tomato soup
Variety vegetable salad with vegetable-herb garnish
Rhubarb delight
Coffee, tea, or other I-O beverage
Snack
Cranberry applesauce
Dinner
Our favorite vegetable soup
Vegetable dinner of acorn squash rings, rice and
    mushroom casserole, honeyed beets
Mango delight
Coffee, tea, or other I-O beverage
Snack
Cranberry-orange drink

TUESDAY

Breakfast
Peach-plum compote

2 melba toast with artificially sweetened preserves
Coffee, tea, or other I-O beverage
Snack
1 tangerine
Lunch
Basic hearty beef-tomato soup
Green salad with grapefruit dressing for greens
Orange-cranberry dessert
Coffee, tea, or other I-O beverage
Snack
Vegetable snacks
Dinner
Chinese vegetable soup
Vegetable plate of Italian tomatoes mélange, broiled
  eggplant, French-style zucchini
Apple tapioca pudding
Coffee, tea, or other I-O beverage
Snack
Lemon cooler

WEDNESDAY

Breakfast
Baked rhubarb
1 slice extra-thin toast with artificially sweetened jam
Coffee, tea, or other I-O beverage
Snack
1 cup grapes
Lunch
Quick pea soup
Spiced celery root salad with apple cabbage slaw
Strawberry-rhubarb sauce
Coffee, tea, or other I-O beverage
Snack
Mushroom snacks
Dinner
Chicken-vegetable soup
Vegetable plate with herbed grilled tomatoes, cas-
  serole of vegetables
Peach-plum compote
Coffee, tea, or other I-O beverage

Snack
   Fruit punch

THURSDAY

Breakfast
   Simple broiled grapefruit
   No-sugar dry cereal with diluted cream (and water)
   Coffee, tea, or other I-O beverage
Snack
   Raw carrot strips
Lunch
   Escarole-spinach soup
   Cucumber-tomato surprise
   Quick rice dessert
   Coffee, tea, or other I-O beverage
Snack
   1 cup cherries
Dinner
   Watercress pepper pot
   Vegetable plate of squash vinaigrette, green beans
      with mushrooms, onioned beets
   No-sugar fruit cocktail
   Coffee, tea, or other I-O beverage
Snack
   Citrus iced drink

FRIDAY

Breakfast
   Spiced cantaloupe
   2 rye wafers with artificially sweetened jam
   Coffee, tea, or other I-O beverage
Snack
   Small banana
Lunch
   Chinese vegetable soup
   Cucumber salad with seasoned coleslaw
   Baked apple à l'orange
   Coffee, tea, or other I-O beverage

Snack
Lemon cooler
Dinner
Thick blender soup
Vegetable plate of whipped vegetable medley, baked
carrots, celery Chinese style
Rhubarb delight
Coffee, tea, or other I-O beverage
Snack
Medium sliced orange

SATURDAY

Breakfast
1 tangerine, segmented
1 slice cinnamon toast
Coffee, tea, or other I-O beverage
Snack
Tangy cocktail
Lunch
Chinese onion soup
Grapefruit shells salad with fresh lemon dressing
Home-style pineapple sherbet
Coffee, tea, or other I-O beverage
Snack
Minted gin or vodka refresher (or grape sparkle)
Dinner
Chinese vegetable soup
Vegetable plate of zucchini treat, vegetables with
mushrooms, sautéed green peppers
Liqueur strawberries
Coffee, tea, or other I-O beverage
Snack
Cranberry-orange drink

SUNDAY

Breakfast
Cloved stewed apricots
1 slice extra-thin toast with artificially sweetened preserves
Coffee, tea, or other I-O beverage

Snack
  2 fresh apricots
Dinner
  Basic hearty beef-tomato soup
  Vegetable plate of baked carrots, Italian zucchini
    with onion, herbed cauliflower
  Apple tapioca pudding
  Coffee, tea, or other I-O beverage
Snack
  White wine spritzer (or party punch)
Supper
  Thick blender soup
  Tossed greens with grapefruit, with spicy all-purpose
    sauce
  Orange-cranberry dessert
  Coffee, tea, or other I-O beverage
Snack
  Spiced tea refresher

Stay-Slim
Eating

ONCE YOU GET DOWN to your desired weight, you can keep that more attractive, healthier figure with Stay-Slim Eating. You may eat a wide variety of foods. However, unlike the Quick Weight Loss and Inches-Off diets, now you count calories—which will become second nature very soon.

You must not eat more calories daily than your body uses up, or you'll become overweight again. You may eat practically any foods you want, as long as you don't exceed your daily maximum calorie intake for your height and desired weight.

All the Quick Weight Loss and Inches-Off recipes can be used for Stay-Slim Eating—so, in effect, every recipe in this book is a Stay-Slim recipe. In addition, the added Stay-Slim recipes on the following pages are created for delicious, healthful eating (but not on the QWL and I-O diets) *and* are low in calories so they won't use up too much of your daily calorie total. Thus, they'll help keep your figure slim, trim, and attractive.

Actually, for Stay-Slim Eating, you may eat any of your favorite dishes—as long as you're careful not to exceed your maximum daily calorie intake to stay at your desired weight. Always keep in mind that one rich, calorie-heavy serving may use up your total calorie allowance for the day!

In the case of any QWL and I-O recipes which combine protein foods with vegetables—such as the QWL recipe for Savory Lamb Stew—you can have both the meat and vegetables, figuring out the approximate calorie count per serving (just a few calories one way or the other aren't significant).

It pays to follow the same basic instructions as given in the QWL and I-O recipes. For instance, removing all possible fat and skin from any serving is better for your overall slimness, good health, and good looks. The same is true for your family and guests.

On Stay-Slim Eating you may add bread, cookies, and other foods that may not be permitted on the QWL and I-O diets—but again, as long as you don't exceed your total daily maximum calorie allowance.

Using the Ideal Weight and Calorie Chart

"Ideal Weight" figures for women and men are based on my experience in 53 years of medical practice as an internist. I have found that these weights are healthiest for most individuals, figured out according to height. (For the teenager's ideal weight, deduct 1 pound for every year between the actual age and 25, as listed in the adult Ideal Weight Chart here.)

These "ideal weight" figures are lower than the usual "average weight" figures in other listings which I consider too high. Most "average weights" have been computed by including many overweights and very few underweights. Thus the figures are in error since the mathematical "average" comes out higher than it should be.

Your ideal weight is likely to be best for you from every viewpoint—health, vigor, appearance, and longer life. If you prefer to weigh a little more, then the higher figure becomes your "desired weight"—the choice is entirely your own. It is interesting that while some might consider our "ideal weights" too low, most of the healthy, energetic national and international beauty contest finalists are *under* our "ideal weights."

However, if you think that you personally look best 5 to 10 pounds more than the ideal weight on the chart, use your judgment to set your desired weight a little higher. I've found particularly that some women over age 50 who are only about 5 feet 2 inches tall or less, prefer being a little over ideal weight in order to have their faces look fuller. But for greatest health and vigor, don't set your desired weight much higher than your ideal weight on our chart.

The *"Daily Calorie Intake" figures* here allow women to eat 12 calories per pound per day, and men to eat 13 calories per pound per day (same for teenagers). If when you're down to your ideal weight, you're still losing weight on your daily calorie allowance, increase your intake until you stay at ideal weight. Similarly, if you're gaining weight on your daily calorie allowance, cut down the amount you're eating until you find the perfect balance for yourself as an individual—since each person necessarily differs somewhat, and *vive la difference.*

IDEAL WEIGHT AND CALORIE CHART

WOMEN (Unclothed) MEN

Height	Pounds Weight	Daily Calories to Maintain Weight	Pounds Weight	Daily Calories to Maintain Weight
4 feet 8 inches	85–93	1020–1120	92–100	1200–1300
4 feet 9 inches	88–96	1055–1155	93–101	1215–1320
4 feet 10 inches	90–98	1080–1180	95–103	1240–1350
4 feet 11 inches	93–101	1115–1215	98–106	1275–1380
5 feet	95–103	1140–1240	100–108	1300–1410
5 feet 1 inch	97–105	1175–1275	105–113	1370–1470
5 feet 2 inches	100–108	1200–1300	110–118	1450–1560
5 feet 3 inches	105–113	1260–1360	115–123	1510–1610
5 feet 4 inches	110–118	1320–1420	120–128	1575–1675
5 feet 5 inches	112–120	1350–1450	125–133	1640–1740
5 feet 6 inches	117–125	1400–1500	130–138	1700–1800
5 feet 7 inches	120–128	1450–1550	135–143	1760–1875
5 feet 8 inches	125–133	1500–1600	140–148	1825–1925
5 feet 9 inches	130–138	1550–1650	145–153	1900–2000
5 feet 10 inches	135–143	1620–1720	150–158	1950–2050
5 feet 11 inches	140–148	1680–1780	155–163	2020–2120
6 feet	144–152	1740–1840	160–168	2100–2200
6 feet 1 inch	148–155	1800–1900	165–173	2150–2250
6 feet 2 inches	153–161	1850–1950	170–178	2210–2315
6 feet 3 inches	158–166	1900–2000	175–183	2275–2380
6 feet 4 inches	163–171	1950–2050	180–188	2350–2450
6 feet 5 inches	168–176	2000–2100	186–193	2410–2510
6 feet 6 inches	173–183	2050–2150	190–198	2470–2575
6 feet 7 inches	178–188	2100–2200	195–203	2530–2630
6 feet 8 inches	183–193	2200–2300	200–208	2600–2710

Tips for Stay-Slim Eating

WEIGH YOURSELF UNCLOTHED EVERY MORNING upon arising. If you are 3 or more pounds over your desired weight (after a heavy eating and drinking weekend, or any other time), go back on the Quick Weight Loss Diet. You'll lose that overweight within a day or two. Use the QWL Diet to adjust your weight downward whenever necessary for the rest of your life. Then cut your daily calorie intake until you know exactly how much you personally can eat to maintain your desired slimness.

To repeat, necessarily, your body is individual and cannot be regulated precisely according to mathematical averages. You must personally learn how many calories per day will keep you at your desired weight. It may be a few calories more or less than the numbers on our chart.

Cut your daily calorie intake by using low-calorie foods. Keep in mind that the more calories you save by substituting low-calorie foods and beverages, the more you can eat of other foods and still stay within your Stay-Slim daily calorie allowance. For example, drinking an 8 ounce glass of no-sugar cola (about 5 calories) instead of a regular cola (105 calories) saves you about 100 calories. That lets you add a piece of fruit, or a cup of vegetable soup, or any other 100-calorie serving, because of the calories you saved on a single glass of soda.

Count the calories in your snacks during the day and evening, otherwise you may be adding hundreds of calories above your daily Stay-Slim calorie allowance, and wonder why you're gaining weight and starting to bulge again. Don't try to fool yourself. Use your good sense, realizing that if you snack on an ice cream soda while you're shopping, you'll be adding about 350 calories. Substituting an iced cupcake and no-sugar cola drink would still amount to about 165 calories, while a snack of a tangerine and black coffee would be only 70 calories—quite a difference from 350 calories for the "shopping snack." It makes an enormous difference in pounds and inches when you choose your snacks according to calorie count, a difference that you can enjoy showing in your slim, trim figure—or try to hide in tent-like dresses.

Combine different types of vegetables in cooking up your own creative tasty combinations, such as tomatoes with green beans, spinach with mushrooms, beets and pearl onions or thin onion slices, and so on.

Don't let yourself be misguided by some menus suggested in other cookbooks and listings which provide far more food than the average adult needs. For example, a menu suggestion in a leading newspaper lists for dinner:

Tomato and onion soup with a poached egg in each bowl
Sautéed flounder fillets in butter
Spinach-stuffed, buttered mushrooms
Boston lettuce salad
Fresh pears and cheese
Beverage

Adding the usual rolls and butter, rich dressings and whole-milk cheeses, this menu (which some so-called experts would say is "a low-calorie dinner") actually piles many hundreds of extra, fattening calories on the diner.

A far more healthful and nutritionally satisfying dinner would be a lean steak, a salad with low-calorie dressing, a serving of artificially sweetened gelatin dessert, and coffee or tea without milk, cream or sugar.

Don't let anyone convince you that it's "unhealthy"

to eat so little. The truth is that the dinner listed in the newspaper provides many more calories than most people can burn up without piling on more weight and threatening good health and life itself.

To save calories, use artificial sweeteners whenever possible instead of sugar, in recipes and in beverages. For instance, suppose you drink about 6 cups of coffee and/or tea daily, with 2 teaspoons of sugar per cupful, as many people do. At 18 calories per teaspoon of sugar, you'd save 216 calories a day just by substituting artificial sweetening, with no difference in taste (according to many impartial taste tests).

Go easy on salt if you have any tendency toward water retention which is sometimes evidenced by swelling of feet, ankles, or legs. Lots of salt causes the body to retain more water, increasing total weight.

Get the Stay-Slim habit of spreading high-calorie additives very thin on crackers or bread. A light coating of jam, butter, or other spreads, can give you the desired flavor without adding too many calories. It's healthier to be a Stay-Slim epicure than a spread-it-thick overweight glutton.

Cut food in small pieces, and chew slowly. By eating small pieces slowly, a smaller portion seems to be larger and more satisfying than if you swallow big chunks quickly. In addition, slow, thorough chewing is better for your digestive processes also.

Decorate dishes with low-calorie garnishes such as cucumber slices sprinkled with a little fresh dill, carrot sticks in curls, fresh herbed parsley, watercress, celery stalks sprinkled with paprika, and so on. You add flavor and food bulk but very few calories.

Don't ever serve huge portions, even of low-calorie dishes. Don't hesitate to leave food on your plate. Either save it for the next meal or throw it away rather than add bulging pounds to your body. Stay-Slim Eating also means Stay-Attractive and Stay-Healthier Eating.

Don't skip an annual or semi-annual medical check-up, even though you stay slim and vigorous. While slimness keeps you generally healthier, and helps pre-

vent a number of medical problems, other disorders
may attack you regardless. You must be examined
regularly by a physician.

For *full details on Stay-Slim eating*, check the other
Stillman/Baker books: *The Doctor's Quick Weight
Loss Diet, The Doctor's Quick Inches-Off Diet,* and
The Doctor's Quick Teenage Diet.

Stay-Slim Calorie Tables

TABLE OF MEASUREMENTS

By volume capacity:
1 cup equals 8 fluid ounces or ½ pint or 16 tablespoons
1 tablespoon equals 3 teaspoons
2 tablespoons equal 1 fluid ounce
1 pint equals 2 cups   1 quart equals 4 cups

By weight:
1 ounce equals 28.35 grams
100 grams equal 3.52 ounces
16 ounces equal 1 pound

Calories may vary a little for specific items in different calorie charts, depending primarily on size variations in fruits, vegetables, and other foods. Such differences usually aren't significant. Your concern is staying slim, and you must judge how your daily calorie intake affects you; if you start to gain weight, cut your calories a little until you find the correct daily total to keep you at your desired weight.

Canned and other packaged foods may vary considerably in calories per ounce, depending on the content of each ounce. Some companies list calorie content on their packages, so always check the printing, especially when shopping.

MEATS AND POULTRY

Meats and poultry here are figured as "lean" and cooked, with no visible fat, all skin removed from poultry, and no extra fats used in cooking. (For your general information, removing all visible fat and skin usually takes off about 60 calories per ounce.) Calories listed are for meat cooked "medium" or served as is; therefore if meats are cooked "rare," add about 20 calories per listed serving; if meats are "well done," take off about 20 calories per listed serving.

	Calories
Bacon, cooked crisp, 2 slices	90
Canadian, cooked, 2 slices	90
Beef roast, lean, 4 ounces	260
Hamburger, lean, broiled, 4 ounces	250
Corned beef, lean, 4 ounces	260
Dried, chipped beef, 4 ounces	230
Liver, 4 ounces	160
Potpie, 8 ounces, average	560
Steak, lean, broiled, 4 ounces	230
Stew beef, 4 ounces, lean	210
Sweetbreads, 3 ounces	165
Bologna, all-beef, 3-inch slice	40
Salami, cooked, 2 ounces	180
Chicken, turkey, cooked, flesh only, 6 ounces	230
Raw, with bones, ready to cook, 8 ounces	190
Breast, with bone, raw, 1 pound	395
Canned, boneless, 6 ounces	340
Livers, 4 ounces	145
Frankfurter, medium, all-beef	150
Ham, cured, lean, 3 ounces	210
Boiled, lean, 3 ounces	200
Canned, lean, 2 ounces	100
Deviled, canned, 2 ounces	150
Lamb, chop, broiled, lean only, 4 ounces	225
Leg, lean, 4 ounces	220
Liver, calf, broiled, 4 ounces	160
Sweetbreads, calf, lamb, 4 ounces	110

	Calories
Pork, roast, lean only, 3 ounces	210
Chop, lean only, no bone, 3 ounces	230
Sausage, average, well cooked, dried, 2 ounces	270
Tongue, beef, cooked, 4 ounces	275
Calf, cooked, 4 ounces	180
Veal, cutlet, broiled, 3 ounces	185
Roast, lean, 4 ounces	260

FISH AND SHELLFISH
(MEAT ONLY)

	Calories
Bass, no fat or skin, 4 ounces	115
Bluefish, 4 ounces	135
Carp, 4 ounces	130
Caviar, sturgeon, 1 ounce, whole eggs	75
Pressed	90
Clams, medium size, each	15
Canned, including juice, 3 ounces	45
Clam juice, clear, 4 ounces	22
Cod, 4 ounces	90
Crabmeat, 4 ounces	105
Canned, 4 ounces	115
Frozen, 4 ounces	100
Croaker, 4 ounces	100
Fish flakes, canned, 4 ounces	125
Fish roe, canned, 4 ounces	150
Fish sticks or fillets, frozen cooked, 4 ounces	200
Flounder, 4 ounces	90
Gefilte, canned or in jars, 4-ounce piece	90
Haddock, 4 ounces	90
Smoked, lean, 4 ounces	115
Halibut, 4 ounces	115
Smoked, 4 ounces	250
Herring, smoked, kippered, 4 ounces	240
Pickled, 4 ounces	250
Salted, brined, 4 ounces	250
Lobster, 1 pound size, whole, no fat	110
Lobster meat only, 4 ounces	110

	Calories
Mackerel, 4 ounces	220
Oysters, medium, each	12
Meat only, 4 ounces	75
Perch, 4 ounces	135
Perch, yellow, 4 ounces	105
Pickerel, 4 ounces	95
Pike, 4 ounces	100
Pompano, 4 ounces	190
Red Snapper, 4 ounces	105
Salmon, fresh or frozen, 4 ounces	135
Canned, undrained, 4 ounces	194
Canned, drained, 4 ounces	160
Roe, 4 ounces	235
Smoked, lean, 4 ounces	200
Sardines, canned, water-drained, 4 ounces	180
Scallops, 4 ounces	125
Sea bass, 4 ounces	110
Shad, 4 ounces	190
Roe, 4 ounces	140
Shrimp, medium, each	10
Meat only, 4 ounces	105
Raw, in shell, 1 pound	285
Smelts, 4 ounces	110
Sole, 4 ounces	90
Sturgeon, smoked, 4 ounces	170
Trout, 4 ounces	125
Tuna, caned in water, 4 ounces	140
Canned in oil, drained, 4 ounces	180
Whitefish, smoked, 4 ounces	175
Whiting, frozen fillets, 4 ounces	90

VEGETABLES

	Calories
Artichoke, cooked, 4 ounces	50
Hearts, 4 ounces	30
Asparagus, medium spear	3.5
Canned, 6 medium spears	20

	Calories
Avocado, medium half	185
Beans, baked, canned, 1 cup	60
Beans, baked, canned, 1 cup	320
Beets, 1 cup	70
Broccoli, 1 cup	45
Brussels sprouts, 1 cup	60
Cabbage, raw, shredded, 1 cup	25
Cooked, 1 cup	45
Carrots, 5½ inch, raw, each	20
Diced, cooked, 1 cup	45
Cauliflower, cooked, 1 cup	30
Celery, 8-inch stalk, raw	5
Diced, cooked, ½ cup	20
Chinese pea pods, cooked, 1 cup	90
Corn, cooked, 5-inch ear	65
Canned, 1 cup	170
Cucumber, medium	30
Eggplant, cooked, 1 cup	40
Raw, untrimmed, 1 pound	92
Endive, raw, 4-inch size, each	5
Escarole, large leaf, each	5
Green beans, 1 cup	35
Kale, cooked, 1 cup	30
Kohlrabi, 1 cup	40
Lentils, 1 cup	220
Lettuce, 5-inch compact head, 1 pound	70
2 large leaves	5
Lima beans, 1 cup	150
Mushrooms, 1 cup	30
½ pound, untrimmed	62
Canned, 4 ounces	19
Okra, 1 cup	50
Onion, raw, 2½-inch diameter, each	40
Cooked, 1 cup	60
Flakes, dehydrated, 1 tablespoon	50
Parsley, raw, chopped, 1 tablespoon	1
Peas, cooked, 1 cup	110
Canned, frozen, drained, 1 cup	120
Peppers, raw, green or red, medium size, each	15
Potatoes, medium, baked with peel, each	105

Calories

Without peel, each	90
Boiled, medium, each	90
French-fried, 2 to 2½ inch, each	15
Mashed with a little milk only, ½ cup	70
Chips, 2-inch medium size, each	11
Radishes, raw, medium, each	3
Sauerkraut, drained, 1 cup	30
Spinach, and other such greens, cooked, 1 cup	45
Squash, summer type, 1 cup	35
Winter type, 1 cup	95
Sweet potatoes, medium size, baked	155
Candied	300
Tomatoes, raw, medium size, each	30
Canned, 1 cup	45
Juice, 1 cup	50
Paste, canned, 6 ounces	140
Sauce, canned, 1 cup	75
Turnips, 1 cup	50
Turnip greens, cooked, 1 cup	40
Vegetable juice, mixture, 1 cup	45
Water chestnuts, 4 ounces	90
Watercress, 1 cup	6
Wax beans, 1 cup	45
Zucchini, cooked, 1 cup	40
uncooked, 1 pound	75

FRUITS

Calories

Apples, raw, medium size	80
Juice, 1 cup	120
Canned, with sugar, ½ cup	120
Canned, no sugar added, ½ cup	50
Apricots, raw, medium size, each	20
Canned, in sugar syrup, ½ cup	120
Canned, no sugar added, ½ cup	45
Dried, raw, each small half	10
Dried, cooked, no sugar added, ½ cup	100
Nectar (juice), no sugar added, ½ cup	30

	Calories
Bananas, medium, each	85
Blueberries, blackberries, 1 cup	85
Cantaloupe, 5 inch, medium half	40
Cherries, fresh, 1 cup	65
Canned, no sugar added, ½ cup	60
Cranberry sauce, canned, sweetened with sugar, ½ cup	200
Fresh, 1 cup	52
Juice, sweetened, 6 ounces	125
Juice, no sugar, 6 ounces	35
Dates, pitted, 1 cup	500
Each, medium	35
Figs, dried, large 1 by 2 inch, each	60
Fruit cocktail, canned in syrup, ½ cup	100
Canned, no sugar added, ½ cup	40
Grapefruit, 5 inch medium, half	55
Juice, fresh, no sugar added, 1 cup	95
Grapes, 1 cup	85
Juice, sweetened, ½ cup	105
Juice, unsweetened, ½ cup	70
Frozen juice, ½ cup	60
Honeydew melon, 2- by 7-inch slice	50
Lemons, medium, each	20
Juice, unsweetened, 1 tablespoon	4
Limes, medium, each	20
Oranges, medium, each	65
Juice, fresh, no sugar added, 1 cup	110
Peaches, medium, 2 inch, each	35
Canned in sugar syrup, ½ cup	100
Canned, no sugar added, ½ cup	35
Pears, medium, 3 inch, each	100
Pineapple, fresh, diced, 1 cup	75
Canned, in sugar syrup, ½ cup	100
Canned, in own juice, no sugar added, ½ cup	60
Juice, no sugar added, ½ cup	70
Plums, 2 inch medium, each	30
Prunes, cooked, unsweetened, medium, each	17
Juice, canned or frozen, ½ cup	100
Raisins, dried, ½ cup	230
1 level tablespoon	30

	Calories
Raspberries, fresh, red, 1 cup	70
Black, 1 cup	90
Strawberries, fresh, 1 cup	70
Frozen, ½ cup	180
Tangerines, medium, 2½ inch, each	40
Watermelon, 4- by 8-inch wedge	110

DAIRY PRODUCTS . . .
BUTTER . . .
CHEESE . . .
EGGS . . .
MILK . . .
MARGARINE . . .
OILS . . .
SALAD DRESSINGS . . .
SHORTENING

	Calories
Butter, ½ pound	1605
1 tablespoon	100
1 pat or square	50
Cheese, American, 1-inch cube	70
Grated, 1 tablespoon	30
Blue cheese, 1 ounce	105
Camembert, 1 ounce	85
Cottage cheese, creamed, 1 ounce	30
Low-fat, diet-type, 1 ounce	25
Farmer cheese, 1 ounce	35
Pot cheese, 1 ounce	22
Skim milk, 1 ounce	22
Uncreamed, 1 ounce	24
Cream cheese, 1 ounce	105
Edam, 1 ounce	105
Gorgonzola, 1 ounce	110
Gouda, 1 ounce	110

	Calories
Liederkranz, 1 ounce	85
Limburger, 1 ounce	100
Mozzarella, part skim, 1 ounce	85
Muenster, 1 ounce	100
Neufchatel, 1 ounce	70
Parmesan, 1 ounce	110
Grated, 1 tablespoon	25
Pizza cheese, 1 ounce	75
Process "Cheese Food," average, 1 ounce	90
Port du Salut, 1 ounce	100
Ricotta, 1 ounce	50
Romano, 1 ounce	110
Grated, 1 tablespoon	25
Spread cheese, average, 1 ounce	85
Swiss, 1 ounce	105
Swiss Process, 1 ounce	100
Eggs, small	60
medium	70
large, cooked without fat, each	80
White only, raw, each	20
Yoke only, raw, each	60
Margarine, ½ pound	1615
1 square	50
1 tablespoon	100
Milk (cow's), whole, 1 cup (8 ounces)	160
Skim, in carton, 1 cup	80
Skim, dry, nonfat, 1 cup	80
Skim,, evaporated, 4 ounces	90
"99% fat free," 1 cup	120
Evaporated, regular, ½ cup	175
Buttermilk, cultured, 1 cup	85
Cream, light, 1 cup	525
Light, 1 tablespoon	35
Heavy, 1 tablespoon	50
Sour cream, 1 tablespoon	30
Imitation sour cream, 1 tablespoon	25
Non-Dairy creamer, 1 tablespoon	11
Oils, cooking, salad . . . vegetable, including corn, cottonseed, olive, peanut, soybean, and vegetable oils, 1 tablespoon	125

	Calories
Salad dressings—French, 1 tablespoon	60
All-purpose, miscellaneous, 1 tablespoon, average	70
Mayonnaise, 1 tablespoon	100
Mayonnaise-type salad dressing, 1 tablespoon	65
Russian dressing, 1 tablespoon	75
Low-calorie, "dietetic," see labels, 1 tablespoon	1–25
Shortening, vegetable, 1 tablespoon	100
Yogurt, plain, 1 cup	130
Fruit-flavored, average, 1 cup	270
Vanilla, 1 cup	200

BREADS AND GRAIN PRODUCTS, CEREALS

	Calories
Breads, all types, average slice, plain, toasted	65
Extra-thin slice	43
Biscuit, 2½-inch diameter, each	140
Melba toast, rounds each	10
Rectangles, each	10
Bread crumbs, 1 cup	400
Breadsticks, average, each	40
Bread stuffing, 1 cup	280
Cereals, cooked, average type, 1 cup	140
Dry cereals, unsweetened, average, 1 cup	110
Presweetened, average, 1 cup	140
Crackers, butter-flavored, average, each	17
Cheese wafers, average, each	11
Graham, medium, each	28
Matzo, sheet, average, each	120
Oyster crackers, small, each	3
Rye wafers, 2 x 3½ inches, each	25
Saltines, soda crackers, average, each	13
Zweiback, each	30
Flour, 1 cup	450
1 tablespoon	28
Cake flour, 1 cup	375

	Calories
Macaroni, spaghetti products, cooked, 1 cup	175
Egg noodles, cooked, 1 cup	190
Muffins, 2¾-inch diameter, bran, each	125
Corn, each	140
English, plain, average, each	145
Pancakes, 4 inch, each	60
Rice, cooked, 1 cup	185
Raw, 1 cup	720
Rolls, medium size (1.3 ounce), each	120
Waffles, average size, each	240

DESSERTS, SWEETS

	Calories
Cakes, angel food, 2-inch sector	110
Chocolate layer, 2-inch sector	420
Cupcake, iced, 2¾ inch, each	160
Plain cake, 3 by 2 by 1½ inch, each	180
Sponge cake, 2-inch sector	115
Candy, caramels, fudge, average, 1 ounce	120
Chocolate, milk or dark, 1 ounce	145
Syrup, thick, 1 tablespoon	50
Chewing gum, regular, 1 slice	8
Cookies, plain, small, average each	25
Fig bar, small, each	55
Ginger snaps, small, each	16
Shortbread, small, each	40
Miscellaneous cookies vary greatly according to types, piece, up to	100
Doughnuts, medium size, plain, each	170
Gelatin dessert, regular, ½ cup	80
Sugar-free, ½ cup	12
Gelatin, unflavored, dry, 1 envelope	30
Honey, 1 tablespoon	60
Ice cream, average type, ½ cup	140
Ice cream soda, average size and type	350
Ice milk, average, ½ cup	110
Frozen custard, average, ½ cup	150

	Calories
Ices, average, ½ cup	135
Sherbet, average, ½ cup	120
Jams, jellies, marmalades, preserves, average, 1 tablespoon	50
Artificially sweetened jams, (check labels), 1 tablespoon	4–25
Apple butter, also peach, apricot, 1 tablespoon	35
Pies, apple, other fruit pies, average, 4-inch sector	330
Custard, pumpkin, cream-type, average, 4-inch sector	270
Lemon meringue, 4-inch sector	300
Popcorn, no butter, 1 cup	40
Puddings, custard, cornstarch, tapioca, average, ½ cup	170
Sugar, granulated, 1 teaspoon	18
1 cup	770
Sugar syrup, plain or maple sugar, 1 tablespoon	55
Sweetener, artificial (varies by brand, calories usually negligible; check individual packages)	

SOUPS

	Calories
Bouillon, broth, consommé, clear, fat removed, 1 cup	8
Borscht, 1 cup	70
Chicken, 1 cup	80
Creamed chicken, 1 cup	170
Clam Chowder, Manhattan, 1 cup	75
New England, 1 cup	140
Minestrone, 1 cup	100
Mushroom, 1 cup	80
Creamed, 1 cup	200
Onion, 1 cup	50
Oyster stew, 1 cup, skim milk (no cream)	150
Pea, 1 cup	150
Rice, noodle, barley in clear soup, 1 cup	115
Schav, 1 cup	15

	Calories
Tomato, 1 cup	90
Vegetable, 1 cup	80

"Low-Calorie," "Dietetic" Soups, see package labels

MISCELLANEOUS—
BEVERAGES . . .
CONDIMENTS . . .
NUTS . . . OTHER

	Calories
Beverages, coffee, tea, plain, no sugar or cream	0
Beer, 12 ounces	160
low-carbohydrate beer, 12 ounces	100
Cocktails, alcoholic, average, 3 fluid ounces	180
Distilled liquor; brandy; gin; scotch; vodka; whiskeys,	
1 fluid ounce, 86 proof	70
94 proof	76
100 proof	82
Liqueurs, 80 proof, 1 fluid ounce	110
Wines, 4 ounces, dry, average	100
Port, 4 ounces	185
Sherry, 4 ounces, dry	150
sweet	185
Vermouth, 4 ounces, dry	140
sweet	180
Carbonated beverages, assorted flavors, average	
8 ounces	110
Ginger ale, dry, 8 ounces	85
Artificially sweetened (check labels), 8 ounces	4
Cocoa, 1 cup	235
Catsup, chili sauce, cocktail sauce, average, 1 tablespoon	18
Mustard, prepared, 1 teaspoon	8
Olives, green and ripe, large, average	8
Nuts, peanuts, roasted (regular or dry), shelled, ½ cup	420

	Calories
Peanut Butter, 1 tablespoon	100
Cashews, pecans, walnuts, et cetera, average, ½ cup	375
Pickles, dill 4 inch, sweet 3 inch, each	18
Relish, average, 1 tablespoon	22
Pizza, plain cheese type, 6-inch wedge	200
Vinegar (various types, average), 1 tablespoon	2
1 ounce	4

HORS D'OEUVRES

These recipes are not only delicious, but they are low-calorie recipes which can be used for hors d'oeuvres and dips in the Quick Weight Loss and Inches-Off sections. Be sure to check and use them as you wish for Stay-Slim eating and general serving.

Caviar Canapés

½ cup cottage cheese
2 tablespoons skim milk
1 cucumber, in thin slices
(retain skin)

2 tablespoons whitefish roe
cavair
Chopped egg (optional)
Chopped onion (optional)

Process cottage cheese and skim milk in blender at low speed for a few seconds, until very smooth. Spoon on tops of cucumber slices and top with caviar. Garnish with chopped egg and/or chopped onion. Makes 4 to 6 servings (245 calories whole recipe).

Tuna 'n Egg Spread

1 medium can tuna fish, water-packed (or oil-packed tuna placed in sieve and cold water run through to wash off oil)
¼ cup low-calorie salad dressing (see recipes)
2 teaspoons lemon juice

½ teaspoon prepared mustard
1 slice medium onion, diced
½ teaspoon salt
¼ teaspoon celery salt
5 hard-cooked eggs, quartered

Place all ingredients except eggs in blender and process at high speed briefly or until blended. Remove to bowl. Chop eggs in blender 5 quarters or so at a time (if you have no "chop" button turn *low* on and off). With fork, toss with other ingredients. Use as spread on melba toast, or as stuffing for celery ribs. (588 calories entire large recipe.)

Beef-Stuffed Mushrooms

1 pound very lean chopped beef, all visible fat removed before grinding
12 large mushrooms (or 16 medium), washed, stems removed
1 egg
1 small onion, chopped very fine
3 tablespoons water
2 tablespoons chili sauce or catsup
Salt and pepper to taste

Chop stems of mushrooms. Using fork, combine with all other ingredients except mushroom caps. Spoon into mushroom caps and bake in 350° oven ½ hour or until stuffing is brown and crisp on top. (95 calories each piece, figuring 12 large mushrooms.)

Celery Canapés

2 small bunches celery hearts
6 tablespoons cottage cheese
1 vegetable bouillon cube
3 tablespoons boiling water
1-inch square Roquefort or blue cheese
1½ teaspoons chopped chives
2 teaspoons chopped green pepper
Dash Worcestershire sauce
Paprika

Wash celery thoroughly and trim. Cut stalks into 1½-inch lengths and place in ice water (leave tiny ones whole). Dissolve bouillon cube in boiling water and blend in Roquefort cheese. Using fork, combine with cottage cheese, chives, green pepper, and Worcestershire sauce. Remove celery from ice water. Dry, fill hollows with mixture and sprinkle with paprika. (220 calories, whole recipe.)

Stuffed Cucumber Slices

1 medium cucumber
4 tablespoons cottage cheese
1 tablespoon chopped
pimiento

Salt (to taste)
Pepper (to taste)
Mixed herbs (to taste)

Carefully cut off ends of cucumber and scoop out center with a long, thin, sharp knife or apple corer, leaving about ¼-inch thick shell. Score green skin with a sharp fork if desired. In blender combine cucumber pulp, cottage cheese, pimiento, salt, pepper, and mixed herbs, and process slowly to a smooth paste. Spoon paste into center of cucumber, then chill well. Slice into ¼-inch slices, and serve as hors d'oeuvres, or as a luncheon dish for 1. (90 calories, whole recipe.)

Tomato Appetizers

6 triangles extra-thin toast
6 slices tomatoes, thick
2 tablespoons finely chopped
green pepper
1 tablespoon chopped chives

1 well-done strip of
bacon, crumbled
Salt
Pepper
Paprika

Place a tomato slice on each piece of toast. Sprinkle chopped green pepper and chives on tomatoes and season with salt, pepper, and paprika. Place under broiler until tomato slices are tender; remove with spatula. Sprinkle crumbled bacon on top. Serve hot. Makes 6 servings (35 calories per serving).

Zucchini Canapés

2 medium zucchini squash
2 hard-cooked eggs
Salt

Pepper
Paprika

Scrub zucchini, trim off ends, and cut into ⅛-inch thick round slices, leaving on skin. Slice eggs into circles, place one slice on each zucchini circle. Sprinkle on salt, pepper, and paprika to taste. (187 calories whole recipe.)

Dippy Vegetables

1 vegetable bouillon cube
1 tablespoon boiling water
1 cup cottage cheese
3 tablespoons chopped chives
¼ cup chopped green pepper
¼ cup grated carrot
2 finely minced radishes
¼ teaspoon paprika
4 stuffed olives, sliced

Dissolve bouillon cube in boiling water and combine with all other ingredients except olives, stirring thoroughly. Spoon into serving bowl and place olive slices over the top. Refrigerate. Serve as a dip for celery, carrot strips, raw cauliflower flowerets, etc., or spread on squares of melba toast. Makes 1½ cups (18 calories per tablespoon).

Blender Tangy Dip

2 cups cottage cheese
3 tablespoons skim milk
2½ tablespoons prepared
horseradish
½ teaspoon Worcestershire
sauce
Dash of tabasco
3 sprigs parsley,
cut up
Dash of salt

Blend all together at high speed until very smooth and creamy. Chill. Use as dip with raw vegetables or on baked potato. Try it with meats and on hot vegetables, too. Makes 8 servings (65 calories per serving).
Variation: Substitute 1½ tablespoons dry prepared salad dressing for horseradish and Worcestershire sauce.

Cucumber Dip

1 large cucumber, peeled,
diced
½ teaspoon garlic salt
½ cup unflavored yogurt
Lemon pepper marinade
1 radish, sliced thin

Process cucumber and garlic salt in blender until smooth. Combine with yogurt and add lemon pepper marinade to taste. Refrigerate. Use as dip, dressing, or relish. Garnish with radish slices. (4 calories per tablespoon.)

Mushroom Dip

8 large fresh mushrooms, chopped
1 teaspoon chopped scallions
1 teaspoon frozen chives
1 tablespoon chopped fresh parsley
Black pepper

Salt
2 drops hot sauce
¾ cup small curd cottage cheese
1 teaspoon crumbled blue cheese
Poppy seeds

Chop mushrooms very fine and add scallions, chives, parsley, pepper, salt, and hot sauce. Process cottage cheese and blue cheese in blender until smooth. Stir into mushroom mixture. Serve chilled, with poppy seeds sprinkled on top. (13 calories per tablespoon.)

SOUPS

Vegetable-Beef Soup

½ pound very lean ground beef
1 clove garlic, minced
4 carrots, quartered
6 small onions, halved
2 cups celery, diced
1 small cabbage, cut in 6 pieces
4 cups boiling water

3½ cups canned tomatoes (#2½ can) with juice
3 sprigs parsley, or ½ teaspoon parsley flakes
2 teaspoons salt
1 teaspoon pepper
2 beef bouillon cubes
1 bay leaf

Stir beef and garlic in no-stick pan over high heat until brown. Cook with rest of ingredients in covered saucepan for 30 minutes or until vegetables are tender. Makes 6 servings (170 calories per serving).

Creamy Borscht

½ cup cottage cheese
2 tablespoons water
½ envelope instant vegetable broth

32-ounce bottle chilled low-calorie borscht (3 calories per ounce)

Process cottage cheese, water and broth in blender at low speed until smooth and creamy (use small blender jar if you have one) to make "substitute sour cream."

Spoon ¼ th of the "sour cream" into each of 4 large mugs or glasses. Pour a little borscht into each. Stir to mix thoroughly with cream. Fill mugs with borscht and stir again. Serve chilled. Makes 4 servings (55 calories per serving).

Onion-Mato Soup

1 can (10¾ ounce) condensed tomato soup
1 soup can water
1 can (8 ounce) minced clams (with juice)

1 can (8 ounce) boiled onions (with juice)
1 tablespoon grated Italian cheese

Combine ingredients and bring just to boiling. Sprinkle each serving with grated cheese. Makes 4 servings (100 calories per serving).

Tomato-Clam Soup

1 can (10¾ ounce) condensed tomato soup
1 can (10¾ ounce) cold water
1 can (8 ounce) minced clams with juice

1 can (16 ounce) stewed tomatoes
1 tablespoon grated Parmesan cheese

Stir all ingredients together in saucepan and bring to boiling point. Simmer 2 minutes and serve piping hot, top sprinkled with grated cheese. Makes 4 servings (98 calories per serving).

What-To-Do-With-Rest-Of-Turkey Soup

(I-O dieters don't eat bits of turkey meat.)

1 turkey carcass, broken up, all fat trimmed off (meat clinging to carcass is a bonus)
6 cups water (or more to cover ¾ height of bones)
2 whole cloves
1 medium onion, quartered (or 4 leeks)
1 white turnip, quartered
2 ribs celery, quartered (with leaves)

2 carrots, quartered
1 bay leaf
3 sprigs parsley
1 tomato, quartered
2 parsnips, sliced
1 teaspoon thyme
1½ teaspoons salt (or more, to taste)
Black pepper
3 tablespoons raw rice

Boil turkey carcass in water in a large kettle for 10 minutes, removing any scum which accumulates on top. Add all other ingredients except the rice, and simmer, covered, for 2 hours. Occasionally skim off fat.

Strain broth into a clean saucepan. Separate turkey bones from vegetables, scrape meat off bones into broth, and discard bones. Pick cloves and bay leaf from vegetables; discard; return vegetables to broth. Add raw rice, cover, and simmer 15 minutes longer until rice is tender. If flavor is not strong enough for you, add 1 or 2 chicken bouillon cubes. Makes 4 servings (168 calories per serving).

Clam Madrilène

1 can (10½ ounce) tomato consommé madrilène
1 can (8 ounce) minced clams (drained, reserve juice)

¼ cup cottage cheese
Hungarian paprika

Chill consommé to jell. Drain clams, reserving juice. Gently fold clams into jellied consommé and spoon into 4 bouillon cups or serving bowls. Process cottage cheese and 2 tablespoons juice from clams in blender at low speed for a few seconds until smooth. Spoon some over each serving and top with a sprinkle of paprika. Delicious for a hot summer evening, or any time. Makes 4 servings (80 calories per serving).

Louisiana Crab Soup

1 can (10¾ ounce) condensed tomato soup	2 ounces dry sherry wine Pinch mixed herbs
1 soup can cold water	1 can (7½ ounce) crabmeat,
1 cup beef bouillon	bones removed

Mix first 5 ingredients in a saucepan, bring to boil and simmer 10 minutes over low heat so flavors combine and alcohol cooks away. Flake crabmeat and add to soup. Cook 1 minute longer to heat crab. (May be prepared instead with shrimp, lobster, or a combination of shellfish, or any cold fish.) Makes 4 servings (110 calories per serving).

Chilled Shrimp Soup

1 can condensed chicken bouillon	1 tablespoon scallions or chives, diced
1 soup can skim milk	½ teaspoon lemon juice
¾ cup cooked shrimp, diced	⅛ teaspoon Worcestershire sauce
¼ cup celery, diced	

Stir soup and skim milk together in saucepan, then add other ingredients. Heat to just under boiling point, pour into three bowls, and refrigerate for at least 4 hours before serving. Makes 3 servings (83 calories per serving).

MEATS

Chicago Beef Stew

2 pounds lean beef (eye round, sirloin roast, London broil, etc.), all visible fat removed
1½ cups tomato juice
¾ green pepper, cut up small
1 cup beef broth
1½ teaspoon garlic salt
1 bay leaf
1 teaspoon paprika
½ teaspoon green pepper
4 carrots, scraped and cut into ¾-inch circles
1 package frozen green beans

Cut meat into 1-inch cubes. Mix all ingredients but green beans and carrots in saucepan, and cook gently, covered, for 2½ to 3 hours, until meat is almost tender. Stir in carrots, cook 15 minutes longer; add green beans, bring to boil again, then cook gently 8 to 10 minutes more until beans are done. Remove bay leaf before serving. Makes 8 servings (265 calories per serving).

Beef with Sauerkraut

1½ pounds lean beef, all visible fat removed, cubed (1½ inch)
2 small onions, quartered
¾ teaspoon salt
⅛ teaspoon black pepper
½ teaspoon paprika
¾ pound sauerkraut
1 bay leaf
1 cup boiling water

Brown meat and onions in bottom of a no-stick saucepan. Season with salt and pepper, and paprika. Add half the water. Cover and cook over low heat ½ hour. Stir in sauerkraut, cover, and cook 10 minutes. Add bay leaf and rest of water, cover again, and cook 1½ hours more. Remove bay leaf before serving. Serve a little horseradish on the side. Makes 4 servings (375 calories per serving).

Beef-Cabbage Casserole

1 pound ground beef, all
  visible fat removed before
  grinding
1 cup chopped celery
½ cup chopped onions
2½ cups tomatoes (No. 2
  can) with juice
2 teaspoons salt

Dash black pepper
¼ teaspoon Worcestershire
  sauce
4 cups coarsely shredded
  cabbage
¼ cup prepared stuffing

Brown meat in no-stick pan. Add celery and onions
and sauté for 5 minutes. Add tomatoes, salt, pepper,
and Worcestershire sauce. In casserole, make 4 alternate layers of cabbage, meat, cabbage, meat. Sprinkle
stuffing on top. Bake in 375° oven ¾ hour. Serve
piping hot. Makes 6 servings (235 calories per serving).

Country Burgers

1½ teaspoons grated onion
¼ cup skim milk
1 pound lean ground beef,
  all visible fat removed
  before grinding
⅓ cup uncooked quick
  or instant rice

1 egg, beaten slightly
¾ teaspoon salt
⅛ teaspoon black pepper
⅛ teaspoon oregano

Combine onion and skim milk and let stand 10
minutes or more.

Using fork, mix all other ingredients together lightly
but thoroughly. Add milk-onion mixture. Form 4 patties and broil about 4 inches from heat source about 6
minutes on one side and 4 minutes on the other for
medium-done burgers. Makes 4 servings (310 calories
per serving).

Meat Loaf Burgers

1 pound very lean ground
  beef, all visible fat
  removed before grind
2 eggs
1 small onion, minced
2 tablespoons catsup or
  chili sauce

2 tablespoons skim milk
2 sweet pickles, chopped
1 teaspoon salt
½ teaspoon dry mustard

Gently mix all ingredients with fork. Form into 4
patties and broil 3 inches from flame in broiler pan 6
or 7 minutes on each side. Makes 4 servings (300 calories per serving).

Tomato-Topped Meat Loaf

1½ pounds very lean
  ground beef
1 cup chopped parsley
1 large onion (or 2 small),
  chopped
1¼ teaspoons salt
¼ teaspoon pepper

1 teaspoon Worcestershire
  sauce
½ cup tomato juice or
  water
1 egg
1 small can tomato paste

Lightly combine all ingredients except last with fork.
Spoon into baking pan and gently shape to form a loaf.
Spread tomato paste over entire top. Bake in 325°
oven for about 1 hour. Makes 6 servings (290 calories
per serving).

Greek Loaf

2 10-ounce packages frozen
  choppen spinach
1½ pounds very lean
  ground beef, all visible
  fat removed before
  grinding
2 eggs, slightly beaten
  (add salt to taste)

½ cup onion, finely
  chopped
½ teaspoon nutmeg
¾ teaspoon salt
⅛ teaspoon freshly ground
  black pepper

Cook frozen spinach following directions on package and drain thoroughly. Mixing with fork, lightly combine spinach with other ingredients. Spoon into loaf pan and bake 1 hour. If desired, pour some heated tomato sauce over before serving. Makes 6 servings (285 calories per serving).

Vary by mixing 1 cup plain cooked rice with above before baking. Will then serve 8.

Deluxe Individual Meat Loaf

1 pound lean ground beef, all visible fat removed before grinding	2 tablespoons snipped parsley
	1 teaspoon salt
	Black pepper
2 tablespoons chopped onion	1 large (or 2 small) tomato, chopped
2 tablespoons chopped pepper	1 teaspoon grated onion
	¾ teaspoon dry mustard
2 tablespoons breadcrumbs	1 tablespoon Worcestershire sauce
1 egg, beaten slightly	
2 tablespoons prepared horseradish	Dash pepper sauce

With fork, mix first 9 ingredients and spoon into no-stick 6-partition muffin tin. Combine other 5 ingredients to make sauce, heat together. Then brush over each meat loaf. Bake loaves 30 to 40 minutes in 350° oven, brushing occasionally with sauce. When serving, pour remaining sauce (if any is left) over meat. Makes 6 servings (310 calories per serving).

Blender Ham 'n Egg Loaf

1½ cups very lean, trimmed, cooked ham	6 eggs
	½ teaspoon salt
1 medium onion, cut in quarters	¼ teaspoon black pepper
1 green pepper, cut in eighths	

Cube ham, and chop ¾ cup in blender, turning "high process" on and off several times if you have no "chopping" button. Remove, and chop remaining ¾ cup ham. Remove ham, and put all other ingredients into blender. Process until pepper and onion are just chopped. Mix with ham and bake all together in no-stick baking pan in 375° oven for 10 minutes, or until egg is set. Makes 4 servings (280 calories per serving).

Beef-Mushroom Casseroles

½ pound fresh mushrooms, washed, trimmed, and sliced
1 large onion, thinly sliced
¼ teaspoon seasoned salt
⅛ teaspoon paprika
⅛ teaspoon marjoram
¼ cup prepared (dry) stuffing
½ cup canned stewed tomatoes

1 pound ground beef round, all visible fat removed before grinding
1 egg, slightly beaten
1 tablespoon chopped parsley
¼ teaspoon oregano (optional)
½ teaspoon salt
Lemon pepper marinade (to taste)

Sauté mushrooms and onions with seasoned salt, paprika and marjoram in no-stick skillet until onions are soft. In bowl, soak stuffing with stewed tomatoes for a few minutes. Using fork, mix in rest of ingredients and taste for amount of seasoning, adding more if desired. Spoon ¼ of mushroom mixture into bottom of each of 4 individual casseroles. Cover with meat mixture and bake in 350° preheated oven for half an hour. Top of meat should be brown and crusty. Sprinkle a little grated cheese over the tops if desired. Makes 4 servings (310 calories per serving).

Eggplant-Beef Casserole

1 medium eggplant	¼ cup prepared (dry)
Juice of 1 lemon	stuffing
1 pound ground beef round,	Oregano (if desired)
all visible fat removed	Salt and pepper to taste
before grinding	Grated cheese

Peel eggplant and slice ½ inch thick. Sprinkle lemon juice on both sides of slices. Combine other ingredients together lightly with fork. Make a layer of eggplant in bottom of no-stick casserole. Cover with one-third of the meat mixture. Repeat process twice, making 3 layers each of eggplant and meat. Top with a thin sprinkling of grated cheese, or with a little more of the prepared stuffing mix. Bake in preheated 350° oven 45 minutes, or until eggplant is tender. Makes 4 servings (305 calories per serving).

Beef-Mushroom Stuffed Eggplant

1 medium eggplant	½ pound ground lean beef,
6 large mushrooms, cut up	all visible fat removed
small (or small can	before grinding
chopped mushrooms,	1 tablespoon parsley,
drained)	chopped
1½ tablespoons onion,	¾ teaspoon salt
chopped	Dash nutmeg
1½ tablespoons green pepper,	2 ripe tomatoes
finely chopped	2 teaspoons grated
1 teaspoon vegetable	Parmesan cheese
margarine	

Bake eggplant in oven until slightly tender to the touch (15 to 20 minutes). Cut in half lengthwise and scoop out pulp, leaving shell intact. Chop pulp.

In no-stick skillet, sauté mushroom pieces with onion and pepper in margarine, until onions are transparent. Stir the meat into this mixture, continue cooking until meat is no longer raw. Add pulp of eggplant, parsley, salt, and nutmeg.

Spoon this mixture into eggplant shells. Remove skin from tomatoes, mash pulp, and distribute over each half. Bake in preheated 350° oven 30 to 45 minutes. Top with sprinkling of grated cheese. Makes 4 servings (175 calories per serving).

Variations: Use 1 cup minced turkey, chicken, ham, veal or shrimp instead of beef. Eliminate nutmeg, if you prefer.

Beef-Stuffed Tomatoes

4 large tomatoes
1 teaspoon vegetable oil
3 tablespoons chopped onions
3 mushrooms, sliced thin
½ pound ground lean beef,
  all visible fat removed
  before grinding
½ cup cooked rice

½ teaspoon garlic salt
¼ teaspoon Worcestershire
  sauce
Dash black pepper
Dash paprika
Hot water to cover baking
  pan bottom ⅓ inch

Remove pulp from tomatoes, reserving shells. Sprinkle salt and pepper inside shells. In no-stick skillet, heat oil, and brown onion and mushrooms in it. Stir in meat, cooking and breaking apart until slightly browned. Add cooked rice, Worcestershire sauce, garlic salt, pepper and paprika to meat, mix with fork, and spoon into tomatoes. Pour ⅓ inch hot water in baking pan. Place stuffed tomatoes in the water and bake at 375° for ½ to ¾ hour, or until tops are brown. Makes 4 servings (190 calories per serving).

Beef-Rice Stuffed Peppers

2 cups cooked rice (white,
  wild, or mixed)
½ pound ground lean beef,
  all visible fat removed
  before grinding

½ teaspoon salt
6 green peppers
Hot water

With fork, mix rice, meat, and salt. Fill peppers. Place in baking dish with a little hot water in bottom. Bake in 350° oven until peppers are tender. Makes 4 servings (240 calories per serving).

Supreme Beef-Stuffed Mushrooms

1 pound ground beef round, all visible fat removed before grinding
¼ cup prepared (dry) stuffing
⅓ cup tomato sauce
½ cup chopped celery
¼ cup chopped green pepper
1 tablespoon minced parsley
1 egg
½ teaspoon salt
¼ teaspoon basil
Black pepper
1 pound large mushrooms, stems removed

Soak stuffing in tomato sauce for a few minutes. Mix together thoroughly, using fork, with all other ingredients excepting mushrooms.

Arrange mushrooms in one layer, hollow sides up, in large shallow baking pan. Mound meat mixture into mushrooms and bake in 350° preheated oven until meat mixture is crusty and mushrooms just tender (about 20 minutes). Makes 4 servings (330 calories per serving).

Meatballs with Celery Julienne

1 pound lean ground beef, all visible fat removed before grinding
1 beef bouillon cube
1 cup boiling water
2 bunches green celery, thinly slivered lengthwise
¼ cup minced onion
1 cup finely chopped fresh or canned mushrooms
1 teaspoon garlic salt
Black pepper
1 can tomatoes (1 pound)

Dissolve bouillon cube in boiling water and cook celery slivers in the bouillon for 10 minutes. Mix beef, onion, mushrooms, garlic salt, and a dash of black pep-

per in a bowl. Lightly shape in 1-inch meatballs. Preheat heavy skillet with 2 tablespoons juice from tomatoes, and brown meatballs all over. Add tomatoes,
draining about half the juice from them first. Partially
cover tomato-covered meatballs and simmer 30 minutes,
stirring occasionally. Drain hot celery, place on serving
platter, and pour meatballs with sauce over it. Makes
4 servings (270 calories per serving).

Mock Pizza

2 English muffins
4 large slices tomato
½ cup very lean ground
  round steak
2 teaspoons grated onion
¼ teaspoon garlic powder

4 thin slices part skim
  mozzarella cheese
⅛ teaspoon oregano
Pinch cayenne
¼ teaspoon salt

Break English muffins into halves crosswise and toast
lightly. Arrange in baking pan and place a slice of tomato on each. Using fork, mix together chopped steak,
onion and garlic, spread over tomatoes. Place a slice of
cheese on each and sprinkle with oregano, cayenne and
salt. Bake in preheated 400° oven 15 minutes. Makes 4
servings (192 calories per serving).

Curried Lamb

3 pounds lean lamb, with
  all visible fat removed, cut
  into serving portions
1 teaspoon curry powder
¼ teaspoon fresh ground
  pepper
1 teaspoon salt
¼ cup chopped parsley
⅓ cup chopped celery
1 teaspoon grated lemon
  rind
1 cup orange juice
  (unsweetened)

1 medium orange, sliced
  very very thin
1 medium lemon, sliced
  very very thin
1 medium-sized fresh pineapple, core removed, sliced
  very thin (or use can of
  unsweetened sliced pineapple, cut up small, without
  juice)
Sliced cucumber and onion
  rings (optional)

Cover lamb with all other ingredients, and simmer on top of stove, covered, for 1½ hours, or until lamb is tender. Serve with thinly-sliced cucumber and thin onion rings, if desired. Makes 8 servings (300 calories per serving).

Lamb with Vegetables

1½ cups leftover lamb, chopped	¼ cup chicken broth
3 large onions, chopped fine	3 medium tomatoes
½ tablespoon olive oil	Salt
1 package frozen green beans	Pepper
	Ground nutmeg

In no-stick pan, stir onions and lamb in heated oil over medium flame until onions are brown. Add the frozen beans and broth, stirring occasionally with fork, and cook covered until beans are tender (about 10 minutes). Cut tomatoes into thick slices and place them over the beans. Simmer 10 minutes more, covered. Add salt, pepper, and nutmeg to taste. Makes 4 servings (225 calories per serving).

Wendy's Greek Lamb

2½ pounds lean lamb shoulder, no bone, (or boned leg of lamb), all visible fat removed	Black pepper
	1 medium can tomato sauce
	1 small eggplant
	1 teaspoon salt
1 teaspoon garlic salt	

Rub garlic salt and pepper into lamb. Place in uncovered casserole and roast at 400° ¾ hour. Drain off fat. Pour tomato sauce over lamb, cover, and bake at 350° 2 hours longer.

While lamb is cooking, slice eggplant into ¼-inch slices, leaving on skin; salt each slice, pile one slice on top of the other, and let stand 1 hour. Wipe eggplant slices with paper towels; cut into large strips.

Add eggplant strips to lamb and tomato sauce 1½ hours before baking time is over. Makes 6 servings (310 calories per serving).

Lamb Kabobs on Grill

1 tablespoon vegetable oil
1 small clove garlic
1 small onion, chopped
2 teaspoons lemon juice
½ cup puréed tomato
2 teaspoons granulated artificial sweetener
1 teaspoon salad herbs
¾ teaspoon salt
Pinch black pepper

1½ pounds lean lamb from shoulder or leg, all visible fat removed, cut in 1½-inch cubes
1 large onion, cut in eighths
1 green pepper, cut in 1¼-inch pieces
1 small eggplant, cut in 1¼-inch cubes
16 cherry tomatoes

Make a marinade by mixing together first 9 ingredients. Alternate lamb, onion, pepper, eggplant, and tomatoes on 4 skewers. Place filled skewers on heavy foil and brush liberally with marinade. Close foil tightly and refrigerate for at least 6 hours, or more if possible.

When ready to cook, remove kabobs from foil (save foil) and place on grill over medium hot fire, browning quickly, turning once or twice. Return kabobs to foil, apply marinade again. Close foil, and cook on grill in closed foil 30 minutes longer. Makes 4 servings (350 calories per serving).

Veal in Mushroom Sauce

1 pound veal scallopini, pounded until ¼ inch thick
1 tablespoon vegetable oil
2 tablespoons onions, minced
½ pound fresh mushrooms with stems, sliced thin

¾ cup white cooking wine
½ cup double-strength beef bouillon
2 tablespoon non-dairy creamer
2 sprigs parsley, minced

Brown veal in oil in skillet. Remove veal, and cook onions, mushrooms, wine, bouillon and creamer together in same skillet, stirring, for 5 minutes. Return veal to pan and heat in sauce. Sprinkle each serving with minced parsley. Makes 4 servings (295 calories per serving).

Ham Danish Style

4 slices extra-thin toast	16 spears cooked or
4 very thin slices lean	canned asparagus
Virginia (or boiled) ham,	4 small slices part skim
all visible fat removed	mozzarella cheese

Put a ham slice on each piece of toast. Then add 4 asparagus spears to each. Top with cheese slices and broil until the cheese melts and spreads. Makes 4 servings (165 calories per serving).

New York Franks

4 all-beef frankfurters	½ teaspoon salt
3 tomatoes, in ½-inch slices	⅓ cup grated cheddar cheese
1 large onion, thin sliced	(Italian grated cheese
1 green pepper, chopped small	may be used instead)

Cut franks into bite-size pieces. Put tomatoes, onion, and pepper in no-stick pan, sprinkle with salt, and distribute franks on top. Cook gently 15 to 20 minutes until vegetables are tender. Sprinkle cheese over mixture and cook, covered, 5 minutes more. Makes 4 servings (235 calories per serving).

POULTRY

Country Chicken

2 pounds chicken fryer
   parts (thighs, drum
   sticks, or breasts)
2 tablespoons chicken
   bouillon
Salt to taste
Pepper
1 clove garlic, chopped

2 medium onions,
   cut in eighths
4 quartered tomatoes
1 medium eggplant, cut
   into 1-inch cubes
   (leave skin on)
2 tablespoons chopped parsley
1 teaspoon dried thyme

Brush chicken parts with bouillon, sprinkle with salt
and pepper, and place in covered saucepan with other
ingredients. Cook over low heat on top of stove until
chicken is tender (about 45 minutes). Makes 4 servings
(240 calories per serving).

Snow-Capped Chicken Breasts

4 small (6-ounce) chicken
   breasts
2 tablespoons vegetable oil
2 tablespoons white
   wine vinegar

Seasoned salt
Pepper
4 thin (1-ounce) slices part
   skim mozzarella cheese
Paprika

Place chicken breasts in shallow baking pan and
brush with mixed oil and vinegar. Season with salt and
pepper. Wrap baking dish in foil and bake in preheated 325° oven 45 minutes. Remove foil, top each
chicken breast with a slice of mozzarella cheese, and
sprinkle with paprika. Return to oven and bake uncovered until cheese melts. Makes 4 servings (245 calories
per serving).

Saffron Chicken with Rice

2½ cups cooked chicken, cubed (no skin)
1 clove garlic, crushed
1 tablespoon vegetable margarine
1 cup uncooked long grain white rice
2 cups chicken bouillon
⅛ teaspoon saffron (or ¼ teaspoon blended saffron seasoning)
½ teaspoon salt
1 package frozen wax beans, thawed

Heat garlic in margarine over low heat in large skillet until garlic is lightly browned. Add rice and continue cooking, stirring until rice is golden. Add bouillon, saffron, salt, and wax beans. Cook, separating beans, 5 minutes. Add cubed chicken, cover, and cook over very low heat until rice is tender (about 14 minutes). All liquid should be absorbed. Makes 4 servings (350 calories per serving).

Crispy Chicken

2-pound broiler chicken, cut into eighths
½ cup evaporated milk
1 cup corn flake crumbs
1 teaspoon salt
¼ teaspoon pepper

Moisten chicken pieces in evaporated milk, then roll each piece in mixture of corn flake crumbs, salt and pepper. Bake in shallow no-stick pan in preheated oven at 350° for about 1 hour, or until brown and tender. Makes 4 servings (265 calories per serving).

Chicken in White Wine

2½-pound broiler chicken, cut in eighths
⅛ cup vegetable oil
1 teaspoon garlic salt
¼ pound fresh mushrooms, sliced, or 1 small can sliced mushrooms
½ cup onion, minced
¼ teaspoon marjoram
⅛ teaspoon black pepper
¾ cup dry white wine
2 tomatoes, cut in eighths
1 tablespoon parsley, minced

Brown chicken slowly in hot vegetable oil in large skillet. Pour off any remaining oil and add garlic salt, mushrooms, onion, marjoram, and pepper. Cook slowly, stirring occasionally, until onion is soft. Stir in wine, cover and simmer slowly about 30 minutes. Chicken should be tender. Skim off fat and add tomatoes, cover and cook 5 minutes longer. Arrange on platter, pour sauce over chicken, and sprinkle with parsley. Makes 4 servings (340 calories per serving).

Citrus Baked Chicken

2½-pound broiler chicken,
  cut in eighths
⅓ cup dry white wine
Juice of 1 lemon
Juice of 1 lime
1 teaspoon garlic salt

¼ teaspoon thyme
White pepper
1 teaspoon vegetable
  margarine, melted
Paprika (optional)

Wash chicken pieces, pat dry with paper towels, and arrange in shallow casserole. Mix together all other ingredients except margarine and paprika, and pour over chicken pieces. Refrigerate for 2 or 3 hours, turning chicken over occasionally. Pour off marinade (save), rearrange chicken into a single layer in casserole, brush with melted margarine, and bake in preheated 400° oven 1 hour, or until tender, basting frequently with marinade. Serve chicken pieces with pan juices poured over them. Sprinkle with paprika if you like. Makes 4 servings (265 calories per serving).

Paprika Chicken on Rice

3-pound broiler chicken,
  cut in quarters
4 tablespoons chicken
  bouillon
1 large onion, sliced
2 teaspoons paprika

¾ teaspoon salt
⅛ teaspoon black pepper
8 ounces buttermilk
2 cups hot cooked white
  rice
Watercress

Place chicken parts in broiler pan, brush with bouillon, and brown in broiler on both sides, brushing with bouillon several times to prevent drying. Brown onions in a little bouillon in a large no-stick skillet. Add browned chicken, and stir in paprika, salt, pepper, and buttermilk. Be sure all ingredients are combined thoroughly and chicken parts are coated. Cover, and simmer 25 minutes. Stir occasionally while cooking. Chicken should be tender.

Serve over hot rice and garnish platter with watercress. Makes 6 servings (275 calories per serving).

Chicken Teriyaki

2-pound broiler chicken, cut up	1 can No. 211 unsweetened chunk pineapple and juice
Salt and peper	1 medium onion, sliced into rings
1 medium green pepper, sliced	

Marinade: (can be refrigerated and used again).

1 cup soy sauce	1 clove garlic, crushed
½ cup granulated artificial sweetener	¼ teaspoon ginger

Soak chicken in combined marinade ingredients 3 or 4 hours. Remove chicken, add salt and pepper, and bake in shallow pan in preheated 350° oven 30 minutes, keeping chicken moist by brushing with marinade.

Turn chicken over and top with pepper slices, pineapple chunks with juice, and onion rings. Return to oven for 30 to 35 minutes longer until chicken is tender, turning again while baking. Makes 4 servings (260 calories per serving).

Mexican Chicken

2½-pound fryer chicken, cut in eighths, (or use your favorite chicken parts)
1 teaspoon seasoned salt
2 large tomatoes, chopped
1 onion, minced
1 green pepper, diced
2 ribs celery, chopped
1 roasted pimiento, diced
¼ cup capers
½ cup pimiento-stuffed olives, sliced
Water to cover

Remove skin from chicken parts and scrape away any visible fat. Place in saucepan with all other ingredients, add water to cover, bring to boil, lower heat, cover pot, and simmer 1½ hours. Occasionally skim off any scum or fat that may rise to top. Makes 4 servings (290 calories per serving).

Chicken Fruit Medley

2-pound broiler chicken, cut up (or 2 pounds chicken parts)
Flour
½ teaspoon salt
Black pepper
¼ cup vegetable oil
1 can (8 ounce) low-calorie peach slices (reserve juice)
½ cup pitted prunes
1 cup no-sugar-added apple juice
¼ cup chili sauce
2 teaspoons cider vinegar
3 tablespoons grated onion
½ teaspoon grated lemon rind
½ teaspoon seasoned salt

Remove skin from chicken. Mix flour with salt and pepper and rub over chicken parts. Brown in hot oil in large skillet. Pour off any remaining oil and blot chicken lightly with paper towels.

Drain peach slices, saving the juice. Combine peach juice with prunes, apple juice, chili sauce, vinegar, grated onion, lemon rind, and salt. Pour over chicken, cover skillet, bring to boil, lower heat and simmer 45 minutes, skimming off any fat which rises to top. Add peach slices; heat 5 minutes longer. Makes 4 servings (350 calories per serving).

Steamed Chicken with Vegetables

2½-pound whole broiler-
    fryer chicken
½ teaspoon salt
⅛ teaspoon pepper
¼ cup vegetable oil
¼ teaspoon thyme
⅓ cup dry white wine
1 can (10½ ounce) con-
    densed chicken broth,
    no water added

4 whole leeks, ends trimmed
1 small head (¾ pound)
    cabbage, core removed,
    cut in eighths
4 carrots, cut into thin discs
Salted boiling water
1 sprig parsley, minced

Sprinkle chicken cavities with salt and pepper and tie wings and legs as for roasting. Brown chicken on all sides in hot oil over medium heat in heavy saucepan. Drain off any remaining oil, and with chicken placed breast side up, sprinkle it with thyme. Pour wine and chicken broth over it, bring to boil, then simmer, covered, for 45 minutes, or until chicken is tender.

Simmer leeks, cabbage and carrots in covered saucepan in salted boiling water about 20 minutes, or until tender.

Place chicken in center of serving platter and surround it with the cooked vegetables. Sprinkle with parsley over all. Makes 4 servings (350 calories per serving).

Aspic Chicken

2½ cups cooked chicken (or
    turkey), cut in small cubes
2 envelopes plain gelatin
¼ cup cold water
4 chicken bouillon cubes
4 cups tomato juice

1 bay leaf
3 whole cloves
2 tablespoons snipped
    parsley
Artificial sweetener equal
    to 1 teaspoon sugar

Soften gelatin in ¼ cup cold water. Heat bouillon cubes in tomato juice, adding bay leaf, cloves, and parsley. Cook gently 8 minutes, then pour through strainer. Combine with gelatin and stir until gelatin dissolves.

Add seasonings and sweetener, and chill until almost set. Add chicken and spoon into mold. Chill until set. Unmold. Serve on lettuce or other greens. Makes 4 servings (200 calories per serving).

Summertime Chicken (or Turkey) Jell

3 cups chopped cooked chicken or turkey (remove skin before chopping)

1 envelope unflavored gelatin

¼ cup cold water

1¾ cups chicken broth

¼ cup low-calorie mayonnaise

Dash hot pepper sauce

½ teaspoon salt

Dash black pepper

½ cup celery, minced

½ cup green pepper, chopped

1 tablespoon chopped chives

Sprinkle gelatin over cold water and allow to soften 5 minutes. Add broth and heat, stirring, until gelatin is dissolved. Cool slightly. Stir in mayonnaise and hot pepper sauce; refrigerate until mixture is slightly thickened. Fold in chopped chicken, salt, pepper, celery, green pepper, and chives. Pour into mold or loaf pan and refrigerate until firm (5 or 6 hours). Unmold on platter circled with salad greens. Garnish with watercress or parsley sprigs. Makes 4 servings (215 calories per serving).

Chicken Livers and Mushrooms

1¼ pounds chicken livers

18 whole mushrooms

Salt

Lemon pepper marinade, or other flavored pepper

⅛ cup white cooking wine

Wash chicken livers and cut in halves, removing fat and membrane in centers. Wash mushrooms, cutting off bottoms of stems. Season mushrooms and livers with salt and seasoned pepper and place in shallow, no-stick broiling pan. Brush tops with some of the wine and broil near heat until livers are brown, about 7 minutes. Turn over, brush with wine, and broil again until brown. Serve piping hot, with juice, if there is any. Makes 4 servings (200 calories per serving).

Turkey Curry

2 cups diced cooked turkey
½ cup chopped celery
½ green apple, chopped
1 medium onion, chopped
2 teaspoons vegetable margarine
1½ teaspoons curry powder (more or less, to taste)
2 tablespoons flour
⅛ teaspoon ginger

2 cups chicken (or turkey) broth, all fat removed
3 tablespoons golden raisins (or dried currants)
½ teaspoon salt
½ cup seedless grapes, halved
1½ cups hot cooked white rice

Sauté celery, apple, and onion in margarine until tender. Add curry, flour and ginger, and cook for 2 minutes, stirring. Stir in broth and bring to boil. Add turkey, raisins and salt; heat through. Stir in grapes with fork. Serve over small portions of hot rice. Makes 4 servings (260 calories per serving).

FISH

Sole Food

1½ pounds sole fillets (or flounder) fresh or frozen, thawed
2 tablespoons minced parsley
⅓ cup celery, chopped
2 tablespoons grated onion
1 small can sliced mushrooms, butter removed, drained

2 tablespoons onion bouillon
¾ cup ready-mixed dry stuffing
½ cup water
½ teaspon salt
1 teaspoon paprika

Wipe fish with damp paper towels. Sauté parsley, celery, onions and mushrooms in bouillon, using no-stick skillet, until light brown.

Moisten stuffing with ½ the water, using fork; mix lightly with vegetables. Sprinkle salt over dark sides of fillets and place some stuffing mixture at one end of each. Roll up fillets with stuffing inside, fasten each with a toothpick, and arrange open side down in a baking dish. Pour remaining water over them. Cover dish, and bake at 350° in preheated oven 10 minutes. Uncover; bake 10 minutes longer. Serve with a sprinkle of paprika on each roll. Makes 4 servings (190 calories per serving).

Variations: Stuff instead with seasoned chopped shrimp, or chopped cooked spinach; may be cooked in tomato sauce instead of water.

Fillet of Sole with Mushrooms

2 pounds fillet of sole	1½ teaspoons salt
2 cups sliced fresh mushrooms (or drained canned)	⅛ teaspoon black pepper or lemon pepper marinade
¼ cup chopped onion	1 tablespoon chopped parsley
1 tablespoon vegetable oil	

Sauté mushrooms and onions in oil until onions are transparent. Sprinkle salt and pepper over fish. In a heavy pan, place the fish in layers, with sautéed mushrooms and onions between and over the fish. Sprinkle parsley over the top. Simmer on top of stove, covered, for 20 minutes. Makes 6 servings (165 calories per serving).

Oven-Browned Fish

2 pounds lean fish fillets (your choice)	Black pepper
Skim milk (very little)	Mixed herbs
Seasoned salt	Breadcrumbs (very small quantity)

Brush the fillets with skim milk, and season with salt, pepper, or other seasonings such as seasoned salt, herbs and spices. Roll in breadcrumbs for very light covering (shake off excess). Place on aluminum foil in baking dish, and bake at about 450°, 4 to 5 minutes per side until crisp and lightly brown. Makes 6 servings (130 calories per serving).

Poached Blue Trout

1½ pounds fresh blue trout (or other small lean fish)
4 cups fish stock or bouillon
1 cup white wine
½ cup white wine vinegar
1 bay leaf

12 peppercorns
1 onion, sliced
2 sprigs parsley
2 carrots, sliced thin
1 teaspoon salt

Boil all ingredients except fish in a saucepan. Submerge fish, lower heat, and simmer 15 minutes. Remove from heat, carefully place fish in casserole. Strain liquid and pour over fish. Reheat, and serve. Makes 4 servings (260 calories per serving).

Poached Halibut with Spinach Sauce

1½ pounds halibut steak
½ cup dry white wine
½ cup fresh lemon juice
Water to cover (if needed)
¼ cup minced fresh onion
1 package frozen spinach
½ teaspoon salt

Water
1 teaspoon instant non-dairy creamer
1 teaspoon grated cheddar cheese
½ cup liquid from cooked fish
2 tablespoons grated cheddar cheese

Place fish in saucepan and pour wine and lemon juice over it. Add water to cover and bring to boil. Cover pan and cook over low heat until fish flakes with a fork (about 6 minutes). Drain, reserving ½ cup of the liquid.

Add minced onion to frozen spinach in saucepan and cook with salt and water according to package directions. Using fork, mix in non-dairy creamer and 1 teaspoon grated cheese. Add ½ cup fish liquid; stir.

Place spinach mixture over fish and top with sprinkling of grated cheese. Bake in 400° oven until heated through. Makes 4 servings (265 calories per serving).

Sea Bass Continental

1 sea bass, 2 pounds (not including head and tail)	5 whole peppercorns
	2 cloves
1 medium onion, quartered	½ bay leaf
2 stalks celery, cut in halves	2 teaspoons salt
6 medium carrots, peeled and cut in serving portions	2 tablespoons lemon juice
	2 tablespoons white vinegar
3 sprigs parsley	

In large pot, boil together, uncovered, all ingredients except fish in 2 quarts of water. Lower heat and add the sea bass. Cover and simmer about 20 minutes or until fish is tender. Let stand 10 minutes. Carefully remove fish and carrots and place on serving platter. Discard rest of ingredients. Makes 6 servings (180 calories per serving).

Baked Salmon with Saffron Rice

1 pound canned salmon	14 ounces (approximate) chicken broth (or dissolve
1 tablespoon butter	
1 medium onion, chopped	2 chicken bouillon cubes in
¼ teaspoon saffron powder	14 ounces of boiling water)
1 clove diced garlic	3 tablespoons chopped
1 cup uncooked rice	parsley

Melt butter in heavy baking dish and in it sauté onion, saffron, and garlic until onion is transparent. Stir in rice until thoroughly mixed. Add salmon liquid, and

chicken broth; bring to boil. Remove from flame. Flake
salmon gently and fold pieces into rice. Bake covered
in preheated 400° oven ½ hour or until rice is tender.
Fluff with fork before serving. Sprinkle with chopped
parsley. Makes 6 servings (250 calories per serving).

Chinese Tuna Dinner

½ cup chopped onions
½ cup sliced green pepper
1 small can sliced mush-
  rooms (drain and reserve
  2 tablespoons liquid)
2 cups diced celery
1½ tablespoon flour
1¼ cups onion broth
¾ cup sliced water chest-
  nuts, drained

1 cup bean sprouts, drained
2 cans (7 ounces each)
  water-packed tuna (or
  regular tuna, drained,
  placed in strainer, and oil
  washed out with cold
  water)
½ teaspoon salt
3 teaspoons no-sugar
  soy sauce

Sauté onions, green pepper, mushrooms, and celery
for 5 minutes in no-stick skillet in 2 tablespoons juice
from mushrooms. Remove from heat and blend in
flour. Add broth, return to heat, and simmer for 10
minutes, stirring. Add water chestnuts, bean sprouts,
tuna, salt, and soy sauce. Bring again to boil, reduce
flame and heat through. Makes 6 servings (100 calories
per serving).

SHELLFISH

In many of these shellfish recipes, you'll find that you
may substitute (or combine) shrimp, crabmeat, scallops, lobster, or lobster tails for the kind listed in the
directions. Most of the recipes list shrimp, but other
species may be used instead. Suit your personal preference, considering also the availability and cost of the
various types of shellfish. When changing the recipe, you
can check the calorie tables, although the different

kinds of shellfish are all quite low in calories. Be sure
to use the delicious low-calorie recipes in the Quick
Weight Loss section for Stay-Slim eating, as well.

Crab Curry

2 cans (7 ounce) crabmeat   3 tablespoons flour
  (or 1 pound fresh   1 teaspoon curry powder
  crabmeat)   1 teaspoon salt
¼ cup onion, chopped small   ⅛ teaspoon pepper
1 tablespoon vegetable   1½ cups skim milk
  margarine

Pull apart crabmeat, removing little bones and cartilage while flaking it. Sauté onion in margarine until
golden. Remove pan from heat and add dry ingredients,
stirring thoroughly. Place in top of double boiler and
blend in skim milk; stir while cooking until thickened.
Add crabmeat to mixture and continue cooking for 5
minutes. Makes 4 servings (185 calories per serving).

Seacoast Crab

1 pound fresh lump or   ¼ teaspoon garlic salt
  frozen crabmeat   ½ teaspoon Dijon mustard
  (or cut-up shrimp)   ½ cup lemon juice
3 tablespoons chopped green   2 finely chopped hard-
  onion or chives   cooked eggs
1 tablespoon chopped parsley   1 teaspoon paprika
1 tablespoon dry tarragon   Salt and black pepper
1 tablespoon polyunsaturated
  oil

With a fork, blend all ingredients except crabmeat in
a bowl. Add the crab (be sure it is picked over for
bones) and gently toss. Heat through; serve in large
seashells or ramekins. Makes 4 servings (185 calories
per serving).

Chinese Lobster

1½ pounds lobster meat, cut into chunks
1 green pepper, diced
1 clove garlic, crushed
10 scallions, minced, including greens
1 can sliced mushrooms, with liquid
2 tablespoons teriyaki sauce
1 can water chestnuts, drained and sliced
1 can bean sprouts, drained
1 package frozen Chinese pea pods, thawed
2 cups hot cooked white rice

Sauté green pepper, garlic, scallions, and mushrooms (with liquid) in a large no-stick skillet in teriyaki sauce for 10 minutes. Add water chestnuts, bean sprouts, and frozen pea pods. Cook 5 minutes longer, or until heated through, stirring. Add lobster chunks, coating them thoroughly with vegetable mixture. Heat again until lobster is hot. Add teriyaki sauce to taste, if necessary. Serve with cooked white rice. Makes 4 servings (185 calories per serving).

Curried Rock Lobster

4 rock lobster tails
2 tomatoes, peeled and diced small
2 onions, minced
1 tablespoon curry powder
1 bay leaf thoroughly crumbled
½ teaspoon garlic salt
2 dashes cayenne (red pepper)
1 tablespoon chopped parsley
¼ teaspoon marjoram
1 tablespoon bouillon

Place frozen lobster tails in boiling salted water, then bring water to boil again and simmer for about 5 minutes. Drain immediately and plunge into cold water. With sharp knife under meat strip all meat from shells, saving shells for serving.

Dice the lobster meat into ½-inch chunks while sautéeing the onions in bouillon in no-stick pan. When hot, stir in the tomatoes and all seasonings, mixing well. Simmer slowly for about 20 minutes, then add lobster pieces and heat thoroughly, mixing well occasionally. Place the mixture in the lobster shells, sprinkle with paprika, and serve at once. Makes 4 servings (145 calories per serving).

Oyster Stew

2 teaspoons butter	2 cups clam broth
⅛ teaspoon Worcestershire sauce	28 raw medium oysters
⅛ teaspoon paprika	2 cups skim milk
	Paprika

In a deep saucepan, heat together butter, Worcestershire sauce, paprika, and clam broth. Just before boiling point, add oysters; continue cooking over low heat. When oyster edges begin to curl, add skim milk. Bring almost to boil; pour into 4 soup bowls, dividing oysters evenly, and sprinkle with paprika. Makes 4 servings (145 calories per serving).

Scallop-Rice Mélange

1 pound sea scallops, in halves if large size	2 tablespoons instant onion broth, double strength
1 tablespoon vegetable margarine	½ teaspoon cornstarch
2 cups hot cooked green beans	2 cups hot cooked extra long grain white rice
1 large red pimiento cut in strips, then in small pieces	

In large skillet, sauté scallops in the margarine about 7 minutes until cooked (test with fork), tender but not overdone. Add to scallops the green beans, pimiento, onion broth, and cornstarch. Combine thoroughly with a wooden spoon, and heat over medium flame for just a few minutes. Serve on a platter ringed with the hot rice. Makes 4 servings (235 calories per serving).

Curried Shellfish

½ pound crabmeat, broken up and cartilage removed

½ pound cooked shrimp, cut into quarters

½ pound scallops or lobster meat, cut into small pieces

1 can (6 ounce) sliced or diced mushrooms, drained and butter, if any, removed

2 tablespoons grated onion

3 tablespoons parsley, minced

1 teaspoon seasoned salt

¼ teaspoon black pepper

½ teaspoon ground ginger

3 teaspoons curry powder (vary amount to taste)

½ cup dry white wine

1 rib celery, diced

Combine crabmeat, shrimp, and scallops with mushrooms, onion and parsley. Simmer rest of ingredients together for 5 minutes and add to seafood mixture. Spoon into a casserole and bake 25 minutes in a preheated 350° oven. Makes 4 servings (200 calories per serving).

S-S Bouillabaisse

1½ pounds boned fish (striped bass or other available fresh fish); separate fish heads, bones and skin from the fish

½ pound raw shrimp, peeled and cleaned

½ pound scallops, bite-size

1 quart water

1 clove garlic, minced

2 onions, minced

1 carrot, thin slices

6 ribs celery, diced

1½ teaspoons salt

1 bay leaf

2 tablespoons bouillon

4 cups canned tomatoes and juice

4 teaspoons chopped parsley

Cayenne (red pepper)

In 1 quart water in a large saucepan, add fish heads, bones and skin (but not fish fillets), ½ of the minced garlic, ½ of the minced onion, carrot slices, 2 celery ribs, ½ of the salt, and the bay leaf. Bring to a boil, then simmer for ½ hour. Strain off the fish stock and place aside. Dispose of the other materials (fish heads, etc.).

In heated bouillon in a small shallow pan, sauté the rest of the garlic and onion until soft, without browning. Place in pot with strained fish stock, tomatoes, remaining celery, and salt, cook until at a boil, then cover and simmer for 20 minutes.

Add the boned fish and simmer over low fire for 10 minutes. Add scallops, shrimp, and parsley, and cook at moderate heat, not boiling, for 8 to 10 minutes or until fish is tender and flakes with a fork. Serve in soup plates. Add a dash or two of cayenne atop each serving. Makes 6 servings (240 calories per serving).

VEGETABLES

For Stay-Slim Eating, you'll be using mostly the satisfying low-calorie recipes in the Inches-Off section. Here are a few additional recipes which contain ingredients such as yogurt, cottage cheese, milk and eggs, which aren't permitted on the Inches-Off Diet.

Curried Broccoli (or Asparagus)

1½ pounds fresh broccoli, heavy stalks removed (or asparagus)
1½ teaspoons salt
Water to cover
1 cup unflavored yogurt
1 tablespoon prepared mustard

1 teaspoon herb-flavored salt
Dash black pepper
½ teaspoon curry (or more, to taste)
2 raw carrots, cut in spears
8 radishes

Wash broccoli carefully and separate into about 8 pieces with tender stalks included. Cook in salted water to cover until tender but crisp. Drain well and refrigerate.

Make a sauce of yogurt, mustard, flavored salt, pepper, and curry. Arrange cold broccoli on serving platter, surround with cut carrots and radishes, and serve with the sauce. Makes 4 servings (75 calories per serving).

Old-World Eggplant

1 medium eggplant
(1 to 1¼ pounds)
1 large cucumber, pared
1 medium onion, chopped
1 cup celery, diced
⅓ cup stuffed pimiento
olives, sliced
½ cup cottage cheese
processed in blender
with 2 tablespoons skim
milk ("sour cream")

either 1 clove garlic, minced,
and 1 teaspoon salt;
or 1 teaspoon garlic salt
1 tablespoon lemon juice
Artificial sweetener equal to
½ teaspoon sugar
Dash hot sauce
Lettuce
2 hard-cooked eggs, sliced
or cut in wedges

Wash eggplant and bake in shallow pan in 450° oven 20 minutes. Cool 10 minutes, then pare and cut into ½-inch cubes into a medium size bowl. Cut cucumber in half lengthwise, then in half again. Remove seeds and slice into bowl with eggplant. Add onion, celery, and olives. In separate bowl, mix cottage "sour cream," garlic, salt, lemon juice, artificial sweetener, and hot sauce. Toss with eggplant mixture, using fork. Serve chilled in bowl lined with lettuce, with egg slices, and more olive halves, if desired, on top. Makes 6 servings (75 calories per serving).

Baked Potato Nests

2 medium baking potatoes
4 tablespoons skim milk
4 tablespons cottage
cheese
¾ teaspoon seasoned salt

Black pepper
2 tablespoons chopped
chives
1 sprig parsley, minced
Paprika

Bake potatoes until tender when gently squeezed. Divide in halves lengthwise. Scoop potato from shells, reserving shells. Mash the potato pulp thoroughly with a fork; combine with all other ingredients except paprika. Spoon this mixture into the half-shells and bake at 350° for 10 to 12 minutes until heated through. Top each half with a sprinkle of paprika. Makes 4 servings (70 calories per serving).

Buttermilk Spinach

1½ pounds fresh spinach	½ teaspoon salt
2 tablespoons water	3 ounces buttermilk
1 medium onion, minced	1 hard-cooked egg, chopped

Wash spinach thoroughly; cook in water with onion and salt until onions are tender, stirring occasionally. Remove from heat, squeeze out liquid, and chop into small pieces. Add buttermilk and reheat over low flame, stirring until piping hot. Sprinkle chopped egg over top. Makes 4 servings (60 calories per serving).

Baked Egged Tomatoes

4 large tomatoes, cut in half crosswise	1 tablespoon tarragon vinegar
2 tablespoons seasoned breadcrumbs	1 teaspoon Worcestershire sauce
1 tablespoon lemon juice	½ teaspoon prepared mustard
2 hard-cooked eggs, chopped fine	1 tablespoon minced parsley

Place tomato halves, cut side up, in shallow baking pan. Mix breadcrumbs and lemon juice, and spread on tomatoes. Bake 15 minues in 375° preheated oven.

Mix chopped eggs with rest of ingredients and distribute over tops of tomatoes. Return to oven for 5 minutes longer, or until tomatoes are tender but not mushy. Makes 4 servings (90 calories per serving).

Variation: Crumble 2 well-done slices of bacon and add to chopped egg mixture (23 calories extra per serving).

Stuffed Zucchini

2 medium zucchini squash	2 tablespoons chopped
Salted water to cover	parsley
1 egg, beaten	1 teaspoon salt
2 small onions, finely	⅛ teaspoon pepper
chopped	Grated Parmesan cheese
¼ teaspoon basil	

Preheat oven to 350°. Cover zucchini with salted water, bring to boil, and cook until slightly tender (about 5 minutes). Cut in halves lengthwise and remove pulp. Combine pulp, egg, onion, basil, parsley, salt and pepper. Stuff shells with this mixture. Sprinkle grated cheese over tops of halves, return to oven, and bake 20 minutes. Makes 4 servings (45 calories per serving).

Variations:

1. Add a few chopped mushrooms to pulp.
2. Top with part skim mozzarella cheese instead of grated cheese.
3. Add cut-up water chestnuts to pulp.
4. Sprinkle crumbled bacon over tops.

SALADS

Here are some favorite salad recipes which contain ingredients such as chicken, fish, and cottage cheese which aren't permitted in the low-calorie salads in the Inches-Off section. Of course, you may add to many of the salads such ingredients as cold meats—but always counting the extra calories in your total daily eating.

Here also are some richer *salad dressings*, containing additional ingredients, to use along with the low-calorie Inches-Off dressings.

Chicken-Bacon-Cheese Salad

1-pound head romaine let-
tuce, washed, dried, and
torn into bite-size pieces
1 bunch watercress, trimmed,
washed, dried
2 slices well-done bacon,
crumbled
1½ cups diced cooked
chicken (or turkey)
2 ribs celery, thinly sliced

¼ cup cheddar cheese
in thin strips
1 tablespoon grated Italian
cheese
2 teaspoons chopped
scallions (optional)
1 tablespoon vegetable oil
1½ tablespoons red wine
vinegar
½ teaspoon salt (or more,
to taste)

Place lettuce and watercress in salad bowl together
with crumbled bacon, diced chicken, celery, cheddar
cheese, grated cheese, and scallions. Refrigerate, covered. Just before serving, add vegetable oil and toss well;
add vinegar and salt, toss well again. Serve immediately.
Makes 4 servings (260 calories per serving).

Chicken Salad Jell

1 envelope unflavored
gelatin
½ cup cold water
1½ cups chicken broth
1 chicken bouillon cube
1 tablespoon parsley, minced
⅛ teaspoon paprika
Juice of 1 lemon

1 hard-cooked egg, sliced
1 cup cooked (or canned)
carrots, sliced
3 cups cooked chicken,
cubed
Lettuce leaves
4 teaspoons low-calorie
substitute "mayonnaise"

Sprinkle gelatin over cold water to soften. Heat
chicken broth to boiling and stir in gelatin mixture and
bouillon cube until dissolved. Add parsley, paprika, and
lemon juice. Place in refrigerator or freezer until mixture is partially set.

Arrange egg slices in bottom of greased mold, place
carrots over them, and then cubed chicken. Pour partially set gelatin mixture into mold and refrigerate for 2

to 3 hours, until firm. Unmold on platter circled with lettuce leaves. Serve with 1 teaspoon low-calorie "mayonnaise" over each portion. Makes 4 servings (300 calories per serving).

Stuffed Tomato Salad

12 ounces cottage cheese or pot cheese
2 tablespoons skim milk
1 cup celery, thinly sliced
¼ teaspoon seasoned salt
2 teaspoons frozen or fresh minced chives
Dash of white pepper
Dash of garlic powder (if seasoned salt does not include garlic)
4 medium-to-large tomatoes
Paprika
Salad greens
Carrot sticks and watercress for garnish

Mix together all ingredients except tomatoes, paprika, salad greens, carrot sticks, and watercress. With sharp knife, cut down into tomatoes almost to bottom to form 6 wedges. Gently pry wedges apart at top. Stuff with cottage cheese mixture. Sprinkle tops with paprika. Serve each stuffed tomato on a bed of greens, garnishing with carrot sticks and watercress. Makes 4 servings (132 calories per serving).

Spring Herring Salad

1 8-ounce jar herrings bits, drained
4 carrots cut in discs
1 medium head lettuce, torn into bite-size pieces
1 tablespoon chopped chives
1 tablespoon chopped parsley
1 medium onion, sliced and separated into rings
8 medium radishes cut in discs
2 tablespoons favorite low-calorie salad dressing
2 hard-cooked eggs, quartered
Paprika

Place all ingredients except eggs and paprika in salad bowl and toss gently with salad fork and spatula. Arrange egg quarters on top decoratively. Sprinkle with

paprika for color. Serve immediately. Makes 4 servings
(147 calories per serving).

Creamy Shredded Cabbage

3 cups shredded cabbage
½ cup cottage cheese
2 tablespoons skim milk
½ envelope instant vege-
    table or beef broth

½ cup grated carrots
    (2 small carrots)
½ teaspoon seasoned salt
    Black pepper

Process cottage cheese, skim milk, and instant broth
in blender at low speed until smooth and creamy, to
make sauce. Combine other ingredients and toss with
sauce. Serve as salad. Makes 4 servings (60 calories per
serving).

Cucumbers in Cream

3 cucumbers, peeled
½ cup cottage cheese
3 tablespoons cider vinegar

½ teaspoon seasoned salt
1 tablespoon fresh dill,
    minced

Slice cucumbers very thin. Process cottage cheese,
vinegar, and salt in blender at low speed until very
creamy. Pour over cucumbers and sprinkle dill on top.
Makes 4 servings (50 calories per serving).

Fruit and Red Cabbage Salad

3 cups raw red cabbage,
    shredded
1 cup seedless grapes, or
    halves of seeded grapes
1 medium apple, diced
2 tangerines, segmented

2 tablespoons low-calorie
French dressing (or your
    choice of low-calorie
    dressings)
1 medium head lettuce,
    separated in leaves

In a bowl combine the red cabbage, grapes, diced
apple, tangerine segments, and dressing and toss gently

but thoroughly. Line a serving bowl with the lettuce leaves, and fill with the salad mixture. Serve immediately. Makes 4 servings (138 calories per serving).

Jellied Cranberry Salad

2 envelopes unflavored
  gelatin
3 cups low-calorie cranberry
  juice
½ cup natural (no-sugar
  added) pineapple juice
½ cup no-sugar added
  crushed pineapple, drained
  (use juice with above)

¼ cup finely diced celery
¼ cup finely diced radishes
1 large carrot, grated
½ cup shredded cabbage
½ cup finely diced apple
  Salad greens

Sprinkle gelatin over 1 cup of the cranberry juice, let soften for 5 minutes, heat, and stir until gelatin is dissolved. Add remainder of cranberry juice and the pineapple juice, stirring. Chill, and when mixture is consistency of heavy cream, fold in crushed pineapple, vegetables and diced apple. Pour into 1½ quart mold. Chill until firm. Turn out and serve on crisp greens. Makes 6 servings (72 calories per serving).

Orange-Carrot Mold

1 envelope unflavored
  gelatin
½ cup unsweetened orange
  juice
1½ cups boiling water
1 teaspoon liquid artificial
  sweetener

1 cup orange sections,
  membranes removed
½ cup carrots, shredded
1 tablespoon grated
  orange rind
  Salad greens

Soften gelatin in orange juice and stir into boiling water until gelatin is dissolved. Add sweetener and chill until partly jelled. Cut up orange sections and add with carrots and orange rind to gelatin mixture. Chill in 4 individual molds until firm. Unmold on greens to serve; garnish with a few carrot curls or mint leaves, if desired. Makes 4 servings (55 calories per serving).

Tomato Aspic

1 envelope unflavored gelatin
¼ cup cold water
¾ cup boiling water
1 small (10¾ ounce) can condensed tomato soup
1 rib celery, chopped

1 teaspoon grated onion
½ teaspoon salt
Artificial sweetener equal to 3 teaspoons sugar
Black pepper
1 bunch watercress

Sprinke gelatin over cold water to soften. Add hot water and stir until dissolved. Mix in all other ingredients (except watercress) and pour into mold. Chill until firm. Unmold and serve on watercress. Makes 4 servings (60 calories per serving).

SALAD DRESSINGS

Blender Mock Sour Cream

1 cup cottage cheese
2 tablespoons skim milk
1 tablespoon lemon juice

Blend ingredients at high speed until creamy and smooth.

Use on very low-calorie wafers for appetizers, or as dip for raw vegetables. Also may be used as sour cream substitute in other recipes. Makes 6 servings (43 calories per serving).

Blender Cucumber "Sour Cream"

1 cucumber, cut up
1 cup cottage cheese
2 tablespoons skim milk

1 tablespoon lemon juice
½ teaspoon salt
Pepper

Blend ingredients at high speed until creamy and smooth. Use on very low-calorie wafers as appetizers, or as dip for celery, carrot sticks, raw cauliflower, etc. Sprinkle snipped chives on top, if desired. Also delicious on hard-cooked egg slices as canapés, and on plain baked potatoes with chives. Makes 6 servings (43 calories per serving).

Low-Calorie Cooked Salad Dressing

⅓ cup water
2 tablespoons flour
½ cup wine vinegar
Artificial sweetener equal
    to 1 teaspoon sugar
½ teaspoon Worcestershire
    sauce

½ teaspoon dry mustard
¼ cup catsup
⅛ teaspoon garlic salt
½ teaspoon paprika
1 teaspoon prepared
    horseradish

In saucepan, cook and stir water, flour, and vinegar together until thick and creamy. Allow to cool, then add other ingredients and beat with electric beater or rotary egg beater until smoothly blended. Chill in jar or bottle in refrigerator, shaking well before each use. Makes 1 cup (160 calories, whole recipe).

Cooked Creamy Salad Dressing

2 cups skim milk
2 well beaten eggs
Artificial sweetener equal
    to ½ cup sugar

1 teaspoon prepared mild
    mustard
¼ teaspoon butter
½ teaspoon salt
⅛ teaspoon pepper

Cook all ingredients together in top of double boiler over hot water (do not boil), until smooth and thickened. (Stir constantly.) Refrigerate, then use on shredded raw cabbage, sliced tomatoes, or sliced cucumbers. Makes 2 cups (about 10 calories per tablespoon).

Pink Salad Dressing

½ cup cottage cheese
2 tablespoons buttermilk
1 tablespoon chili sauce
½ teaspoon seasoned salt
2 tablespoons chopped onion, or onion flakes
½ teaspoon paprika

Combine ingredients in electric blender and process until very smooth. Will serve 4 individual portions of salad. (40 calories per serving.)

Tomato Dressing

1 can (15 ounce) tomato sauce
1 cup small-curd cottage cheese
¼ cup water
2 tablespoons grated onion
1½ tablespoons fresh lemon juice
½ teaspoon basil leaves
1¼ teaspoons salt
1 teaspoon dry mustard
⅛ teaspoon black pepper

Combine all ingredients in a large bowl and stir until well mixed. Serve chilled on salad greens or raw vegetables. Will keep for a week or so if well refrigerated in a covered bowl or jar (8 calories per tablespoon).

Buttermilk Dressing

¾ cup buttermilk
¾ tablespoon prepared white horseradish
1 teaspoon prepared mustard
1½ teaspoons lemon juice
Salt
Black pepper

Shake all ingredients together in a small jar. Chill. Use on salad greens, or with shrimp, crabmeat, salmon, tuna fish, cottage cheese, etc. (7 calories per tablespoon).

Creamy Salad Dressing

1 cup plain yogurt	2 teaspoons prepared mustard
¼ teaspoon grated onion	¼ teaspoon liquid
¼ teaspoon salt	artificial sweetener
1 teaspoon lemon juice	2 teaspoons bacon bits

Combine all ingredients in a covered jar and shake well. Chill. Shake before each use. Makes 1 cup (10 calories per tablespoon).

Low-Calorie Cocktail Sauce

2 tablespoons fresh lemon juice	1½ teaspoons white horse-radish (squeeze out juice and discard)
3 teaspoons unsweetened apple juice	¼ cup catsup
3 teaspoons tomato juice	

Mix all ingredients together and use sparingly as sauce for shrimp, crab, lobster, etc. Makes 1 cup (5 calories per teaspoon).

DESSERTS

You'll also use the delicious low-calorie desserts in the Quick Weight Loss section, and the Inches-Off fruit and dessert recipes (of course, many people skip desserts entirely).

Rich, high-calorie, high-fat recipes for cakes, pies, and other desserts are purposely excluded from this book. If you wish to have any such servings on your Stay-Slim Eating, be sure to include the number of calories in your total daily calorie allowance—lest you gain weight rapidly.

Sponge Cake

7 eggs (at room tempera-   ½ teaspoon vanilla
  ture), separated   2 tablespoons lemon juice
½ cup cold water   1½ cups sifted cake flour
Liquid artificial sweetener   ¼ teaspoon salt
  equal to ½ cup sugar   ¾ teaspoon cream of tartar

Beat yolks of eggs until thick (5 minutes). Add
water, sweetener, vanilla and lemon juice to eggs and
beat 10 minutes longer, until fluffy and thick. Sift cake
flour and salt together a little at a time into egg mixture, gently folding in.

Beat egg whites until foamy, then add cream of tartar
and continue beating until stiff peaks form. Fold batter
lightly into beaten egg whites and pour into greased
9-inch tube cakepan. Bake in preheated 325° oven 65
minutes. Makes 12 servings (90 calories per serving).

Mock Danish Pastry

4 pieces extra-thin-sliced   2 teaspoons granulated
  white bread   artificial sweetener
8 tablespoons cottage cheese   8 drops no-sugar
¼ teaspoon cinnamon   strawberry flavoring
¼ teaspoon vanilla   Nutmeg

Toast bread lightly in toaster. Stir together remaining
ingredients except nutmeg and spread on toast. Broil
for a few minutes, 5 inches from heat until heated
through. Sprinkle with a little nutmeg if you like.
Makes 4 servings (85 calories per serving).

Coffee Custard

6 egg yolks   Artificial sweetener equal to
2 cups skim milk   ⅓ cup sugar
                                  1 teaspoon instant coffee

Beat egg yolks until lemon colored and thick. Scald milk, mix in coffee and sweetener. Add to eggs slowly, stirring. Pour into 6 small custard cups. Place custard cups into a pan of hot water, cover with foil, and bake in preheated 325° oven about ½ hour. A knife inserted into custard should come out clean. Serve chilled. Makes 6 servings (90 calories per serving).

Variations: May be prepared with 1 teaspoon vanilla or ½ teaspoon almond extract instead of instant coffee, if desired.

Orange-Banana Jell

1 envelope plain gelatin
¼ cup cold water
½ cup hot water
1 tablespoon sugar

1 cup orange juice
2 teaspoons lemon juice
1 teaspoon vanilla extract
1 banana, sliced

Sprinkle gelatin over cold water to soften, add hot water and sugar, and stir until gelatin is dissolved. Add orange juice, lemon juice, and vanilla, set in refrigerator to chill until almost jelled. Whip with rotary beater until fluffy. Fold in sliced bananas, return to refrigerator to chill until firm. Makes 4 servings (67 calories per serving).

Prune Custard

8 large prunes (canned or cooked, pitted)
2 tablespoons lemon juice
2 egg yolks, whipped

2 pinches of salt
½ teaspoon granulated artificial sweetener, more or less, to taste

Place all ingredients in blender, and process at moderate speed until fluffy. Chill thoroughly, then serve. Makes 4 servings (75 calories per serving).

Raisin Rice Pudding

4 tablespoons uncooked rice	artificial sweetener equal
3 cups skim milk	to ⅓ cup sugar
1 stick cinnamon	⅛ teaspoon salt
½ cup raisins	1 teaspoon vanilla
1 egg	Cinnamon or nutmeg

Cook first 3 ingredients together 45 minutes in top of double boiler. Add raisins and cook 10 more minutes. Remove from heat and discard cinnamon stick. Beat together lightly egg, sweetener, salt and vanilla. Stir into rice, return to heat and cook 3 minutes more in double boiler. Serve hot or cold, with cinnamon or nutmeg sprinkled over each portion. Makes 4 servings (165 calories per serving).

Stay-Slim Custard

2 cups skim milk	1 teaspoon vanilla
3 medium eggs	Nutmeg
Artificial sweetener equal	
to ½ cup sugar	

Scald skim milk. Combine all other ingredients except nutmeg. Add scalded milk slowly, mixing well. Pour into 5 custard cups. Set custard cups in a pan of hot water, and bake in preheated 300° oven about 1 hour. A knife inserted in custard should come out clean. Serve chilled, with nutmeg sprinkled on top. Makes 5 servings (80 calories per serving).

Apple Spice

6 large eating apples	¼ teaspoon nutmeg
¼ cup water	¼ teaspoon salt
⅓ cup granulated	3 eggs
artificial sweetener	2 tablespoons skim milk
¼ teaspoon cinnamon	1½ teaspoons cornstarch

Peel apples, cut in quarters. Cook in water, covered, until very soft. Add sweetener, spices and salt; stir. Let cool 10 minutes. Beat together eggs, milk, and cornstarch and add to apples. Pour into shallow no-stick baking dish and place in moderate (325°) oven for about 20 minutes. Serve hot. Makes 8 servings (110 calories per serving).

Creamy Citrus Mold

2 envelopes unflavored
　gelatin
¼ cup cold water
1½ cups boiling water
Liquid artificial sweetener
　equal to ½ cup sugar
¼ cup no-sugar-added
　lime juice

¼ cup no-sugar-added
　lemon juice
Green food coloring,
　just a little
⅓ cup ice water
⅓ cup nonfat dry milk

Soften gelatin in cold water. Add boiling water and stir until gelatin is dissolved. Add sweetener, lime and lemon juice. Chill until almost set. Add a few drops of green food coloring. Beat ice water and nonfat dry milk at high speed in mixer until like whipped cream, and fold gently into gelatin. Place into 4-cup mold or into 6 small individual molds. Chill until set. Makes 6 servings (40 calories per serving).

Quick Blender Fruit Fluff

2 envelopes unflavored
　gelatin
¼ cup nonfat dry milk
1 tablespoon lemon juice
⅓ cup water
Artificial sweetener equal
　to 1 cup sugar

½ cup no-sugar-added
　pineapple juice
1-pound can no-sugar-added
　sour cherries, drained
2 cups crushed ice

Into blender put gelatin, dry milk, lemon juice, water, sweetener, and pineapple juice. Process at medium speed 1 minute. Add cherries and ice, blend 1 minute longer. Spoon into 8 parfait or sherbet glasses and allow to set in refrigerator until serving time. Makes 8 servings (56 calories per serving).

Creamy Lime Dessert

1 envelope unflavored
    gelatin
¼ cup cold water
¾ cup boiling water
½ tablespoon green crème
    de menthe
¾ cup no-sugar lime juice
    (fresh or prepared)

Liquid artificial sweetener
    equal to ½ cup sugar
¼ cup ice water
¼ cup nonfat dry milk
½ tablespoon crème de
    cacao

Soften gelatin in cold water. Add boiling water and stir until gelatin is dissolved. Add crème de menthe, lime juice and sweetener. When chilled and firm, force gelatin through a sieve. Beat ice water and nonfat dry milk in small bowl at high speed in electric mixer until like whipped cream, then blend in crème de cacao. In 3 parfait glasses, alternate gelatin and whipped milk in layers. Chill until served. Makes 3 servings (60 calories per serving).

Strawberry Whip

1 envelope unflavored
    gelatin
½ cup cold water
1 teaspoon liquid artificial
    sweetener

1 tablespoon lemon juice
1 pint unsweetened frozen
    strawberries, crushed
2 egg whites, beaten until
    stiff

Using the top of a double boiler, soften gelatin in ½ cup cold water. Add sweetener and lemon juice, and cook, stirring until gelatin is dissolved. Remove from heat and add the strawberries. Let stand until mixture thickens, then beat with electric mixer until fluffy. Fold in egg whites and chill in 1½ quart mold or 6 small molds. Makes 6 servings (35 calories per serving).

Variations: Use canned no-sugar pineapple chopped in blender, frozen no-sugar-added pitted cherries chopped in blender, or puréed stewed pitted plums or apricots.

Strawberry-Blueberry Surprise

1½ cups strawberry ice milk   ½ cup fresh blueberries
1 envelope unflavored   1 tablespoon grated lemon
   gelatin   rind
½ cup fresh strawberries

Combine all ingredients in a blender, and process until smooth. Spoon at once into 4 prerefrigerated shallow dessert glasses. Place a strawberry in center of each serving and scatter a few blueberries over the top. Makes 4 servings (135 calories per serving).

Stay-Slim Menus

CONSULT THE IDEAL WEIGHT CHART to find out how many calories you can eat daily and still maintain your desired weight. If you find it necessary after a few days, you can adjust your calorie total to stay at your personal balanced weight. For Stay-Slim Eating, either follow the recipes in this book, or plan your own eating with any foods and recipes of your preference, *making sure always that you stay within your daily total calorie allowance.*

All the Quick Weight Loss and Inches-Off recipes may be used, since any recipe in this book is, in effect, a Stay-Slim recipe; just check and add the calories per serving.

The menus listed here are for an individual who can maintain her or his desired weight by eating about 1400 calories per day. These menus are general guides only, to show how you can arrive at your totals. You can select, shift, and shuffle foods as you see fit, as long as you don't eat more calories than you burn up each day on the average.

If you are permitted over 1400 calories for your height, add to these (or your own) menus accordingly. If your daily total allowance is less than 1400 calories per day, you may either cut some items or the size of servings to bring you down to your total.

Remember that it is very important to weigh yourself unclothed each morning upon arising, and to make whatever eating adjustment is necessary.

Realize that it's impossible to be precise in judging

the size of individual portions in some cases. *What counts is your weight on the scale, and staying at your desired weight.* Add or cut out foods, or adjust the sizes of servings, according to your morning weight.

Again, if you gain 4 or more pounds, go right back on the Quick Weight Loss Diet or Inches-Off Diet, whichever you prefer, until you're back at your desired weight. Then you may return to Stay-Slim eating of a variety of foods. You can use this on-and-off technique healthfully for the rest of your life. The little ups-and-downs don't hurt you—*as long as you don't stay up!* Your constant goal is to keep off unhealthy, bulging fat.

Stay-Slim Eating means just what the name states: *eating that keeps you slim* once you're down to your desired weight. Calorie counting this way soon becomes automatic and is not a chore if you really care about your good health and looking your most attractive.

Menus such as the following provide delicious eating as well as desired weight maintenance. If you wish to make any substitutions, as you will, just add or deduct the correct number of calories. For instance, for each 1-ounce alcoholic drink, you'd have to deduct about 80 calories, such as skipping an 80-calorie dessert or other 80-calorie (a little more or less) serving. The calories in everything you eat must be added that day to arrive at the correct total.

If you go over your calorie allowance one day, try to keep under your allotment by about the same amount the next day. Soon you'll learn how to balance out your calories. Your concern is not just calorie counting as such, but maintaining your desired weight. If you load up on a weekend, for example, and gain some pounds, don't weep and wail and scold yourself. Instead, do what works—go right back on the Quick Weight Loss or Inches-Off diets until you're down to your desired weight again in no time.

In checking servings in the menus here, you'll find that some Quick Weight Loss and Inches-Off recipes are used. Calories per portion are based on the recipes as listed in these pages, and the calorie tables. Coffee and tea are figured with artificial sweetener, if any, and black with no more than a dash of skim milk or non-dairy creamer; if you use sugar and cream or whole milk, add the calories accordingly.

Reminder: Be sure to take your daily vitamin-mineral pill, worthwhile for Stay-Slim Eating, and a *must* on the diets.

STAY-SLIM MENUS

MONDAY

	Calories
Breakfast	
4 ounces orange juice	55
Half cantaloupe	40
2 ounces cottage cheese	60
Coffee or tea	0
Lunch	
1 cup chicken broth	12
Chicken-bacon-cheese salad	260
1 slice extra-thin toast with artificially sweetened jam	50
Apple spice	75
Coffee or tea	
Dinner	
Half grapefruit	55
Chicago beef stew	265
Garden vegetable salad with low-calorie dressing	130
Sponge cake	90
Coffee or tea	
	1092
Snack	
Drinks, additional servings	300
Day's total	1392

TUESDAY

	Calories
Breakfast	
4 ounces no-sugar grapefruit juice	55
1 cup dry cereal	110
½ cup skim milk	40
Coffee or tea	
Lunch	
4 ounces clam juice	22
Sole food	190
Curried broccoli	75
Coffee custard	90
Coffee or tea	
Dinner	
Creamy borscht	55
Beef-Rice Stuffed Peppers	240
Old-world eggplant	75
Baked egged tomatoes	90
Orange-banana jell	67
Coffee or tea	
	1104
Snack	
Drinks, additional servings	300
Day's total	1404

WEDNESDAY

	Calories
Breakfast	
4 ounces tomato juice	23
2 slices Canadian bacon	90
1 slice extra-thin toast with artificially sweetened preserves	50
Coffee or tea	
Lunch	
Vegetable-beef-soup	170
Stuffed tomato salad	132
Stay-Slim custard	80
Coffee or tea	

Calories

Dinner

½ dozen clams with cocktail sauce	100
Curried rock lobster	145
Creamy shredded cabbage	29'
Tomato, sliced	30
Creamy lime dessert	110
Coffee or tea	
	959

Snack

Drinks, additional servings	450
Day's total	1409

THURSDAY

Calories

Breakfast

4 ounces orange juice	55
1 cup cooked cereal	140
½ cup skim milk	40
Coffee or tea	

Lunch

Onion-mato soup	100
Vegetable plate of baked potato nest, buttermilk spinach, Italian broiled tomato	180
English muffin with artificially sweetened jelly	155
½ cup no-sugar pineapple cubes	60
Coffee or tea	

Dinner

Caviar canapés	60
Tomato-topped meat loaf	290
Curried asparagus	75
Stuffed zucchini	45
Raisin rice pudding	165
Coffee or tea	
Day's total	1365

NOTE: *no allowance here for snacks or drinks. However, as an example of your figuring method, if you cut out the raisin rice pudding, you could have a 2-ounce drink of Scotch, or anything else totaling about 150 to 200 calories.*

FRIDAY

	Calories
Breakfast	
Half grapefruit	55
1 slice cinnamon toast	60
Coffee or tea	
Lunch	
Vegetable beef soup	170
1 slice extra-thin toast thinly spread with butter	65
Spring herring salad	147
Artificially sweetened cherry gelatin dessert	12
Coffee or tea	
Dinner	
Tomato appetizer	35
Sea bass continental	180
Italian egged spinach	50
Green beans with mushrooms	56
Bibb lettuce salad	67
½ cup no-sugar fruit cocktail	40
Coffee or tea	
	947
Snack	
Drinks, additional servings	450
Day's total	1387

SATURDAY

	Calories
Breakfast	
4 ounces no-sugar grapefruit juice	50
Herbed omelet	190

	Calories
1 slice extra-thin toast with artificially sweetened jam	50
Coffee or tea	

Lunch

1 cup thick blender soup	40
Paprika chicken on rice	275
Creamy shredded cabbage	60
Strawberry whip	35
Coffee or tea	

Dinner

Zucchini canapés	50
Steak flambé	300
Simple broiled mushrooms	20
Fruit and red cabbage salad	55
Creamy citrus mold	40
Coffee or tea	

	1174

Snack

Drinks, additional servings	300

	Day's total	1474

SUNDAY

	Calories

Breakfast

Half cantaloupe	40
Spanish omelet	140
Mock Danish pastry	85
Coffee or tea	

Dinner

Turkey curry	260
Cranberry applesauce	85
Baked potato nest	70
Frenched green beans	20
Strawberry-blueberry surprise	135
Coffee or tea	

Supper

Medium orange, sliced	65

	Calories
What-to-do-with-rest-of-turkey soup	168
Multi-leafed salad with low-calorie dressing	60
Quick blender fruit fluff	56
Coffee or tea	
	1184
Snack	
Drinks, additional servings	200
	Day's total 1384

Fair warning: you must be honest with yourself if you wish to stay slim. For instance, if you choose for your salad regular Russian dressing (75 calories per tablespoon) instead of low-calorie dressing (10 calories per tablespoon, check recipe or package label), you must add to your day's calorie total 65 calories per tablespoon. Similarly, if you add a tablespoon of butter to your vegetables, you must add 100 calories, and so on.

Keep in mind that all the recipes in this book are comparatively low-calorie recipes. Thus, as another instance, if the "creamy borscht" you serve were made with real cream (50 calories per tablespoon) or sour cream (30 calories per tablespoon), you'd have to add calories accordingly in your figuring. If you don't make such realistic additions, you'll go over your Stay-Slim daily calorie allowance, and you'll become overweight again, to your horror.

The tendency with most overweights, a very human failing, is to blame the diets or the Stay-Slim system, instead of themselves. Never forget—*these diets and the Stay-Slim system work wonderfully,* as many thousands of happy ex-overweights have proved for themselves. Play fair, and they'll work "miracles" for you—think about it, then follow instructions exactly (not overeating, not consuming over-large portions)—and you can't help but slim quickly and beautifully, and stay that way.

To Your Slim, Healthier,
Happier Tomorrows . . .

PLEASE ALWAYS KEEP in mind these basic rules of good health and good eating, as provided for you in the instructions, menus, and recipes in this book:

1. Take off overweight quickly and surely.
2. Keep eating "thin" to stay slim.
3. Never overeat.

This sound advice is backed by medical authorities everywhere. The editor of a noted medical journal, in naming three of the top public health problems in the United States, headed the list with: "SUICIDE BY EATING TOO MUCH."

With your cooperation, this book cannot fail to help you slim down and stay at your most attractive, healthiest best. It instructs you in the simplicity and benefits of low-fat eating, and can revolutionize your eating habits.

It is our hope that the many hundreds of low-fat, lower calorie recipes here will become your constant guide. More digestible servings, coupled with the detailed instructions in the proved Quick Weight Loss and Inches-Off diets, alternated with Stay-Slim Eating, will surely help you and yours to slim down, and to stay trim.

As we were finishing this book, a letter arrived—similar to many thousands of others from Quick Weight Loss and Inches-Off dieters. It is reproduced here exactly as received, with the thought that it will provide proof and inspiration for you, as it does for us:

Dear Dr. Stillman,

You are the greatest doctor this side of heaven—and I love you! I saw you on the Mike Douglas Show and rushed out to buy your book. Everything—but everything—you said has come true for me, and I feel great —simply great! I only wanted to lose about 15 to 20 pounds, and thanks to you, I have. It's the easiest, fastest, and most gratifying feeling in the whole world. Thank you—

Mrs. R. L.

Our best wishes to you and yours for all your slim, healthier, happier "Tomorrows!"

Index